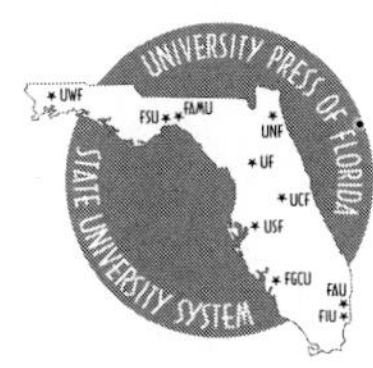

Florida A&M University, Tallahassee
Florida Atlantic University, Boca Raton
Florida Gulf Coast University, Ft. Myers
Florida International University, Miami
Florida State University, Tallahassee
University of Central Florida, Orlando
University of Florida, Gainesville
University of North Florida, Jacksonville
University of South Florida, Tampa
University of West Florida, Pensacola

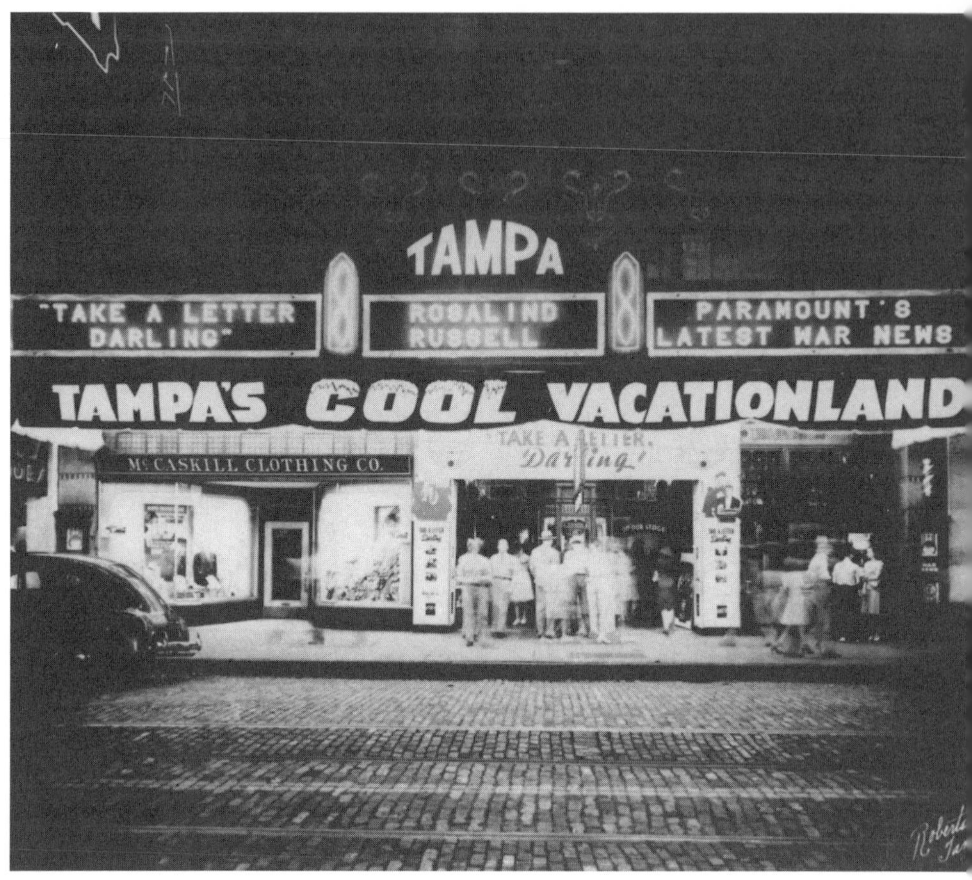

University Press of Florida

Gainesville Tallahassee Tampa Boca Raton Pensacola Orlando Miami Jacksonville Ft. Myers

Claudia and Lodovico,
Thank you for
supporting the
Tampa Theatre
Janna Jones

The Southern MOVIE PALACE

Rise, Fall, and Resurrection

Janna Jones

08 07 06 05 04 03 6 5 4 3 2 1

This project was supported by a grant from the Graham Foundation for Advanced Studies in the Fine Arts

Library of Congress Cataloging-in-Publication Data
Jones, Janna.
The southern movie palace: rise, fall, and resurrection / Janna Jones.
p. cm.
Includes bibliographical references and index.
ISBN 0-8130-2605-9 (cloth: alk. paper)
1. Motion picture theaters—Conservation and restoration—Southern States. 2. Urban renewal—Southern States. I. Title.
NA6846.U6 J66 2003
725'.823'0975028—dc21
2002040905

The University Press of Florida is the scholarly publishing agency for the State University System of Florida, comprising Florida A&M University, Florida Atlantic University, Florida Gulf Coast University, Florida International University, Florida State University, University of Central Florida, University of Florida, University of North Florida, University of South Florida, and University of West Florida.

University Press of Florida
15 Northwest 15th Street
Gainesville, FL 32611-2079
http://www.upf.com

For Mark Neumann

Contents

List of Figures ix

Acknowledgments xi

Introduction 1

1 From Glory to Ruins: The Early Years of the Movie Palace 13

2 The Decline of the Southern Downtown Movie Palace 40

3 Rescuing the Past from the Wrecking Ball 80

4 Creating the Illusion of a Material Past 119

5 The Discursive Past 188

6 The Transformation of the Downtown Movie Palace 232

Notes 275

Photo Credits 285

Index 287

Figures

1. Tampa Theatre auditorium 2
2. Tampa Theatre exterior in 1926 15
3. Carolina Theatre exterior in the 1920s 16
4. Alabama Theatre interior 21
5. Tampa Theatre mezzanine 24
6. Saenger Theatre exterior in 1929 27
7. "Colored" theater entrance 28
8. Rex Colored Theatre 31
9. Protestors at the Carolina Theatre in 1962 51
10. Demonstrators who rushed the lobby door at the Carolina Theatre in 1962 54
11. Orpheum Theatre exterior in the 1970s 67
12. Faded Orpheum marquee 69
13. Current state of the Lyric Theatre 111
14. Organ at the Lyric Theatre 117
15. Fox Theatre's proscenium and auditorium 126
16. Fox Theatre's jewel drop 132
17. Tampa Theatre lobby today 158
18. Alabama Theatre's restored auditorium 166
19. Saenger Theatre's restored marquee 176
20. Saenger Theatre's original interior 179
21. Decorative detail in Saenger Theatre's lobby 181

22. Saenger Theater's end caps 183
23. Orpheum Theatre's Czechoslovakian crystal chandelier 219
24. Exterior of the renovated Orpheum Theatre 221
25. Fox Theatre, from the corner of Ponce de Leon and Peachtree Streets 247
26. Restored exterior of the Alabama Theatre 252
27. Restored exterior of the Saenger Theatre 256

Acknowledgments

This book was made possible by the generosity of many people. In particular, I would like to acknowledge the Graham Foundation for Advanced Studies in the Fine Arts, the University of South Florida Research and Creative Scholarship Council, and the University of South Florida College of Arts and Science Research Grant Council. Their generous support enabled me to conduct research at the movie palaces and libraries in Atlanta, Birmingham, Biloxi, Durham, and Memphis.

Much of this book is based on interviews that I conducted at various theaters around the South. Many people took time out of their busy schedules to answer my questions articulately, honestly, and passionately. In particular, I would like to thank Steve Martin, Pepper Fluke, and Monte Moses at the Carolina Theatre; John Bell and Tara Schroeder at the Tampa Theatre; Cecil Whitmire at the Alabama Theatre; Lee Hood at the Saenger Theatre; Lara Mathes, Dawn Chapman, and Lila King at the Fox Theatre; and Pat Halloran and Deana Satterwaite at the Orpheum Theatre.

This book began as my dissertation at the University of South Florida, and I thank Valerie Allen, Elizabeth Bell, Elizabeth Bird, David Payne, and Gilbert Rodman for guiding my thinking about the ways that contemporary culture translates the past.

I also thank Bruce Cochrane and Spencer Cahill in the Department of Interdisciplinary Studies at the University of South Florida, for understanding that I needed some time to write this book. I am thankful for the help of Karen Oberne, who looked after me and my grants without complaint.

I am completely indebted to one of my oldest friends, Julie Beasley, who heroically transcribed hours upon hours of interviews.

I also appreciate the support and insightful comments provided by members of my writing group—Lisa Birnbaum, Bill Cummings, Ella Schmidt, and Mark Neumann.

I am indebted to my friends and shopping therapists—Robin Jones, Alexandra Murphy, and Laura Smith.

I thank Carroll Van West and Thomas Graham for their instructive insights and their support for this project.

I am deeply indebted to Meredith Morris-Babb, editor-in-chief at the University Press of Florida. She has been an enthusiastic supporter of this project from the very beginning. Her patience and sense of humor guided me through this entire process. I also appreciate the guidance of Gillian Hillis. I am grateful for the help and wisdom of Sharon Damoff.

I am thankful for all of the love and support that my parents, stepparents, and the rest of my family have given me. I especially appreciate the early lessons in both aesthetics and restoration that my mother provided me.

But most of all I thank my husband, Mark Neumann. Since the first day that I discovered the Tampa Theatre, he has been by my side, both challenging and supporting my thinking. He has helped to shape many of the ideas in this book—all the while making me believe they were all my own. His love, kindness, intelligence, and good humor inspire my work and, more importantly, my life.

Introduction

It is late, so late that the few hundred people who came to the Tampa Theatre for the second showing of *Before Night Falls* (Julian Schnabel, 2000) have already stuffed their empty popcorn bags and cups into trash cans, slid into their automobiles, and headed home through the quiet of the sleepy downtown. Maybe a few of them first stopped at The Hub, a smoky old bar on Florida Avenue behind the theater. It is not much of a place, but it is the only open spot around the theater on a Saturday night.

But I am still in the theater, experiencing it in a way that I have not done before. I am alone on the stage, lying on my back in the darkness. It is a little odd to see the theater this way. The only light comes from the glow of the electric stars on the ceiling. Wisps of cumulus clouds slowly and mechanically rotate around the ceiling, as if they were drifting across a midnight sky. I can barely make out the statues that sit in alcoves around the proscenium. The rows upon rows of seats are empty shadows. As I look back to the ceiling to watch one of the brighter stars flicker, I think about all of the people in the last seventy-five years who have filled those seats and noticed this same sparkling electric star. While being here alone in the darkness is magical and mysterious, this place was not created for solitude. It was built for lots of people—more than 1,000 people, actually—to sit in the semidarkness and dream together and alone. That is what crowds of people have been doing here since 1926, stargazing and daydreaming for a couple of hours, while the rest of the world goes about its business.

1. A 1926 image of the fantasy-inducing auditorium at the Tampa Theatre. Burgert Brothers Photographic Archives, Tampa-Hillsborough County Public Library System, Tampa, Florida.

While the universe beyond the doors of the Tampa Theatre has changed quite a bit over the years, this place not only continues to function in much the same way as it did in the 1920s, it also looks pretty much the same as it always has. That in itself seems like magic, and in a way it is. The theater appears to have escaped the effects of time by way of an illusion called preservation. It is an effect as remarkable and pleasurable as the flickering electric stars on the ceiling. As a result of the imaginative wizardry of preservationists, the Tampa Theatre and other movie palaces around the country continue to capture our imaginations. If not for their efforts, this book would be about the death of the movie palace—an opulent kind of movie theater lost to us forever. Fortunately, that is not the case, for this book is about its evolution and the many ways movie palaces remain vital and extraordinary places.

Recently I spoke to a women's group whose members ranged in age from fifty to ninety or so. It was a successful presentation, as far as those kinds of talks go, because they did most of the talking. Nearly every one of them had a story to tell about going to the movie palace in the town or city where they were raised. Late for another meeting, I tried to make my way to my car after the presentation, only to have four or five women follow me out the door—still telling me stories. It was clear that their memories of going to the movie palace were important, for many of their childhood and young adult social interactions took place there. They knew my research subject in a way that I never will know it because by the time I was going to movies in the 1960s and 1970s, movie theaters were plain and sterile—the only fantasies were projected on the screen.

I was not surprised by their passionate response to my presentation. I had quickly learned as I began my research that old movie theaters produce powerful feelings of nostalgia. Few old downtown buildings create a similar reaction, and so it is no surprise that an assortment of coffee-table books on the market lament the demise of the theaters and the era that produced them. The famous photograph of Gloria Swanson dressed in a long black gown, holding her black-gloved arms to the sky as she stands amid the rubble of the razed Roxy Theatre seems a campy lament to the death of both the movie palace dream and downtown civility. It is a powerful image, to be sure, but like the books that mourn the end of the picture palace era, the photograph suggests there is no more story to be told.

What Gloria Swanson could never have imagined as she stood amid the Roxy ruins in 1960 is that, a little more than a decade later, individuals motivated in part by their memories would begin figuring out how to save the movie palaces that still stood in the cities where they lived. Some of the theaters remained open, showing pornographic movies to a few people who were not afraid to go downtown; some of them had been closed for years, their owners waiting for the highest bidder to come and take the white elephants off their hands. The theaters were a casualty of the deterioration of the downtown districts in the 1950s and 1960s, caused in part by suburban development, misguided urban renewal, and bitter racial conflicts. City centers were often left for dead by the beginning of the 1970s. But, with the growing popularity of historic preservation during the mid-1970s in the United States, some of the remaining movie palaces began to cause a bit of a stir. A few innovative people began to wonder if it would be possible to rehabilitate the old theaters. Would it be possible, they wondered, to bring them back to life? Could their resuscitation bring people back downtown? Trying to find answers to these questions ultimately led to the rebirth of the downtown movie palaces in some cities.

The story that mourns their demise still exists of course, but there are new chapters to add to the chronicle—stories of near extinction and subsequent rescue by people who refused to believe that life would be better without the big old theaters. It is their near death and renaissance that are of particular interest to me, and it is the second life of the movie palace that is the focus of this book.

I have been studying downtown movie palaces since 1995. My interest in the subject began when I was a doctoral student at the University of South Florida in Tampa. Desiring to discover the interesting niches of the city where I had recently moved, I stumbled upon a newspaper advertisement for a behind-the-scenes tour of the Tampa Theatre. I had been there once or twice already, as it was the only theater in Tampa that exhibited foreign and alternative movies, and I found the building both quirky and exotic. During an afternoon tour, Tara Schroeder, our tour guide, told me and a handful of tourists how the theater had once been the center of community life in Tampa. She explained that the theater fell into disrepair during the 1960s and that the City of Tampa bought the theater for one dollar in the 1970s. Taking us to the balcony, she showed us some of the more recent preservation efforts and made a somewhat low-pressure pitch for us to donate to the preservation fund. Throughout the tour, I felt an underlying and somewhat indescribable sense of loss. Preservation, it seemed to me, was a peculiar form of mourning.

By the time the tour was finished, I was hooked, and soon after, the early history and the subsequent preservation of the Tampa Theatre became the subject of my doctoral dissertation. I discovered that the restoration of the theater was a way to reconstruct the past so that future generations could feel nostalgic for a time that they never experienced. Preservationists, I soon learned, were jugglers of time. Because they wanted future generations to experience a lost era, they attempted to drag the theater back in time while simultaneously constructing bulwarks so that the present could not sneak back into the theater. I was also intrigued by the idea that preservation was more than a matter of paint and plaster repair. As my research continued, I discovered that the theater had a rich and at times troubling social history, yet only its most charming history was preserved. I became interested in better understanding the choices that theater preservationists made when they selected past themes and stories to highlight to the public. From this investigation I began to question the ways in which contemporary culture both disregards and holds on to the past.

As I studied the social history of the Tampa Theatre, it did not take me long to discover that the theater's successes and failures were closely connected to the fortunes of downtown Tampa. By tracing the history of the Tampa Theatre, I uncovered many economic, political, and cultural conditions of downtown Tampa throughout much of the twentieth century. As I interviewed former patrons and employees, preservationists, and city politicians about the theater's decline and rebirth, I realized that in many ways the theater was a microcosm of downtown Tampa. The struggles that downtown Tampa faced during the second half of the twentieth century—racial integration, urban renewal, and downtown revitalization—were the same ones that the theater had confronted. Tampa's premier picture palace was designed to elicit passionate feelings in its city's residents when it was opened in 1926, and the old theater had continued to evoke emotional responses during the rest of the century. Those reactions helped me to shed light on much larger cultural and political issues, and I felt that the ways in which the Tampa Theatre fell into disrepair and then was saved exemplified many of the complexities of contemporary urban life.

I knew that the preservation of the Tampa Theatre was not unique. During my research I discovered many other cities with preserved downtown picture palaces, and I was curious about the motives behind their rescue and preservation. I was aware that many other southern cities had followed the same development patterns as Tampa. Generally understood to be suburban, southern cities did not experience high-density development during the Industrial Revolution, as did those in the North. However, they did have downtown regions that reached their developmental zenith during the 1920s and began their decline as early as the mid-1950s. Southern urban regions flourished in the mid-twentieth century with the onset of widespread automobile ownership and ambitious highway construction. As a result, today's southern cities are largely car centered, which casts a shadow of doubt upon the idea of revitalizing a "city center." They are also spread over large geographical areas, and their populations are less concentrated than those of northern cities. Despite massive central-city annexations, many southern cities have experienced their most rapid growth in their suburbs, especially during the last few decades. Presently, many cities in the South are struggling to lure residents (and their money) away from the suburbs and back to old city centers by revitalizing downtown districts.

Had theater preservationists in other southern cities imagined that the preservation of a movie palace could jump-start their downtown revitalization? How did they remember and imagine both the pasts of their theaters and their city centers? As the American South is most often identified with segregation and racist practices toward African Americans, it is a region that carries a heavy burden of painful history. I knew that theater segregation had been a standard practice in cities across the South, and I wondered if other picture palace preservationists had chosen to include this fact in their stories about the theaters' pasts. What, I wondered, were the stakes of remembering and then including the story of movie palace segregation in cities where racial conflicts had been even more dramatic than they had been in Tampa? It seemed to me that if I would extend my analysis to other southern movie palaces, I would have a unique venue for interpreting the ways in which modern-day people in the South imagine and then go about reconstructing significant elements of the past.

It was not long before I began calling movie palace directors in cities across the southeastern part of the United States. Some did not return my phone calls. Others seemed uninterested in answering my first few provisional questions. But others answered my questions both articulately and passionately. Of those, a few would have kept talking for several hours if I had not stopped them. From the pool of passionate directors who were willing to let me come to their theaters and do extensive interviews and study their archives, I chose six movie palaces in six different states. I selected the Fox Theatre in Atlanta because it is one of the largest and most well known preserved picture palaces in the country. I chose the Saenger Theatre in Biloxi, Mississippi, because it is rather small and has not yet been completely restored. I was interested in the Orpheum Theatre in Memphis and the Alabama Theatre in Birmingham because of their reputations as particularly well run and nicely restored theaters. But I also wanted to learn more about them because they were situated in cities that had been hotbeds of racial conflict during the Civil Rights movement. I chose the Carolina Theatre in Durham because I was curious about how preservationists had conceived of the building's renovation, as I knew that an entirely new building had been added to the old one during its restoration. And of course the Tampa Theatre was selected because it had already chosen me a long time ago.

Over the course of a year and a half, I traveled twice to Atlanta, Biloxi, Durham, and Memphis and once to Birmingham. In each city, I interviewed theater administrators, employees, and volunteers. I spoke extensively with preservationists, craftsmen, theater patrons, city planners, arts council members, city officials, and downtown merchants. I combed theater archives and worked in each city's public library to find information about the theater from the time that it was built to the present day. I researched each city's urban renewal programs, its later attempts at downtown revitalization, and its history of racial segregation, racial conflicts, and ultimate integration. I attended movies and live productions at the theaters and spent time simply hanging around them. I tried to understand the present rhythm of each downtown by meandering through the streets, browsing in shops, eating in restaurants, talking casually with clerks and pedestrians, and always staying in downtown hotels. I also traveled to New York City and interviewed Jeff Greene, who is widely regarded as one of the country's leading restoration experts. At the Tampa Theatre, I continued to conduct interviews with preservationists, and I also remained, of course, a faithful film watcher.

While this book chronicles the twentieth-century practice of movie exhibition, downtown development, and racial conflict in the South, at its center is an analysis of historic preservation. Most of us have enjoyed touring a historically preserved building in our own cities or while we are on vacation. A great deal can be learned about the history of a house or public building on such a tour, but it is rare to learn about the decisions and practices that led to its preservation. As with other forms of leisure, such as going to a play or attending a theme park, many logistics and behind-the-scenes activities remain hidden when one visits a historically preserved building that is open to the public. I am not suggesting that preservation is some sort of conspiracy; rather, I am proposing that preservation is a kind of magic. As with a play, we know that what appears before us is not real, but we suspend our disbelief for a few hours in order to enjoy what has been created for us. By pulling open the back-stage curtain of preservation, I do not intend to ruin the pleasurable illusion of preservation; I only hope for readers to have a clearer understanding of the cultural implications of what it means to preserve the past.

In recent years some interesting cultural criticism has been published about historic districts in the United States. The critiques tend to dismiss preservation as a commodity that strips away any "real" sense of the past.[1] While elements of such criticism have helped me form my own analysis, such critiques are inadequate because historic buildings and districts are read and analyzed as finished projects or as if they were texts. The problem with such an approach is that preservation is, as I have said, an illusion, and by merely observing the surfaces, we cannot understand how and why the illusion is created and how it is sustained. To provide more than a surface interpretation, this book details and interprets theater archival materials, hours of conversations with preservationists, and the twentieth-century history of the downtown districts where the theaters are located. This broader scope leads us to a better understanding of the various political, cultural, and aesthetic struggles that preservationists face and what happens to the past when it is redesigned for use in the present. By interpreting the multiple meanings of preservation and the various roles that it plays in our culture, this book helps us to have a more detailed understanding of what the past means to contemporary people and how they use it to make sense of the present and to envision the future.

I begin by characterizing the conditions of the movie palaces and downtown districts from the 1920s through the 1960s. Chronicling the 1920s success story of the picture palace, I focus on the ways in which the theaters helped to manage patrons' public behavior and helped to foster class and racial distinctions—even though theater owners and architects proclaimed that the movie palaces were a new kind of urban democratic space. Turning to the decline of the theaters, I account for the various reasons that their national reign over movie exhibition and the city was so short-lived. Because the movie palace's success or failure (in both its first and second life) is closely related to the vitality of the city center where it is located, I also explain the reasons why downtown districts across the country deteriorated in the 1950s and 1960s.

The material conditions, social climates, and desegregation efforts in the downtown districts of Birmingham, Durham, Atlanta, Memphis, Biloxi, and Tampa go hand in hand with the circumstances of ruin and restoration for each of these six theaters. In order to better understand the complicated logistics facing preservationists at each theater, I use the second chapter to provide a brief synopsis of how each of these theaters was poised at the brink of destruction in light of the broader urban historical and cultural context surrounding it. In the following chapters, I describe how each one was ultimately saved from the wrecking ball.

Focusing on the Tampa Theatre, the Fox Theatre, the Carolina Theatre, and the Alabama Theater, I chronicle the methods of persuasion and preservation that people employed to save these theaters from destruction. The rhetoric used to gain public support for saving the movie palaces was sometimes couched in a collective nostalgic vision that prodded city residents and officials not only to put up a fight, but also to link the movie palace to a broader belief that the restoration of the movie theater was tied to economically jump-starting failing downtown areas. At the same time, preservationists also argued that saving a picture palace could help to protect the city's architectural heritage and the legacy of cinema in the city. And while preservationists make strong cases for the public good, I found that their intentions for saving movie palaces were also fueled by personal motives and desires that would ultimately find shape in a public arena.

Once a building is saved from destruction, the hard work begins, because then preservationists must attempt to restore the theater's material past. Detailing and interpreting their practices and philosophies, I concentrate on how preservationists understand and use the past for present-day purposes. I reveal the efforts and concerns of the Fox Theatre preservationists who struggle to conserve the original "authentic" atmosphere of the picture palace. Turning to the Tampa Theatre, I provide an analysis of the ways in which preservationists re-create an illusion of the past and the methods and tactics that they use in order to create an illusion of authenticity. The Alabama Theatre's restoration provides a view of preservation as a convincing replication of the past that also accommodates contemporary aesthetic sensibilities. The plans for restoration of the Saenger Theatre enable us to understand the priorities and frustrations that theater directors face as they begin imagining a major restoration, particularly when financial support for the project is limited.

Preservation means more than restoring and re-creating the material past. Paint and plaster are an integral part of resuscitating an old movie theater, but the material past is intertwined with what I call "discursive preservation." The Carolina Theatre and the Orpheum Theatre offer an interesting set of contrasts and lessons for understanding how particular communities and institutions deal with issues of remembering and forgetting the events of the past. I suggest that peculiar struggles and potential benefits are at stake for cities, theaters, and residents when the guardians of preserved movie palaces acknowledge the various economic and cultural transitions that have taken place in their respective cities and theaters during the past seventy-five years.

Despite the gargantuan efforts of preservationists, curators, and the many volunteers who keep the doors open at each of these theaters, all of these movie palaces tell a larger story of southern cities that remain in the midst of transformation. Regardless of whether a theater has been designated to a national historic registry or whether millions of dollars have been spent replicating a color scheme from the 1920s, each preserved theater has something to tell us about the present. Aspiring to remain relevant to the people, the cities, and the communities where they stand, each of these theaters faces a new century in which entertainment and information have proliferated beyond the bounds of what theater designers and planners could have imagined when they were building them. Today, we find each of these theaters attempting to contribute to the goal of a vibrant downtown. But can the busy and bustling downtown of the 1920s (or our fantasy of that era) ever really be reclaimed? In different ways, each of these theaters—in their successes and failures, in their struggles and their particular fates—suggests an answer to that question. Each theater offers us a lesson about what happens when the art of preservation, the architecture of entertainment, and the hope for a cohesive public life are intertwined.

The National Trust for Historic Preservation listed "Historic American Movie Theaters, Nationwide" as the most endangered historic place for the year 2001. While this book details some theater preservation success stories, old movie theaters across the country continue to be threatened by the wrecking ball. Saving and then restoring a theater is both costly and difficult to do, but for reasons both rational and emotional, people around the United States continue to fight to keep the old movie palaces around. With that tenacious spirit in mind, let's go downtown.

Chapter 1

From Glory to Ruins: The Early Years of the Movie Palace

I doubt that there will be anything as opulent or glamorous in movie theater architecture and presentation as the urban picture palace that dominated motion picture exhibition from the late 1910s until the stock market crash in 1929 and the subsequent Depression. The financial and artistic success of D. W. Griffith's *The Birth of a Nation* in 1915 forever changed cinematic viewing, resulting in higher ticket prices, reserved seating, scheduled film showings, and longer runs. Consequently, the popularity of feature-length films and the space and respectability of movie houses began to change. Only centrally located picture theaters could accommodate and afford to show multi-reel films. At first, feature-length film exhibitors colonized old vaudeville houses, but by the end of 1915, theater owners were building new, more luxurious theaters in order to attract the fledgling middle-class audiences that were beginning to regard moviegoing as a socially acceptable activity.

The highly profitable movie palaces provided the bulk of the movie industry's revenue and were the most profitable enterprises in the film industry during the period. Between 1914 and 1922, 4,000 new theaters (of various architectural styles) opened in the United States. By 1926 an average of 50 percent of America's film audiences attended the 2,000 movie palaces in seventy-nine cities.[1] The birth and subsequent popularity of the movie palace coincided with the consumer revolution and the meteoric growth in industry, urban population, and transportation in the United States. Public transportation lines such as the trolley and the streetcar and promotional advertising helped to establish the popularity of downtown shopping districts where fashionable department stores and chain stores that stocked standardized goods flourished. The post-war economic boom and the growth of American cities, as architectural historian Maggie Valentine explains, created a tremendous market for entertainment: "America had emerged as a world power politically and *the* world power in terms of film production. Every major city soon boasted a place worthy of the nation's and the movies' new prominence."[2]

While the movie palaces often represented profit to their owners, they symbolized much more than earnings to city officials and city dwellers. The fantasies that the films promised paled in comparison to the dreams and potential offered by the theaters themselves. The construction and opening of a picture palace, often the most expensive and opulent structure in a city center, marked the moment when a city and its inhabitants had "arrived." As cities began to grow in population and flourish economically, more and more white Americans found themselves living within and aspiring to middle-class standards. Movie palace investors had enough confidence in their city's economy and the disposable income of the new middle class to believe that their city could support a deluxe movie theater with thousands of seats. Representing the pinnacle of urban development during the boom years of the 1920s, the movie palace was a symbol, particularly for a small city in the South, of a sense of confidence, cosmopolitanism, and sophistication.

The Alabama Theatre souvenir program distributed to patrons on the theater's opening night on December 26, 1927, for example, proclaimed that the arrival of the theater to Birmingham was emblematic of the city's significance to Alabama. "Like Birmingham itself," the pamphlet exulted, "the Alabama Theatre is destined to occupy a place of conspicuous importance to the development of Alabama. The spirit of its conception and its influence will be an inspiration to thousands."[3] In almost identical language, the Tampa Theatre's souvenir program given to patrons on its opening night on October 15, 1926, proclaimed the theater's significance to Florida. "Like Tampa itself, the Tampa Theatre is destined to occupy a place of conspicuous importance in the development of Florida," the opening program predicted. "The need is here. The people are here."[4] Obviously the theaters represented more than sites

2. A nearly completed Tampa Theatre in 1926. Notice that the all-important marquee had not yet been placed on the theater. Burgert Brothers Photographic Archives, Tampa-Hillsborough County Public Library System, Tampa, Florida.

3. This 1920s image of the Carolina Theatre illustrates the dramatic visibility of the picture palace marquee. Durham Photographic Archives, Durham County Library, Durham, North Carolina.

CAROLINA
CAROLINA
SODA
SHOP
CAROLINA
NOW SHOWING
THE CUCKOOS
CAROLINA

for movie exhibition; from their inception the movie palaces helped create an identity of glamour, success, and fantasy for the cities where they were situated. Naturally, that identity extended to the people who attended or were employed by the theaters.

Located in prime downtown locations, the theaters were generally situated next to a trolley or streetcar stop and were close to restaurants and department stores, enabling residents to spend their leisure hours and their disposable income in a high-traffic, commercial area of the city. The theaters' ornate box offices, surrounded by a sea of terrazzo, extended out onto the sidewalk, while bas-relief and stone figures marked the period-revival exteriors. Often movie palaces were named after the city or state of their locations and were christened with attention-getting phrases that suggested their regional prominence. The Saenger Theatre, for example, was dubbed the "The Gem of the Gulf Coast." Enormous signs illuminated by hundreds of lights and neon letters that spelled out the name of the picture palaces implied that these were their cities' flagship theaters. Double-faced, twenty-eight feet high and six feet wide, the Saenger Theatre sign incorporated various colored and flashing lights. The *Daily Herald* boasted that the sign gave "Biloxi and this particular corner a very metropolitan appearance."[5] The extravagantly decorated and highly eclectic historic modes of the theaters' exteriors distinguished them from nearby buildings, explains Charlotte Herzog, while also giving them a stamp of legitimacy.[6] The scale of the theaters was compatible with the surrounding banks and office buildings, but the huge neon signs formidably marked the theaters. Valentine suggests that theaters "exploited the psychology of design as a marketing tool."[7]

While the movie palaces' exteriors were an elaborate mix of popular and historic architectural designs, the real razzle-dazzle was reserved for the interiors. The reason for the elaborate and innovative designs was that from the beginning, the movie palaces, not the films exhibited, were the main attraction. As the renowned movie palace owner Marcus Loew, whose theaters eventually covered half of the country, explained, "We sell tickets to theaters, not movies."[8] The theaters were designed to be so flamboyant that patrons would buy movie tickets just so they could revel in the atmosphere of the palaces. Samuel "Roxy" Rothapfel, the well-known manager of several New York movie palaces, believed that people were searching for the exotic, and he played on their curiosity and desire by intentionally dramatizing opulent interior spaces.

Fashionable box office ticket takers, uniformed ushers, and doormen welcomed patrons as they entered the theaters' lobbies. The imposing and expansive interiors often included velvet curtains, balconies, mezzanines, crystal chandeliers, fountains, classical statues and artwork, dramatic lighting, handsome furnishings, full orchestras, completely outfitted organs, and seating for approximately 1,500 to 6,000 spectators. The Alabama Theatre proclaimed itself "the Showplace of the South" and featured an anteroom with a two-story hall of mirrors, accented by two eight-foot candelabra and a star-shaped chandelier. A huge multicolored chandelier in the lobby hung from the gilded coffered ceiling. Moorish arches framed the room while exotic columns, multicolored glass sconces with sunburst reflectors, and large velvet chairs provided eclectic accents. On the second floor, in Peacock Hall, a refined space outside the auditorium, patrons found original works of art and furnishings purchased from a Spanish castle. Enormous paintings in ornate gold frames and classical marble busts were displayed throughout the hallways, lounges, and alcoves. The gold-domed auditorium featured a giant proscenium arch with a floral design of leaves and vines and 2,500 red velvet seats.

Distinctions at the Movie Palace

Such fantastic design was not unique to the Alabama Theatre. Each movie palace strove to create a wildly flamboyant and eclectic public space that in no way mimicked the traditional European styles of architecture that residents were more accustomed to seeing in their cities. David Nasaw contends that the owners, architects, and builders deliberately set out to create a new type of public space: "The heterogeneous crowd assembled in the movie palaces required its own fantastic environments, its own stylized amusement spaces. Nothing that smacked of the class-bound, ethnically divided, gender stratified everyday world would do."[9] In fact, the audiences of the new movie palaces were an amalgam of the working class, the middle class, unaccompanied women who worked at or frequented the downtown retail shops and department stores, tourists, traveling businessmen, and patrons of the legitimate theater. Picture palace developers created a public space that for the first time dramatically mixed various classes of picture show fans. This was no doubt motivated by the desire for high profits; however, many of them proclaimed that they had created a democratic space of leisure. John Eberson, for example, a prolific movie palace architect and designer of the Tampa Theatre, exclaimed, "Here we find ourselves today creating and building supercinemas of enormous capacities excelling in splendor, in luxury, and in furnishings of the most palatial homes of princes and crowned kings for and on behalf of His Excellency—the American Citizen."[10] Movie palace owners Balaban and Katz proclaimed that their palaces were built for "all of the people all of the time," rather than the few who wanted to appear more aristocratic than the rest.[11]

This democratic philosophy may have brought more ticket sales, but it was not entirely anti-elitist. Design elements and structures built into the palaces were intended to enforce acceptable public behavior. Obviously the theater owners wanted customers to aspire to the behavior of the highest common denominator because they could not afford to offend and then lose the patronage of the middle class and the elite. The picture palace, promoted by architect George Rapp as a shrine to democracy, brought together design elements that signaled to many of the theaters' patrons that they had entered a refined public space, and generally they behaved accordingly. In his unpublished autobiography, Richard M. Kennedy, an influential theater owner and manager in the South, suggested that the Alabama Theatre had a humbling effect on its patrons:

> There were about a quarter of a million dollars of objects of art and chandeliers in this fine new theatre, and it was indeed a thing of beauty. One of its problems, however, was the fact that the public was not as sophisticated then, as it is now, and the few people who attended the great shows at the Alabama, were dwarfed by its magnificence, and as they did in libraries, they spoke in hushed voices within its ornate walls. A theatre should be cleaner and more attractive than the homes of its patrons, but this one was just overwhelming and caused the average layman to be embarrassed and awed by it. Sidney Dannenburg asked me, before he threw in the sponge and returned to Toledo, what was the matter with his theatre. He laughed and thought it was funny when I told him that he should cover his marble floors with sawdust and take down some of those expensive and beautiful oil paintings, but I knew the Birmingham public better than he did and my recommendations were more worthy than they seemed to him.[12]

4. Opulent and dramatic interiors such as this one at the Alabama Theatre both awed and intimidated early picture palace patrons. Copyright 1994, M. Lewis Kennedy, Kennedy Studios, Birmingham, Alabama.

Patrons managed their own behavior because of the dignified settings that were similar in ambience to the grand stage theaters and other elite gathering places. The atmosphere of high culture indicated to movie patrons that they should replicate the standards and codes of civility associated with stage theater that had been established in the middle of the nineteenth century. When live theater began catering to various social classes, the theater became a place for training the new audiences how to behave in public, as the private manners of the genteel parlor overtook the public behavior of the theatergoers. Individuals were taught to keep their private bodily matters to themselves, Lawrence Levine explains, and to remain as inconspicuous as possible within the public realm of the theater, as well as on the street.[13] While the theater entertained and tutored its new audiences, the notion that stage entertainment was something for the wealthy never really diminished. Movie palaces' designs served as markers of social status to the growing middle-class populations. Theater owners, Douglas Gomery contends, were able to fashion patrons of their choice, rather than the other way around, helping to reposition the consumer culture in the United States.[14]

In the years before the movie palace became prominent, moviegoing was primarily a working-class activity. Nickelodeons, located on side streets where rent was cheap, were accessible to overworked and underpaid workers and their families. The five-cent movie house was not only inexpensive entertainment, it also showed short movies continuously so that it accommodated tight schedules and budgets. As a result, the nickelodeon became a central working-class institution, Roy Rosenzweig explains, much like the saloon, the church, and the fraternal lodge.[15] The first picture show in Biloxi, for instance, was a vacated storeroom. Sitting at a piano, a man sang, played, and interpreted the pictures as they were exhibited. Reading the movie's advance literature and interpreting the captions that appeared on the screen, he explained the story of the movie as it was shown to the audience.[16] The conditions of the inexpensive movie house frequently paralleled the realities of working-class life. Floors were dirty, the air was stagnant, and rats were almost as plentiful as spectators. "Spartan, and even unsanitary, conditions made little impression on working class movie goers; such surroundings were part of their daily lives," Rosenzweig writes, "but middle class commentators reacted with horror."[17] Part of their shocked reaction was caused by the presence of a large group of working-class people who looked different and smelled different from themselves.

In order to attract middle-class patrons, then, movie palace owners and managers consciously differentiated their theaters from working-class venues by eliminating working-class signifiers, foregrounding symbols of the elite, and enforcing appropriate middle-class behavior—all while simultaneously expounding upon their theaters' democratic aims. Since working-class theaters were characterized by foul-smelling and unhealthful conditions, movie palaces distinguished themselves from such venues by installing air-conditioning systems. Such systems were advertised as solutions that provided odorless, sanitary conditions. The Tampa Theatre's opening night program, for example, dedicated a half-page description to its "Air Cooling and Dehumidifying System." The description boasted that the system "not only keeps new and fresh air in constant circulation but removes all foul air and odors instantly." While the air-conditioning system did cool the air in a city characterized by semitropical heat and humidity, it also helped to eliminate any traces of working-class odor, circulating only the apparently less offensive smells of the middle class.

Military-like uniformed ushers and attendants, who were usually handsome, well-schooled young men, helped to monitor the behavior of the audience, furnished a feeling of security for audiences, and provided a way to control the movement of thousands of people a day. In the early years of the picture palace, patrons did not necessarily enter the auditorium before the beginning of a movie. At times they were seated in the middle of the film; they watched the second half and then stayed and watched the first half of the movie before leaving. This created a need for ushers to guide hundreds of people to their seats in the dark twilight of the auditorium, while a film was running. The military-style performance of the ushers was necessary to maintain physical and moral order in the large auditoriums. Their performances, which included a changing of the guard when it was time to change shifts, suggested to audiences that the ushers were both dignified and prepared for any contingency that might occur. The authority of an usher was rarely challenged, for he was "the king of the aisles, the cop on the beat, and the monitor of our morals while in the balcony," quipped one longtime patron of a movie palace.

The ushers were not the only service providers to theater patrons.

5. Extravagant tapestries, lighting, furnishings, and artwork, such as these in the mezzanine at the Tampa Theatre, provided lessons in high culture to early-twentieth-century patrons. Burgert Brothers Photographic Archives, Tampa-Hillsborough County Public Library System, Tampa, Florida.

Doormen, maids, and porters were also of prominent importance to the atmosphere of the theaters. While the ushers and doormen were white, attractive men, theater managers hired African American women and men to fill the positions of maids and porters. While the white attendants were dressed in military costumes, the African Americans dressed in servant clothing. Such distinctions mirrored the roles that service employees performed in wealthy private homes and exclusive public spaces enjoyed by the country's elite families. The public space of the movie palace was the only place where obedient and respectful theater employees served predominantly middle-class patrons for the cost of a movie ticket. This enabled patrons to see themselves as part of the leisure class for a few hours, like the Hollywood stars that they saw on the screen.

The tapestries, statues, and oil paintings that decorated theaters helped foster an atmosphere of high culture. While the movie palaces provided popular, middle-brow film entertainment, the surroundings within the theaters suggested not only that theater patrons should behave in a manner appropriate for the stage theater, but also that they should become familiar with the language and artifacts of high culture if they were not already. Theater programs generally instructed patrons about the art objects and reproductions of classic art found within the theaters. At the Tampa Theatre, for instance, many of the program's pages were dedicated to explaining the reproductions of classic statues. Such tutelage suggests that the "democratic" public space of the picture palaces not only made social distinctions but also was intended to attract an audience who desired such distinctions.

A 1929 article in Biloxi's *Daily Herald* suggested that Biloxi's new Saenger Theatre was created for its citizens who were already well schooled in the habits of the elite. The article describes the Saenger's opening night as if it were a private party for the city's nobility rather than the opening of a public movie theater. "The foyer, with its quantity of flowers and formal furniture, might have been the salon of some hostess," the article boasted. "Mrs. H. S. Orr, wife of the manager, was lovely in a pale green beaded chiffon evening frock, and greeted many friends from all the Coast who, in honor of this auspicious occasion, were gowned in beautiful evening frocks, and men were in formal evening attire."[18]

The most troubling construction of distinction within the public space of the movie palaces was the exclusion or segregation of African

6. Biloxi's Saenger Theatre as it looked when it opened its doors to patrons in 1929. Biloxi Public Library, Biloxi, Mississippi.

7. This 1939 photo taken in Mississippi is a stark reminder of the overt racism that existed at theaters during the first half of the twentieth century. Photo by Marion Post Wolcott. Library of Congress, Prints and Photographs Division.

American patrons. In fact, the theaters' maids and porters were the only African Americans who were allowed access to all or most of the space within the theaters. A 1937 article in the *Memphis World,* for example, boasted in its headline that "colored" patrons were welcomed under the new management at the Orpheum Theatre. The only theater in Memphis with a "colored" balcony, the article explains that every reader of the *Memphis World* could now make the Orpheum Theatre a weekly habit.[19] But African Americans who wished to attend an Orpheum production were expected to use a separate entrance and staircase to find their seats in the uppermost balcony of the theater. The 600-seat section was known as the "peanut gallery." Similarly, a 1926 *Durham Morning Herald* article describing Durham's new city auditorium (later renamed the Carolina Theatre) appeased its white readership by explaining that "a person on the first balcony cannot go to the second balcony without first coming to the orchestra floor and taking a different flight of stairs."[20] Such a spatial configuration assured white patrons that they would not encounter African Americans while at the movie palace. Even in 1927, when the North Carolina College for Negroes brought black contralto Marian Anderson to Durham's city auditorium, the lower floor of the auditorium was reserved for the white audience.[21]

Nasaw contends that the exclusion or segregation of blacks was a result of "the black image in the white mind." In the mid-1910s, popular songs and films shifted from depicting African Americans as happy-go-lucky to portraying them as menacing people to be feared. In fact, *The Birth of a Nation,* the film that had revolutionized the culture of movies, had also helped to create a dangerous image of African Americans. Part of the allure of the movie palace was that there was no reserved seating or elite boxes for wealthier customers. In addition, it was understood that the palaces were safe places for unescorted white women and children. Because palace managers assumed that their white audiences feared African Americans, and because they wanted to maintain an environment that would continue to attract white middle-class patrons, blacks were either excluded altogether or guided to their seats in the uppermost balconies through a separate entrance. "It was imperative that palace managers guard their white patrons against a possible insult or injury from black customers," Nasaw writes, "who, no matter how refined they might appear to be, it was now assumed, were genetically prone to violence and incapable of restraint."[22]

The segregation or exclusion of African Americans ensured white middle-class patrons that they were in a palace of "discriminating" standards. Besides protecting white patrons from black patrons, the segregation within the palaces helped to perpetuate the idea of a democratic public space that nevertheless felt aristocratic because it made a distinction between black and white. Many African Americans did not accept the segregation policies of the movie palaces. In most cities, African Americans built and operated their own movie theaters. However, these theaters were generally small neighborhood movie houses that in no way rivaled the picture palace. African Americans were not allowed free access to the theaters, particularly in the South, until segregation policies were ruled unconstitutional as a result of the Civil Rights Act. In some cases, however, movie palace owners dismantled the segregation policies before it became legally imperative to do so, because they were motivated by a desire to increase profits, because civil rights demonstrators helped to persuade theater owners to desegregate, or because the theaters were in more progressive cities where integration was not considered such a threat.

The Decline of the Movie Palace

Movie palaces around the country prospered throughout the 1920s, but the stock market crash in 1929, followed by the Depression, caused many theaters to close, with others barely surviving. Some theaters, like the Tampa Theatre and the Alabama Theatre, which opened in 1926 and 1927 respectively, were able to enjoy a few years of prosperity before the stock market crash; others were not so fortunate. The Fox Theatre opened on Christmas Day 1929, just a few months after the crash. By 1932 the Fox Theatre Corporation had declared bankruptcy, and the theater was temporarily closed. Although it reopened a few months later, by the end of the year, the control of the Fox went to the City of Atlanta for nonpayment of taxes.

The motion picture industry, as well as the theaters, was hit hard by the economic downturn of the 1930s. The average weekly attendance fell from 90 million in 1930 to 60 million in 1932.[23] Some 8,000 theaters closed during the same period, leaving only 14,000 theaters open. Movie palace managers attempted to keep their theaters running by introducing such promotional efforts as the double feature, Bank Night, Bingo, and Dish Night. Such promotions as Bank Night encouraged

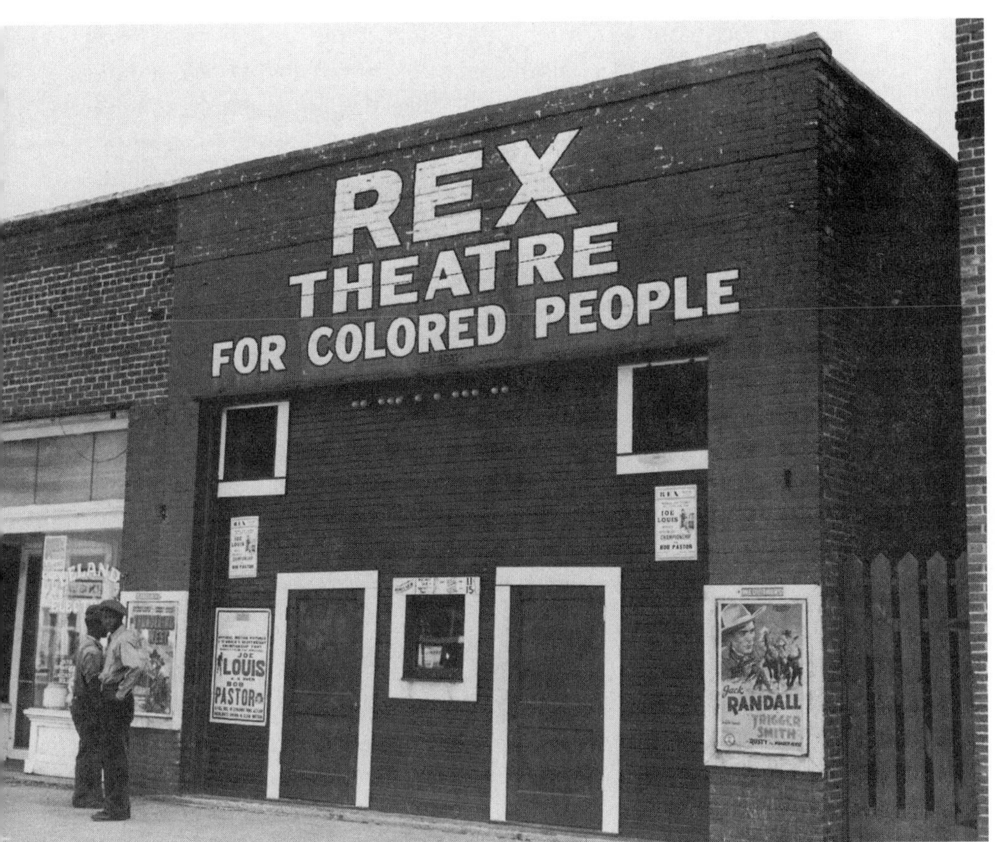

8. Rather than suffering the indignities of sitting in the upper balconies of segregated theaters, many African Americans opened their own theaters, such as the Rex, located in Mississippi. Library of Congress, Prints and Photographs Division.

movie palace patrons to continue to associate the theaters with luxury, status, and excitement, and it offered them the possibility of temporarily rising above their economic situation by winning cash, groceries, or merchandise. A longtime Tampa resident, for instance, recalled that when she won ten dollars on Bank Night at the Tampa Theatre in the summer of 1937, she spent the entire sum on a new dress, a handbag, a pair of shoes, some cosmetics, and a trip to the beauty shop. "Instead of doing the courteous thing, and inviting my date to share refreshments 'on me' after the show," she explained, "I was too exhilarated with my new riches to be that thoughtful and considerate."[24]

Theater owners also began cutting costs by eliminating the personal attention of the doormen and the brigade of ushers. Patrons began seating themselves, and much of the formal atmosphere of the movie palaces dissipated. "From this era on," Gomery contends, "what joy and pleasure the theatrical movie- viewing experience offered were more and more restricted to the screen itself. Talking to your companions suddenly became acceptable, and no one thought it offensive to get up during the middle of the show to get some popcorn."[25]

After the Depression, when construction of movie theaters started again, a new kind of theater, much different from the picture palace, appeared. Moviegoing by the mid-1930s had become a socially acceptable form of leisure, and movie theaters no longer relied on a dubious rhetoric of civility and democracy that the movie palace promoters had touted in the 1920s. After the Depression, picture palace architecture went out of vogue; new movie theaters were based on efficiency and scientific innovation and employed a pragmatic style rather than the ornamental and ostentatious designs of the movie palace. The new, smaller theaters' orientation toward function rather than fantasy was more affordable for theater owners to build; thus, they could erect more theaters and place them near housing developments. The neighborhood houses, both independent and chain operated, helped to shift the attendance habits of movie patrons. Movie customers now had a choice between going downtown to the movies or staying closer to home.

Although movie palaces continued to operate, their reign was already over—only a decade or so after they had captured the imagination of American audiences. Downtown movie palaces did experience a renaissance during World War II as a result of war bond drives and the exhibition of newsreels, but the revival lasted only as long as the war. To promote attendance, to help the war effort, and to collect much-needed metal, the Carolina Theatre, for example, would at various times charge an admission price of ten tin cans per person. War bonds sold at the theater also helped maintain business and profits. But after the war the attendance at the Carolina Theatre, as at other big theaters around the country, declined. In 1948 a new air-conditioning system was installed at the Carolina Theatre in the hope that it would draw more people to the theater; however, there were far too many other economic and cultural factors affecting the declining popularity of the Carolina Theatre for the air-conditioning system to make a drastic difference in ticket sales.

Movie palace status and profitability continued to erode as postwar affluence during the 1950s changed the way Americans lived. Neighborhood theaters contributed to the eclipse of the movie palace, but the widespread growth of television, drive-in theaters, and suburban development also helped to put an end to their popularity. In addition, the subsequent decline of downtown districts, ill-conceived urban renewal, and racial desegregation created an inhospitable environment in and around the remaining movie palaces for white middle-class patrons. The popularity of television, which blossomed during the 1950s, radically shifted spectatorship in America. In 1946 only 8,000 households had television sets. Thirteen years later, in 1959, Americans owned 44 million televisions.[26] Similarly, in 1945 there were nine television stations operating in the United States. By 1952, 2,000 stations were broadcasting to homes across the country.[27] Advertisements during the 1950s and 1960s suggested that television, with its sharp picture and clear sound, was like going to the movie theater. The difference was that television watchers did not have to leave the safety and comfort of their homes.

Television, explains Loren Baritz, "swept away all competition in mass culture, and reduced attendance at movies, baseball games, and restaurants. Because the viewers watched, they did not do other things."[28] A 1955 *Fortune* magazine survey revealed that postwar Americans were spending 2 percent less of their disposable income than they had in 1947. A loss of interest in public entertainment, particularly in movies, was largely accountable for the decline.[29] In 1953, 40 million people attended movie theaters each week, a 55 percent drop from the peak of 90 million spectators per week in 1946 through 1948. Theater attendance reached an all-time low of 39.6 million per week in 1958.[30]

Yet television was only one factor that contributed to the decline in movie theater attendance in general and movie palace attendance specifically. Movie palaces lost financial support when the Supreme Court in 1948 voted unanimously that Paramount and four other major studios constituted an illegal trust. Paramount, Loew's, Twentieth Century–Fox, Warner Brothers, and RKO concurred to divest themselves of their theaters under court order. As a result, theater ownership and management were independent of the studio sovereignty, but they no longer had the economic assistance of the studios to help absorb the costs of movie rentals, advertising, initiating major repairs to theaters that were experiencing wear and tear, and constructing new, extravagant theaters. Consequently, in 1952 the price of a movie ticket had doubled from 1948, the year of the Supreme Court ruling.

Independent movie theater managers and owners attempted to keep afloat in the 1950s by introducing wide-screen and directional-sound novelties such as Cinerama, CinemaScope, Stereophonic Sound, and 3–D projection. Such curiosities not only required new projectors, speakers, and screens, they also often required remodeling. Movie palaces still in business frequently cut away at ornate prosceniums, side murals, and organ grilles to make way for wider screens. A 1953 *Birmingham News* report explained that while the Alabama Theatre was still waiting for its 42-foot-wide CinemaScope screen, nineteen enormous crates of sound equipment had already arrived in order to exhibit the "magnificent CinemaScope production of Lloyd Douglas' bestseller, *The Robe*."[31]

Although the novelties of film exhibition aroused the curiosity of ticket buyers who apparently were not overly concerned with the changing aesthetics of the theaters, downtown theaters and picture palaces continued to suffer because they were located in the center of the city, rather than in the suburbs that had become the economic and social center for many middle-class Americans during the postwar years. Suburban flight solidified the peripheries of a city; neighborhood movie houses, drive-in theaters, shopping malls with convenient parking, and grocery stores built near suburban housing developments contributed to the deterioration of downtown areas in cities across the country. City centers, developed before the proliferation of automobiles, simply could not accommodate the onslaught of cars. Increasingly, the parking inconveniences of downtown areas made it difficult to attract suburbanites and their purchasing power.

While the neighborhood theater became popular after the Depression, the drive-in theater flourished after World War II. Inspired by Americans' fascination with their cars and a dramatic growth in streets and suburban development, drive-in theaters were the only theaters that prospered during the 1950s and 1960s. Drive-in theater attendance accounted for half of the movie ticket sales during the summers in the 1950s.[32] Six drive-in theaters, for instance, were constructed in Memphis in a two-year period between 1949 and 1951. Inexpensive to construct and operate, drive-in theaters were usually located on inexpensive land on the outskirts of suburban developments. Drive-in theaters were convenient (since they were close to suburban developments), family friendly, and oriented around the car. Lee Duncan, the person most responsible for saving the Tampa Theatre from destruction, remembers that his family all but quit going to downtown theaters after a drive-in theater was built in Tampa because it was easier to go to the drive-in theater with growing children. With the children asleep in the backseat of the car, parents could enjoy a double feature and visit with friends, without having to pay a baby-sitter.

Nevertheless, the fascination with drive-in theaters did not persist like America's love of television. As Americans spent more of their time in cars commuting to work and driving to shopping centers situated farther and farther from the city center, the notion of spending an evening sitting in the car came to appeal mostly to teenagers. In addition, as suburbs expanded, the drive-in theater property that had once been on the outskirts of the city became increasingly valuable for shopping malls and industrial parks, enabling theater owners to sell their land for substantial profits. Ironically, there is presently a movement to preserve defunct drive-in theaters, the very theaters that helped to close the doors of Main Street theaters.

The Decline of Downtown Districts

While spectatorship was changing in the United States during the 1950s and 1960s, the most significant factor to alter movie palace attendance was a shift in how and where middle-class Americans wanted to live. The preoccupation with television and drive-in theaters paralleled middle-class Americans' fixation with the suburbs and their automobiles. All over the country, developers built suburban stretches like

Levittown, which supplied homes to 70,000 white middle-class Americans. By 1955, 4,000 families a day were leaving American cities and moving to the suburbs, where a quarter of the nation already lived. By 1970, 74 million people resided in the suburbs, with more people living in American suburbs than in cities or on farms.[33] Part of the reason for the suburban expansion was the unprecedented number of births during the period. Postwar parents sought good schools, fresh air, pleasant surroundings, and safety for the explosion of children who became the baby boom generation. When the $100 billion Interstate Highway Act of 1956 increased highway development, suburban home developments grew even faster.

The swift construction of new roads and an explosive increase in automobile ownership helped to carry white middle-class taxpayers to the safety of the suburbs and away from central cities, which were increasingly associated with crime, blight, and the underclass. Suburban dwellers were able to separate themselves from minorities and the urban poor, who were perceived as potential threats to middle-class domesticity. "The middle-class image of the suburbs as a peaceful refuge," writes historian Clifford Clark, "was further reinforced by the use of restricted covenants to exclude blacks and other minorities, who were identified, through newspaper coverage, with urban crime and disorder."[34]

The urban sociologist Herbert J. Gans proposed that the most harmful effect of suburbanization was the increasing class and race polarization of city and suburb.[35] The divide not only caused racial separation, but it also helped to accelerate urban decay. The movement to the suburbs left many of America's central cities to low-income people, blacks, Hispanics, and new immigrant groups who were generally excluded from the benefits of suburban living, such as jobs that paid acceptable wages, adequate and safe living conditions, and functional educational systems. The departure of the white middle class, according to Robert Beauregard, left cities with lower property values and tax revenues, increased crime, poorer health, social and economic dependency, and larger government expenditures.[36] The cities were left with a declining population base that often found themselves in precarious economic circumstances. As the population turned over and cities aged, urban infrastructure deteriorated, and human problems and social conflicts intensified.[37]

While the white middle class may have turned their backs on downtown districts during the 1950s, by the mid-1960s, urban blight and dissatisfaction of inner-city residents had grown so great that it was impossible to ignore. Frustrated by woefully insufficient attention to their living conditions, inner-city residents participated in racial riots and disorders. "In both Negro and Puerto Rican neighborhoods in inner cities across the country," writes Beauregard, "grievance after grievance accumulated so that some single, seemingly isolated incident was enough to unleash despair and send hundreds and thousands to the streets to chant demands, confront police, loot and burn stores, and articulate in raw terms the Black Power that the more radical Negro leaders were pursuing by other means."[38] The 1965 Watts riot in Los Angeles, which resulted in thirty-four lives lost and $50 million in property damage, was followed by a series of riots throughout the country. An even more destructive riot in Detroit in 1967 resulted in forty-three deaths and $22 million in property loss and damage. When Martin Luther King Jr. was assassinated in Memphis on April 4, 1968, riots erupted in 125 cities during the following week. Across the country, thirty-nine people were killed; more than 3,500 people were injured; and property damage exceeded $45 million.

Riots such as these caused all of America to take notice of the plight of urban residents, but suburban dwellers perceived such uprisings as further evidence to stay clear of downtown districts. Many downtown retailers and other city-center enterprises that had attempted to weather the suburban storm prior to the racial uprisings could no longer withstand the economic losses. Many proprietors went out of business or boarded up their buildings and followed their customers to the suburbs. These closings made matters even worse, as empty streets created more fear and discouraged potential customers from going downtown at all.

More than a decade before the period of racial upheaval in America's inner cities, the federal government implemented an extensive urban renewal strategy. The Housing Act of 1949 was intended to ameliorate the urban blight and the social injustices that had permeated the country's inner cities. However, while urban renewal funds were to be used for clearing blighted or deteriorating areas in the city, many city renewal directors around the country searched for the "blight that's right," meaning that many of the residential buildings that were torn down were not necessarily substandard but were in a good enough area to attract developers. Rather than rebuilding the core of American cities, urban renewal actually tore cities nearly to the ground. Rather than helping inner-city residents, urban renewal razed long-established African American and Latin communities that were adjacent to downtown districts. It also built new highways that cut through the middle of minority neighborhoods. Thus, urban renewal systems fractured and disrupted community life and displaced hundreds of thousands of inner-city families around the country. Through 1967, in fact, urban renewal dispossessed more than 400,000 families, and urban highway construction uprooted 330,000 more families.[39]

The most profound effects of urban renewal were the human victims that it left behind, but the architectural devastation was also substantial. In the mid-1960s, federal and city officials were not in the business of concerning themselves with the historical significance of old buildings, and an unprecedented number of them were razed throughout the country. The Housing Act of 1954 allowed 10 percent of federal grants to be used for nonresidential projects as long as there was "a substantial number" of substandard houses in the area. By 1965, 35 percent of the federal grants were used for nonresidential projects. "Backed by influential coalitions, reinforced by expert judgment that downtown was obsolete, given the power of government to take private property and the budgets of two federal programs to pay for it," Bernard Frieden and Lynne Sagalyn explain, "ambitious renewal chiefs were soon pulling down buildings by the hundreds in the hearts of cities."[40] The result was not only the tremendous loss of interesting and historically important architecture, but downtown districts that lay in rubble.

Federal rules for urban renewal maintained a strict separation between city agencies and potential developers. Cities, therefore, were responsible for urban renewal projects until after the land was cleared and became ready for development. Developers who did not participate in advance planning were not necessarily interested in developing the land once it was cleared; thus, city officials were often left with blocks of vacant lots for years before construction began. Such urban renewal strategies remained in place until 1974, when community development block grants were enacted and federal regulations were cut to a minimum. "Cities were still free—freer than ever—to use federal community development funds for downtown projects," Frieden and Sagalyn write. "But the downtown coalitions could no longer get those funds designated in advance for the projects they wanted."[41] After twenty-five years the urban renewal program was finally over, leaving in its wake the rubble of minority communities and skeletons of the once-thriving downtown districts.

Movie palaces did not escape the wrecking ball. Hundreds of them across the country were razed during the urban renewal period. Many others that survived were boarded up or in complete ruins. The architectural and cinematic fantasies of the 1920s were bulldozed over in the hopes that downtown districts could be revitalized in the process. For picture palace enthusiasts, one of the worst insults was the transformation of Detroit's Michigan Theater into a parking garage. "An auto ramp now runs through Rapp and Rapp's palatial foyer," wrote picture palace expert David Naylor in 1981. "The fragmented plaster of the ceiling coves and the proscenium arch loom above the third parking level. Inexplicably, the movie screen remains in place, giving the former theater the appearance of the world's first triple-decker drive-in."[42]

Clearly, the movie palace was the hallmark and the promise of a vital downtown district during the 1920s. However, the huge downtown movie palaces depended on the population density and economic health of the city center for its sustenance. While the movie palace business nearly folded during the Depression, it was actually the post–World War II economic boom that caused many palaces to be razed, closed, or reduced to B-movie houses. The advent of television, drive-in theaters, and suburban developments and the subsequent decline of downtown districts, followed by urban renewal, left the picture palace limping. Yet there was another factor that also affected their decline. Desegregation had a tremendous impact upon the southern movie palace. The Civil Rights movement allowed African Americans, for the first time, complete access to downtown businesses. This freedom meant the end of segregated balconies, stairways, and entrances for African Americans who wished to attend movie palaces. However, many of the middle-class whites who continued to patronize movie palaces during the late 1950s and early 1960s had little interest in patronizing the integrated theaters. The fact is that few of the theaters ever reached an integrated status because as soon as African Americans were no longer confined by segregation, many of the palaces became chiefly black movie houses.

CHAPTER 2

The Decline of the Southern Downtown Movie Palace

Much of the artifactual history of the six southern movie palaces on which this book focuses disappeared when the private owners of the theaters sold them; thus, we do not have the benefit of that information. However, newspaper accounts, public documents, and interviews with people who remember the theaters during the 1960s and 1970s help us to understand what preservationists faced when they first imagined rescuing the theaters. While the following depictions attempt to characterize specific and varied conditions prior to the renovation and preservation of the six movie palaces, the efforts of civil rights activists, the trend of suburbanization, urban renewal efforts, the decline of the downtown district, and the material and financial state of each movie palace share many common characteristics with one another. Taken together, these depictions portray the general state of many southern downtown districts and the movie palaces that remained standing from the late 1960s to the early 1980s.

Birmingham and the Alabama Theatre

Any mention of the city of Birmingham in the 1960s brings to mind some of the most traumatic and violent images of the Civil Rights movement. Birmingham's civil rights conflicts put an end to the city's segregation practices, but they also scarred middle-class perceptions of the downtown district. By the 1970s Birmingham's downtown was failing because of the white middle-class exodus to the suburbs. In part, this exodus took place because the downtown area had gained a reputation as a dangerous place as a result of the violent encounters between law enforcement officials and civil rights activists.

Prior to the uprising in 1963, African Americans who lived in Birmingham generally lived, according to Lee Bains, within two concentric circles of segregation. "One imprisoned them on the basis of color," Bains explains, "while the other confined them within a separate culture of poverty."[1] From 1900 to 1910, Birmingham's population grew by 245 percent, which helped the city earn the title of the "magic city." The growth of the steel industry was chiefly responsible for the increased population, and cheap labor of African Americans was mainly responsible for the development of the steel industry. Racial segregation was fostered by housing construction that was designed with segregation in mind. Housing developments in Birmingham evolved into a binary market with no transitional areas.[2] This pattern of complete segregation did not begin to change until the late 1940s, when an attorney for the local NAACP branch, Arthur Shores, challenged the unconstitutional racial zoning laws that relegated African Americans to blighted and confined areas of the city. Later, during the 1960s, the largest urban renewal project in Birmingham, the medical center expansion, displaced 1,000 black families. As a result of the expansion project, African American families began to acquire housing within traditionally white neighborhoods, and white families began moving outside of Birmingham proper.

During the years prior to the Civil Rights movement, most of the city's white residents who were deeply ensconced in southern traditions held to the belief that segregation was natural and logical. A 1962 editorial in the *Birmingham News* told readers that the "overwhelming majority of Southerners believes segregation of the races not only is desirable, they can prove that beyond this region it is a natural impulse of most peoples to keep race to race."[3] Thus, the city was really composed of many disunited communities, for African Americans were placed within separate enclaves, scattered throughout the city. To ensure this separation, local laws prohibited blacks and whites from coming together in activities as benign as playing cards, dominoes, checkers, or basketball. Birmingham's 1951 Racial Segregation Ordinance, for example, explicitly decreed segregation for many activities:

> It shall be unlawful for any person in charge or control of any room, hall, theatre, picture house, auditorium, yard, court, ballpark, public park, or other indoor or outdoor place, to which both white persons and negroes are admitted, to cause, permit or allow therein or thereon any theatrical performance, picture exhibition, speech, or educational or entertainment program of any kind whatsoever, unless such room, hall, theatre, picture house, auditorium, yard, court, ball park, or other place, has entrances, exits and seating or standing sections set aside for and assigned to the use of white persons, and other entrances, exits and seating or standing sections set aside for and assigned to the use of negroes, unless the entrances, exits and seating or standing sections set aside for and assigned to the use of white persons are distinctly separated from those set aside for and assigned to the use of negroes, by well defined physical barriers, and unless the members of each race are effectively restricted and confined to the sections set aside for and assigned to the use of such race.[4]

Birmingham African Americans began organizing against the social, economic, and political subjugation during the late 1940s; however, organization was difficult because the state of Alabama declared the activities of the NAACP illegal. Rev. Fred L. Shuttlesworth, a black Baptist minister, who would become a leader in the Civil Rights movement, helped to form the Alabama Christian Movement for Human Rights (ACMHR). The ACMHR had two primary goals: to end discrimination in accommodations and to have equal access to employment.[5] The white community generally resisted the ACMHR's attempts to change the injustices of Birmingham. Blacks who were openly involved with the ACMHR were fired from jobs, were jailed, and were threatened with and suffered from acts of violence such as bombings and physical assaults. Shuttlesworth's home was bombed on December 25, 1956. Although the Shuttlesworths' home was in ruins and two of his children were injured, the explosion did not deter the efforts of the ACMHR. The following day 250 African Americans rode in the white section of Birmingham buses. Yet it took two more years of effort by the ACMHR before the city ordinance that authorized segregated seating was determined to be unconstitutional.[6]

Following the lead of the student movement for civil rights that was spreading in other cities in the South, Shuttlesworth helped to coordinate a direct action challenge in downtown Birmingham on March 31, 1960. Ten black college students requested service at five lunch counters. As a result of the sit-in, the students and Shuttlesworth were arrested, crosses were burned throughout the city, and the national media began paying attention to Birmingham's racist practices. "Unlike Montgomery and Little Rock," writes Glenn Eskew, "Birmingham had successfully—and amazingly—dodged the national spotlight on unsavory race relations, but with the student movement that changed."[7] Preceding the infamous demonstrations and retaliations that took place in Birmingham in April and May 1963, the ACMHR continued their activities by boycotting segregated retail establishments in downtown Birmingham and sending petitions to the city commissioners, requesting the desegregation of public facilities.

The day after a state circuit judge issued an injunction barring civil rights leaders from participating in or encouraging any kind of protest or sit-in, Martin Luther King Jr. willingly violated the injunction on April 12, 1963. During his eight-day imprisonment, King wrote the now-famous "Letter from Birmingham Jail," in which he responded to the objections of white clergymen against the direct action program. "When King came [to Birmingham], the eyes of the nation and world were fixed upon Birmingham," writes sociologist Aldon D. Morris. "White segregationists could no longer beat, jail, and kill black people in the dark. They had to do it on the world stage. And they did."[8]

On May 2 and 3, 1963, thousands of Birmingham's African American children walked through the streets of Birmingham in a protest organized by the SCLC and the ACMHR. Hundreds of young people were arrested, and on May 3, Bull Connor ordered police dogs, clubs, and high-powered water hoses to be used on the young protesters. "With the first blast of water," writes Eskew, "the students, aged thirteen to sixteen, covered their heads with their hands but held their ground. As the pressure increased, they dropped to their knees, then grasped each other, bonding bodies with souls to withstand the force."[9] Americans all over the country, tuning in to the nightly news, were horrified to see the actions of Bull Connor and his officers. What had been indifference to or a lack of knowledge of the racial discrimination and violence in Birmingham quickly turned into a near international outrage.

During the weeks of the intense demonstrations in April and May 1963, white downtown retail merchants, who were suffering financially as a result of the turmoil and the continuation of the black boycott, began meeting with one another in order to devise a way to negotiate with black leaders. They turned to the Senior Citizens Committee, a group of Birmingham business leaders, who were able to negotiate with black leaders and come to a morally binding agreement on May 10, 1963. The final terms included the "desegregation of lunch counters, rest rooms, fitting rooms, and drinking fountains in all downtown stores within ninety days; the placement of blacks in clerical and sales jobs in stores within sixty days; the release of prisoners on low bail; and the establishment of permanent communications between white and black leaders."[10]

The victory in Birmingham propelled civil rights protests in cities across America, and it became evident to the Kennedy administration that federal action was necessary to achieve desegregation in the South. Many civil rights scholars and activists believe that Birmingham was the turning point of the Civil Rights movement that made possible the Civil Rights Act of 1964. "The televised scenes of the dramatic events of the 1963 demonstrations in large measure convinced President Kennedy, the Congress, and millions of American voters that major legislation in the area of civil rights should and could be passed," explains historian Andrew Manis.[11] Wyatt T. Walker, chief of staff of SCLC and the architect of the Birmingham marches in April and May 1963, writes, "Birmingham became the germ-center of a human rights struggle that would claim international attention and forever change the landscape of both social and political demographics of the entire South."[12]

The civil rights activism that placed Birmingham squarely on the media map in the early years of the 1960s not only rid the city of segregation practices but essentially ended the vitality of its downtown district. The number of white middle-class families that moved to the suburbs in Birmingham was sizeable; in the 1970s the white population in the city of Birmingham decreased by 28 percent.[13] Kathy Gilmore, the director of the Metropolitan Arts Council, remembers that the unfavorable press that Birmingham received helped to vacate the downtown area. "Birmingham just happened to be the flash point because Martin Luther King came over, and the whole scene was very focused on Alabama and Birmingham. Birmingham just got the really bad press," she assured me. "It hurt the progress here. I think that's when the dissipation of downtown and white flight and all that started occurring." While Gilmore believes that the downtown area is presently experiencing a renaissance, she is aware that Birmingham and its center city still carry the burden of its discriminatory past. "When you say 'Birmingham,' because of the bad press, it's kind of like a girl in high school with a bad reputation, you can never erase that," Gilmore said. "No matter how old she gets, you'll always know her from high school and that she was a slut. That's the way Birmingham is; it has a black mark."

Birmingham's highly publicized racial riots certainly had an impact on the decline of activity in the city center, which was battling the same problem that city centers all across the county experienced: the migration of middle-class dollars to the suburbs. White flight accounted for more than 50 percent of the decline in the white population of Birmingham during the 1970s, while annexations accounted for more than 30 percent of the increase in the African American population. Between 1970 and 1980 the proportion of the white population declined from 40 to 28 percent, while the proportion of the black population increased from 60 to 70 percent.[14] The movement of whites to the suburbs shifted the focus of their retail and leisure pursuits from the city center to the suburban shopping malls and movie theaters. In the 1970s and early 1980s downtown Birmingham lost most of its smaller retail merchants and its department stores.

Michael Calvert, president of Operation New Birmingham, a public-private partnership that works to redevelop the downtown area, explained that by 1979 the downtown district was suffering because the entire city was in a transitional period as a result of steel mills and heavy manufacturing being replaced by banking and service industries; downtown merchants moved to the suburbs because white middle-class residents were fearful of the city's downtown district, and the first black mayor had been recently elected. White Birmingham residents feared that the African Americans were taking over the city. "Some of them had good reason to be scared," Calvert said, "the way they had treated black people." Cecil Whitmire, the director of the Alabama Theatre, remembers that by the late 1970s downtown Birmingham was collapsing. "They kept building shopping centers, and shopping-center stores became more and more important to the ladies. The big department stores began to close up," Whitmire explained. "The Loveman's next door closed in '77 and was a major blow to downtown. Some of the smaller ones, Blach and Parisian, hung on for a while, but they eventually closed. The downtown was fast becoming a ghost town after five o'clock."

In the midst of the decline of downtown Birmingham, the Alabama Theatre struggled to stay alive. By the end of the 1970s, white middle-class residents had more and more reasons to stay away from the Alabama Theatre. They had suburban movie theaters close to their homes; there were only a handful of stores and restaurants in a nearly empty downtown area that was perceived as dangerous; and the quality of the movies and the physical conditions at the Alabama Theatre was diminishing. While other southern picture palaces lost white middle-class patronage after the theaters were integrated, the Alabama Theatre did not attract a substantial black audience.

There are several possible reasons why blacks did not begin attending the theater in great numbers after the federal government ended segregation.[15] For one, before integration African Americans had never been allowed access into the theater. As at the Tampa Theatre, there was not a separate balcony and entrance for blacks; it was completely off limits to them. Whitmire believes that older blacks in Birmingham were resentful that they had not been allowed in the theater and did not wish to begin patronizing it once they had access to it. He remembers, in particular, the way the influential African American Dr. A. G. Gaston, the founder of Booker T. Washington Insurance Company, Smith and Gaston Funeral Home, and Citizens Federal Savings Bank, felt about attending the theater. "I was at the bank once getting some change, and I said, 'Dr. A.G., we've got a nice show at the theater, why don't you come tonight,'" Whitmire recalls. "He said, 'Sonny, for most of my life it was against the law for me to go to your theater and now that I can go, I won't.'"

If some African Americans, like Gaston, stayed away from the theater on principle, others may have chosen to stay away even after federal law provided them access because they did not feel welcome or comfortable there. Opened in 1927, the Alabama Theatre had catered to the generations of white middle- and upper-class Birmingham residents who had understood the separation of races as natural and logical. Richard M. Kennedy, the owner and manager of numerous theaters across the South, including the Alabama Theatre, characterizes the way many whites in the South perceived the integration of blacks and whites. If his perception of integration is any indication of the inhospitable climate African Americans faced, it is hardly a wonder that blacks were not eager to attend the theater once it was opened to them. In his unpublished autobiography, Kennedy recalls that he, along with fifty other theater owners from around the country, was called to a meeting with Attorney General Robert Kennedy, who Richard Kennedy believes was "the biggest threat to the harmony of the United States since Franklin D. Roosevelt." In the meeting the attorney general requested that the theater owners discontinue the practice of segregation in their theaters before they were forced to. Richard Kennedy remembers rising and asking the attorney general, "Do you mean to say that you have invited us to come to Washington to ask us to cooperate with you while, at the same time, you are telling us that you are going to make us do something that we do not want to do?" Kennedy recalls that the attorney general replied, "Yes, if that's the way you want to put it."

The attorney general then assured the owners that there would be no demonstrations at the theaters before schools and restaurants were integrated. "After he had given this assurance," Kennedy writes, "I inquired what he would do in case negroes demonstrated at our theaters before a civil rights law was passed and before our schools and cafes had been made to serve blacks. 'If you will telephone me, should this be done at any of your theatres, I will immediately see to it that the demonstrations are terminated.' He could just as easily have said, 'I am in charge of all of these unlawful protests and any that I do not authorize will be stopped.'"

Although Kennedy resisted integration in his theaters, particularly his Greensboro, North Carolina, theater, he did ultimately concede. He recalls, "The Civil Rights Law was passed shortly after our confrontation with Bobby Kennedy and the south conformed, although it was distasteful to a great majority. The northern people were quick to censure the people of the south for their treatment of all blacks and they rejoiced over the fact that this new law would correct many injustices. Those very same people who condemned the south the most for its so called animosity toward black people are the ones who seem to be having the most trouble now with the negroes."[16]

While some Birmingham blacks were unwilling on principle to go to the theater after integration, others, faced with an inhospitable climate such as the one expressed by Kennedy, or a feeling of indifference toward a theater with a history of whiteness, chose instead to patronize the five black theaters within three blocks of the Alabama. The fact that the entire downtown area—and not merely the theater—had become integrated provided reason enough for many white middle-class residents to turn their backs on the theater as well.

While the theater stayed afloat with the help of a $100,000 renovation in the 1970s that included new seats, drapes, carpets, and modernized rest rooms, it was not enough to attract a large audience.[17] A 1978 newspaper article explained that the theater had several forces working against it: "The Alabama must fight television, suburban theaters with plenty of parking for a mobile America, the reputation that downtown is troubled with prostitutes and other undesirables after dark. More than that, it must fight the movie distributors. Nobody wants to see his baby go into a downtown movie house anymore. That's regarded as the kiss of death. And not many producers want to kiss millions good-bye."[18]

The Alabama Theatre went through a series of ownership changes during the late 1970s and early 1980s. Before the theater closed in 1982, it was a one-dollar movie house. "It was awful," Whitmire remembers. "They didn't even advertise the movies. They just had a sign up: Movies: $1. You could come in here and stay all day for a dollar." Like other movie palaces that had not closed down, the Alabama Theatre managed to stay open by exhibiting black exploitation, martial-arts, and soft-porn films, while video games met ticket buyers as they entered the lobby. The theater was purchased in 1981 by Costa and Head, an ambitious downtown development corporation, who had more imagination than money. Their development plan stalled, and the theater went dark, remaining closed for four years. "They were going to use the Alabama Theatre as the keystone for nighttime shopping and things like that," Whitmire explained. "So they kept buying buildings, and as the story goes they went one building too far, and then there was no money. Their dream collapsed and they went bankrupt—reorganization at first—but all the buildings were over-mortgaged to the point that there was no way to come back. So they finally went Chapter Seven, which meant everything had to be disposed of." The bankruptcy proceedings in 1986 meant that the Alabama Theatre would be either demolished or sold at auction. It appeared that Birmingham's "Showplace of the South" would go the way of so many other movie palaces around the country.

Durham and the Carolina Theatre

While Birmingham, Memphis, and Montgomery are the cities that are primarily remembered for the impassioned efforts to desegregate the South, Durham was also a hotbed for racial uprisings in the early 1960s. The Carolina Theatre, located in downtown Durham, was at the center of the protests that took place in the city. Like Birmingham, the downtown district and its flagship theater were profoundly affected by the efforts to integrate the theater. In Durham, however, the city was directly involved in the conflict to integrate the Carolina Theatre because the building itself was owned by the city and leased to a private company that ran the theater business. The fact that the city owned the building made the Carolina Theatre a conspicuous target for desegregation protests. In fact, the protests to desegregate the theater are the most thoroughly documented of all of the movie palaces discussed here because it is the only theater building that was not privately owned at the time of the Civil Rights movement.

From its beginning in 1926, the Carolina Theatre (then called the Durham Auditorium) was the only theater in Durham that allowed admission to African Americans. To maintain strict segregated areas, blacks were required to enter through a side door and sit in the second balcony. Again, such seating arrangements were advertised in the newspaper, assuring patrons that the races would not come into contact with one another while attending the theater. This practice remained in effect from 1926 until 1963.

Lawyer and city councilman Howard Clement, an African American who participated in protests to integrate the Carolina Theatre, remembers the racial climate of Durham when he moved to the city in 1960:

> Much to my chagrin, I found out that black Boy Scouts could not wear their scout uniforms on this side of town. I remember I could wear my uniform all over town in Charleston, but they told me there was a railroad track that ran through and still runs through the center of Durham, that on one side you could wear your uniform, but when you crossed that track, you couldn't wear the uniform; this was 1960. That was my real first brush with what I thought was wrong with Durham. I knew about segregated buses; I knew about the segregated theaters. But this thing with the Boy Scouts—a Christian organization? I couldn't understand that. And the Boy Scouts seemed to have accepted it.

Before the protests at the Carolina Theatre began, Clement did not attend the theater, because of its segregation policies. "I wouldn't go to a segregated theater in Durham," Clement explained. "When I was in school in Washington, there was no such thing as a segregated theater, even though there was segregation in Washington. The black theaters, Booker T., the Lincoln, the Republic—they even had a theater called the Howard—there was no segregation. I could sit anywhere I wanted. The audience was 99.9 percent black, but it was still open. That was the issue—that you can sit anywhere you want." Meeting and being influenced by the hard work of Martin Luther King Jr. and Thurgood Marshall, Clement said, were the catalysts for his consciousness-raising. But closer to home, Clement remembers that his aunt who lived in Durham encouraged him to participate in the protests at the Carolina Theatre. Clement explained that his cousin, a talented musician, had been denied access to a public-funded training program associated with the Carolina Theatre. "She never forgot that, even though she became a county commissioner, well respected in the community, chairman of the Board of Education," Clement said. "That slight. That offense. She never forgot."

Prior to the efforts to desegregate the Carolina Theatre, Durham activists began participating in store boycotts and sit-ins at lunch counters in 1960. By the end of the year, Durham's lunch counters were integrated. During the winter of 1961, members of the NAACP Youth Chapter began picketing the Carolina Theatre, protesting the fact that African Americans still were required to sit in the balcony and enter the theater through a side door. They also staged a march on the city hall, marching from the North Carolina College campus, where they presented requests to desegregate the theater to the city council. But it was not until March 1962 that the conflict between the theater's management, the city council, and the NAACP culminated.

Toward the end of February 1962 the Durham Youth Chapter of the NAACP petitioned Durham's city council, calling for it to order the integration of the Carolina Theatre. The NAACP members felt that the theater should be integrated because the building was leased from the city. On March 1, 1962, the *Durham Sun* reported that the Human Relations Committee that had attempted to negotiate with the management of the theater and the NAACP had failed in its efforts. The article explained that the theater management said that "the integration question is 'not negotiable now.'"[19] On March 5 sixty college students from North Caro-

9. Durham's fire captain warned protestors at the Carolina Theatre to clear the exits, while Milo Crawford, the theater manager, held back another group of protestors in 1962. Jim Thornton, *Herald-Sun*, Durham, North Carolina.

lina College and Duke University went to a city council meeting to make statements about the failed negotiations. The city council went on record "'as not opposing integration of the Carolina Theatre' and 'respectfully requested' the management to negotiate the matter through the Mayor's Committee on Human Relations."[20] The council chose such noncommittal wording, in part, because they felt that they had no authority to a force a change in policy because it was a privately run operation in a city-owned building. However, more telling perhaps, at the same meeting council members discussed the economic impact of integration. The *Durham Morning Herald* reported, "In a discussion of the economic effect integration would have on the theater, [council member] Stewart said that Woolworth's and other firms here (which have since integrated lunch counters) felt the same way, but that none of them have suffered any economic loss."[21]

On March 9 the North Carolina Civil Rights Advisory Committee issued a report that called upon the citizens of North Carolina to aid in removing compulsory segregation statutes by legislation rather than through the courts. The committee's report stated that the statutes and city ordinances should be overturned by the same agencies, the legislature and city councils, that enacted them. Such segregated public spaces as prisons, amusement parlors, weenie shops, and taxicabs were named; the Carolina Theatre was specifically named in the report.[22]

Charles Abercrombie, the Carolina Theatre's owner, on March 13 turned down the city council's request that he meet with the NAACP representatives in order to negotiate the question of integration at the theater. His letter to city officials stated, in part:

> We are convinced that if we attempt to operate the Carolina Theater as the only moving picture theater in Durham operated on an integrated basis, we would not be able to carry on our business from a financial standpoint, and believe we would have to go out of business. . . . We understand that the negotiations would not be concerned with whether to integrate, but how to integrate. You either do integrate or you do not, and since we are not convinced that we could successfully operate as an integrated theater and since the question seems to be how, rather than whether to integrate, we can see no basis for an approach which would be mutually satisfactory to both sides.[23]

Clement remembers that the process of desegregating the theater was complicated by economics; white people refused to go to an integrated theater, and Abercrombie was afraid of losing revenue. Clement also claims that there was some opposition in the black community as well. "There were some folks in the black community that didn't see anything wrong. I remember some of them telling me that the best seats in the house were upstairs in the balcony," Clement said. "For various reasons they thought that those were the best seats in the house."

Durham city council's halfhearted proposal and Abercrombie's response led more than 200 African Americans to stage a protest at the theater the following two evenings. According to the *Durham Morning Herald,* the demonstrators assembled at North Carolina College and marched single file from the campus to the theater. Then, for three hours, the protesters walked single file up to the box office and requested to buy a ticket, reading from a mimeographed sheet of paper. Following the script on the paper, the protesters asked, "Are you refusing to sell me a ticket because I am a Negro?" The box office cashiers answered each question, saying, "I cannot sell you a ticket." After hearing the cashiers' responses, the demonstrators wrote down the cashiers' answers on their mimeographed papers.

Finally some of the demonstrators rushed the doors leading into the lobby. The newspaper report explained, "The 'round robin' demand for tickets had become a monotonous parade, but the sudden entry into the theater pushed the barometer of excitement to its peak. That peak held steady until the large group of Negroes left the lobby after 9 P.M. While theater manager Milo Crawford barred the Negroes in the lobby, he asked them repeatedly to leave, and offered them refunds; both suggestions were refused by the Negro students."[24]

The following evening the protests continued at the Carolina Theatre. Again, some of the African American demonstrators rushed the lobby door with the help of white protesters who held side doors open for them. While Durham police directed traffic at the demonstration, they did not arrest any of the protesters. In fact, their only action was to order away from the theater a handful of white teenagers who were throwing eggs at the protesters and attempting to block demonstrators from the sidewalk leading up the theater.[25]

Although the protests were conducted peacefully and the Durham police did not hinder the demonstrations, the following day the protests

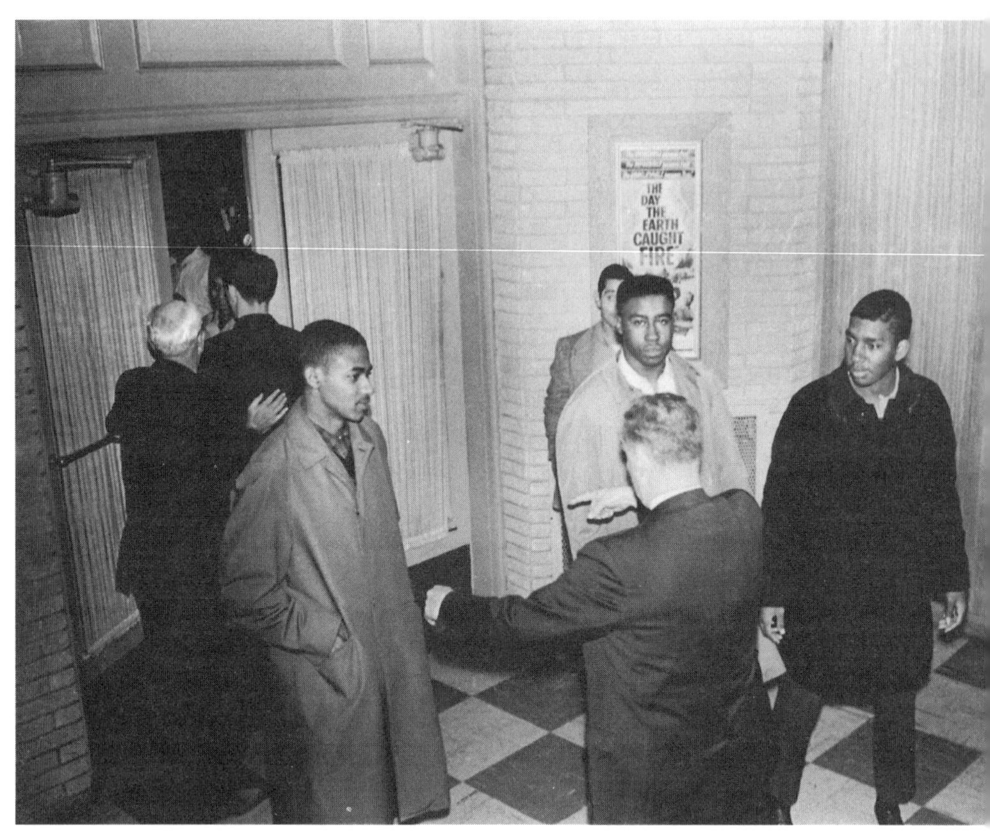

10. Some of the 1962 demonstrators were able to rush the lobby door at the Carolina Theatre. Behind them, a poster for the movie *The Day the Earth Caught Fire* is prominently displayed. Jim Thorton, *Herald-Sun,* Durham, North Carolina.

were halted by a superior court judge who signed a temporary restraining order against thirty-four of the NAACP members. The order, requested by Abercrombie Enterprises, forbade the demonstrators to enter the Carolina Theatre without permission from the management and prohibited them from interfering with the operation of the theater.[26] The restraining order effectively ended the protests at the Carolina Theatre.

Although the theater protests came to a halt, Durham activists continued in their efforts to desegregate downtown Durham. After the arrest of 130 protesters on May 18, 1963, the NAACP and CORE (Congress of Racial Equality) announced that beginning on May 20, there would be thirty days of mass demonstrations. Durham's mayor, Wense Grabarek, negotiated with the activists, promising them that he would immediately respond to their complaints if they would halt their plans for mass demonstrations. Grabarek initiated the Durham Interim Committee for the purpose of resolving and reconciling Durham's racial differences. The eleven-member Interim Committee asked Durham's food-service businesses to adopt a policy of serving customers of any race. Within the next few weeks many of Durham's restaurants were integrated.[27] In June the city voluntarily integrated its swimming pools and other public facilities. And by the fall of 1963, all the city's theaters (with the exception of drive-in theaters) were integrated, including the Carolina Theatre.

Following the integration of the theater, theater management dropped a false ceiling, covering the balcony that had seated Durham's African American patrons since the theater opened. St. Clair Williams, a longtime Carolina Theatre supporter, explained that the theater management dropped the ceiling for two reasons: the theater had heating problems, and after integration neither white nor black patrons wanted to sit in the balcony. "They put a false ceiling in from the edge of the balcony, to the top of the proscenium, and hung drapes all the way around—for the films," Williams said. "It messed up the acoustics as far as the stage was concerned because they put all of the return air from the heating system—the heat came in from the ceiling—under the stage. So when we put operas in here, the audience could not hear the music from the orchestra pit if the air-conditioning was on, so we had to cut the air-conditioning off." Pepper Fluke, a community activist and important contributor to the preservation of the Carolina Theatre, explained that the false ceiling completely covered the theater's proscenium arch work and the entablature. "The new generation that was born after this false ceiling was dropped had no idea about this second balcony," Fluke explained. "There are even people in this community today who will say, 'There's only one balcony in the Carolina Theatre.'"

The integration of the Carolina Theatre, along with the integration of other public spaces in downtown Durham, was one of the factors that put an end to the vitality of the downtown district. Of course, there were other factors that contributed to its decline. Steve Martin, the Carolina Theatre director, explained that the development of shopping centers outside of Durham was the breaking point for the downtown area. "As the city moved outwards into suburbs, the downtown core was basically decimated," Martin said. "The people who had come to the theater were going to suburban theaters; therefore, this theater went downhill. The fewer people, the less they had to keep the building up—which meant the less people and less money downtown, and people just got out of the habit of going downtown." Other downtown theaters—such as the Rialto, the Center, the Uptown, and the Criterion—were demolished. Naturally, downtown restaurants and department stores, which depended in part on the flow of people attending movies downtown, either went out of business or moved to the suburbs as well.

Fluke remembers that Durham's Historic Preservation Society was organized as a result of the decline of downtown Durham and the many significant buildings that were demolished. "Durham was losing so many incredibly wonderful buildings that never should have been torn down," Fluke said. "In retrospect, everybody now says, 'Oh, we lost our museum; we lost our this; we lost our that.' Urban renewal and the freeway took the black historic district right out of being. It wiped out their business district, which was another hard pill for the black community to swallow." Monte Moses, who along with his wife, Connie, was the primary rescuer of the Carolina Theatre, remembers that the degeneration of downtown Durham was crystallized for him with the closing of the Rialto Theatre. The high-rise building that the theater had to give way to was never built. "One by one we saw the symbolic and real landmarks of Durham go," Moses wrote in a 1978 proposal, "to be replaced by parking lots and empty space: the Washington-Duke Hotel and Belk's among others."[28]

As buildings fell around it, the Carolina Theatre's physical condition was deteriorating, as was its popularity. Fluke explained that the area around the theater was in near ruins. The theater sat across the street from an old automobile tire business that blocked the facade of the movie palace, and around it were empty lots that were what was left of several buildings being torn down. At a financial crisis point by the mid-1970s, the theater, like other downtown picture palaces that managed to remain open, exhibited black exploitation and martial-arts films and, briefly, X-rated films. In June 1977 the City of Durham, which still owned the building, asked to be released a year early from the contract with Abercrombie Enterprises. While the city wanted to close the theater immediately, a compromise was made by creating the Crawford-Carolina Corporation. An interim measure, the corporation kept the building occupied while city officials decided what they wanted to do with the building. Durham citizens who were aware of the creation of the Crawford-Carolina Corporation became concerned that the building would be demolished to make way for a parking lot to accompany the construction of a possible civic center and a hotel. It seemed like it was only a matter of time before the Carolina Theatre would go the way of the other downtown movie theaters in Durham.

Atlanta and the Fox Theatre

The Fox Theatre sits on Peachtree Street, Atlanta's most famous street, as it has for nearly a century. Like the city where it is situated, the theater has withstood many changes and turbulent times and has genuinely flourished during the last two decades. Today young African American college graduates (as well as whites) flock to Atlanta so that they can live in one of the country's most progressive cities. Part of Atlanta's attraction is its reputation as an oasis in the South, for it is a forward-thinking city that maintains and promotes harmonious race relations. However, the city was not always so forward thinking. The race riot of 1906 that left dozens of people dead remains the city's worst outbreak of violence since the Civil War.

In the third week of September 1906, Atlanta newspapers began reporting incidents of black men insulting and assailing white women. After a headline reported that a black man had kissed a white woman's hand, an estimated 10,000 rioters roamed the streets, stabbing and beating black men to death. For two hours mobs of whites preyed on any blacks that they could find. Police turned water hoses on the crowds, but the attacks did not end until it began raining. Only 16 whites were charged following the incident; more than 130 blacks were arrested for fighting back.

Black residents of Atlanta prior to the Civil Rights movement experienced the same sort of indignities as African Americans in other southern cities. Public spaces such as department stores, restaurants, public transportation, and movie theaters were routinely segregated. In the oral history *Living Atlanta,* longtime Atlanta residents recall their frustration at the city's segregation policies in the 1930s and 1940s. "Oh it was just terrible," one woman recalled. "I can still remember how you would go into a dime store to be waited on, and some cracker would come up and you'd just have to wait. You know, Christmas rush, you were buying these little presents for family and friends, and you could not get waited on, because they waited on the whites first."[29] Another woman, who had been a domestic worker, remembered the indignities of riding the streetcar after work. "You couldn't sit with a white person. If they didn't feel like moving, plainly speaking if they were just too mean to move, you had to stand there, unless you wanted to fuss. And I never understood. Look, you're going to their house, cooking for them, cleaning their beds, cleaning their house, doing everything, and then you couldn't sit by them. This is what I never could understand."[30]

Theaters were no different than other public facilities in Atlanta. Black entertainers were not able to perform at the vast majority of theaters in the city, and all but one theater had segregated seating. The only theater in the city that did not segregate African Americans to an upper balcony was the 81 Theatre, which had white ownership but served primarily African Americans. Because the Fox Theatre was the city's premier theater, it was particularly nettling for African Americans to have to use a separate box office, entrance, and staircase that was entirely separate from the white facilities. An impenetrable wall prevented African Americans seated in the black section (which was known as the gallery) from entering any other part of the theater. Until the theater was integrated, nannies of white children were the only blacks permitted to enter any part of the theater other than the gallery.

One black Atlantan remembers his discomfort at the Fox's segregation policy. "My wife and I went to the Fox Theatre once to see a picture that we wanted to see. And we went upstairs. You had to climb an enormous flight of stairs on the outside to get to the black balcony upstairs. We sat down, but we were so uncomfortable, we left. We just felt ashamed."[31] Many black residents of Atlanta did not attend the theaters at all, except for the 81. Students who attended Morehouse College were discouraged from going to theaters where segregation was practiced. In

1940 the new president of Morehouse, Benjamin Hays, said, "I wouldn't go to a segregated theater to see Jesus Christ himself."

Sunshine Tucker, the current manager of the Fox's box office, recollects sitting in the balcony at the Fox Theatre in the late 1950s and early 1960s. "We used to come here to see Disney movies. They had a box office on Ponce de Leon that is near the stage door, now," remembers Tucker. "It was earmarked 'colored box office' and that's where we bought our tickets. To us it made no difference; we were kids. We were sitting in the balcony, and we had the best seats in the house. When you think about it, when you're older, you think, 'I used to come here and had to sit in the back of the balcony,' but it's come a long way from that time." Tucker remembers that at times when she was standing in line to purchase movie tickets, young white teenagers drove by and yelled racial slurs at her. "You were pretty much with all of the people you knew, so it wasn't that frightening to me," Tucker explained. "Somebody might yell out of a window and call you an unpleasant name, but I've never been in a situation—and I'm happy about it—that I was threatened or scared."

By the late 1950s African American intolerance of civil rights violations had reached a breaking point. Like other racial activists around the South, Atlanta protesters were inspired by the actions of the four North Carolina Agricultural and Technical College students who violated the law by sitting down at the segregated lunch counter in Greensboro's Woolworth's on February 1, 1960. Within days of the Greensboro sit-in, twenty college students in Atlanta formed the Committee on Appeal for Human Rights (COAHR). The activists initiated a plan for conducting sit-ins at five-and-dime stores and participated in workshops and seminars on the techniques of nonviolence. Acting upon a suggestion from Benjamin Hays, the students drafted a statement entitled "An Appeal for Human Rights," which was an appeal for basic civil liberties. The primary purpose of the appeal was to create a plan for protesting the inequalities in public accommodations, employment, and land use in Atlanta.[32]

By the summer of 1960, COAHR activists had conducted sit-ins at eating facilities, grocery stores, and department stores. COAHR participants, with the help of Rev. Martin Luther King Jr. staged a sit-in at eight downtown department stores on October 19, 1960. Along with fifty-one other protesters, King was arrested for violating the state's anti-trespass law. Although the other protesters were released from jail after an agreement was made that the demonstrations would cease for thirty days while negotiations took place regarding the desegregation of eating facilities of all downtown department stores, King was retained. Accused of violating his probation in an earlier traffic ticket case, King was not released until Robert Kennedy made a personal appeal for his discharge.

The negotiations between white and black leaders were not concluded within the agreed-upon thirty-day time period, and demonstrations began again. It was not until late September 1961 that lunch counters in Atlanta were desegregated.[33] Inspired by and in cooperation with King, COAHR and NAACP activists continued demonstrating, negotiating, and litigating for the purpose of desegregating Atlanta hospitals, churches, hotels, and restaurants during the early years of the 1960s.

The movie theaters in Atlanta underwent their own process of desegregation as a result of pressures from members of COAHR, the NAACP, the Young Adult Group of the Unitarian Church, and the Atlanta Council on Human Relations. When theater owners refused to acknowledge the requests to desegregate Atlanta theaters and also declined to attend several meetings in which negotiations were to take place, COAHR members conducted demonstrations at theaters during the Thanksgiving and Christmas holidays of 1961. In December 1961 two meetings between theater representatives, members from the protest organizations involved in theater desegregation, Mayor William B. Hartsfield, and the chief of police resulted in an agreement to desegregate some of Atlanta's theaters after a "cooling off" and "control" period.

Because the Metropolitan Opera was to appear in Atlanta before a desegregated audience for the first time during the week of May 6, 1962, it was agreed that theater desegregation would take place after the opera example had been set. The "cooling off" period meant that there would be no attempts to desegregate the theaters before June 1, 1962. The "control" period meant that between May 6 and June 1, theater managers would allow at least two African American patrons per week at the four downtown theaters. The rest of the agreement was left to "common sense and the police." After the agreed-upon date, the services of the police were never requested, and the theater managers did not limit African American attendance to only two per week. By May 15 the *Atlanta Journal* reported that the downtown theaters had begun a controlled desegregation plan.[34]

After President Lyndon Johnson signed the Civil Rights Act in 1964, the city of Atlanta was still not a fully integrated city. White business and city leaders did not entirely respond to the pressures of African American leaders until they realized that continued segregation would be disadvantageous to the city's reputation and economic prosperity. The Civil Rights movement placed Atlanta's African American activists at the center of the city's political process. While white leaders at first resisted the growing political power of the black community, by the mid-1980s African Americans held the majority of Atlanta's elected political positions, and there was a strong coalition between white business and civic leaders and African American political leaders. One of the biggest issues that the coalition faced was the decay of Atlanta's downtown area.

Downtown Atlanta experienced the same kind of decline and neglect as other urban centers during the 1960s and the 1970s, and the Fox Theatre suffered greatly from the abandoned buildings and empty lots that surrounded it. Tucker remembers that the empty buildings around the Fox kept people away from the theater. The Fox Theatre's location in a declining area was a problem, but the theater had a unique handicap, for unlike the few thousand empty seats at most downtown theaters, the Fox had 4,500 seats that it could not fill. "With the development of the multiplex theaters and urban flight, it became relatively unprofitable for a 4,500-seat theater to enter into long-term contracts that were required," explained Ed Neiss, the general manager at the Fox. "The theater became somewhat of a white elephant. By the mid-1970s it basically had to cease operating."

The Fox Theatre's premier status had diminished so much that at the very end of its reign, it was exhibiting exploitation films. In fact, the last film shown at the theater was *The Klansman* (Terence Young, 1974) in the weeks after the Fox was purchased by Southern Bell. After the last showing of the film, which depicted a melodramatic rivalry between Ku Klux Klan members and black activists in a small southern town, the theater manager gave a final tour of the theater and then turned off the lights and chained the doors. Joe Patten, the man primarily responsible for saving the Fox, remembers that rocky period of time. "You could tell the end was near," Patten explained. "People were trying to cart off the furnishings. One time, I caught them loading some Egyptian throne chairs in the back of a pickup. I took the sofas and chairs and tables down to the basement and locked them up."

In the early 1970s the Fox Theatre was owned by Mosque Incorporated, a conglomeration of the Loews Corporation, Georgia Theaters, and the Atlanta Shriners. Because Southern Bell was looking for a location for its new headquarters, and three-quarters of the block on which the Fox Theatre was situated was for sale, Bell officials negotiated with Mosque to purchase the theater (on the other one-quarter of the block) so that they could have the entire block on which to build their new headquarters. On the Fourth of July weekend of 1974, word got out that Southern Bell had purchased one of Atlanta's most cherished landmarks. It seemed that the Fox Theatre's days were numbered, and the fact that a large, powerful corporation had purchased the theater made the situation seem even worse.

Memphis and the Orpheum Theatre

The city of Memphis today still struggles to overcome the stigma of the racial violence of the 1968 city sanitation strike. Dr. Martin Luther King Jr., who had come to Memphis in April of that year to lead a march protesting the workers' conditions, was assassinated on the balcony of the Lorraine Motel, located in downtown Memphis. The Orpheum Theatre sits only a few blocks from the Lorraine Motel, which is now the National Civil Rights Museum. Today both buildings stand as monuments to distinct periods in Memphis's history. The Orpheum commemorates the economic and cultural boom of downtown Memphis during the first half of the twentieth century. The Lorraine Motel, which memorializes the death of one of the nation's leaders, also unintentionally marks the period when downtown Memphis fell to ruin. The riots and fires that followed King's assassination, combined with the trend toward suburbanization and the radical urban renewal that destroyed much of downtown Memphis, left the area in decay. Today, however, the downtown district is a vital center of the city.

At the end of the 1950s and early 1960s, Memphis was beginning to struggle with the same kind of racial controversies confronting other southern cities. Fearful of the potential violence that could accompany desegregation efforts, Lucius Burch, a white lawyer and liberal Democrat, helped to create the Memphis Committee on Community Relations (MCCR) in 1959. The committee members were visible business and professional leaders who believed that voluntary desegregation was the best way to initiate integration and avoid NAACP demonstrations in Memphis.

Before the MCCR was able to initiate voluntary desegregation in Memphis, however, young activists began challenging the violation of their basic civil rights in March 1960. The first demonstration occurred at the McLellan's variety store lunch counter on March 18. One of the activists, sitting at the white counter, asked the manager for a cup of coffee. The manager told the demonstrator that he would be happy to serve him at the other counter. When the demonstrator replied that he wanted a cup of coffee at the white counter, the manager closed the lunch counter, and the incident was over without arrests or violence.[35]

Less than a week later several other events began occurring that pushed the city commission to end segregation on public buses, in libraries, at the zoo, and at other public facilities by the following autumn. Until desegregation, African Americans were allowed to go to the Memphis public library or the zoo only on "black Thursday" of every week. On March 22, 1960, demonstrators from LeMoyne College arrived at the Brooks Memorial Art Gallery and Cossitt Library to protest the segregation policies of the gallery and the library. They were subsequently arrested for loitering, disturbing the peace, disorderly conduct, and threatening to breach the public peace. After the arrests, pickets and boycotts such as the "Stay Away from Downtown Days," a boycott of downtown businesses every Monday and Thursday, were initiated.[36] LeMoyne College students participated in other demonstrations in the following months. Five students, for example, were arrested for sitting at the Walgreen's lunch counter in May, occupying seats that were reserved for white customers.[37]

The MCCR persuaded the city commissioners to desegregate some of the downtown lunch counters and the theaters in the fall of 1960. After the desegregation of much of downtown Memphis, racial relations in the city seemed fairly complacent during the early 1960s. "Whites congratulated themselves for solving racial problems at a time when other cities like Birmingham, Alabama, were in turmoil," writes Michael Honey. "Blacks also hoped a new form of government would give them more political power."[38] In 1967 blacks in Memphis obtained three out of thirteen seats on the new city council; however, in the same election segregationist Henry Loeb was elected mayor. Honey explains that the election of Loeb signaled a "hardening by the city's white residents against further racial change," and it also polarized the city of Memphis.[39]

The racial struggles of the 1960s are epitomized by Memphis's sanitation strike of 1968. On January 30, 1968, more than 100 sewer and drain workers reported for work, but African American employees were sent home because rain made it impossible to work in the sewers. They were given two hours of pay, but that was far less money than they typically earned in a day. Whites were not sent home and received full pay for the day. Then, on February 1, as the American Federation of State, County, and Municipal Employees (AFSCME) organizers were meeting with city officials to demand the lost wages for the employees, two unclassified city employees were caught in an automatic compressor on a garbage truck and were killed. The deaths fueled workers' rage at the horrific working conditions. After the sanitation employees failed to receive payment for the lost wages on the following payday, the union demanded union recognition, a dues checkoff, and an increase in hourly wages. The demands were rejected, and the members of AFSCME voted to strike.

The strike magnified the division between the white and black communities in Memphis. After several mediation efforts failed, African Americans and community activists began boycotting downtown businesses, and whites sympathetic with the injustices toward blacks in Memphis joined forces with the union strikers. However, Honey explains that most whites did not support the strike. They carried their own garbage to the curb, and some took jobs as strikebreakers. "Not only the Loeb administration," Honey explains, "but almost the entire white community seemed intransigently opposed to an expansion of black power or union power."[40]

In the middle of March, national NAACP officers came to Memphis, marking a national effort to support the strike. Martin Luther King Jr. gave a speech on March 18, urging 10,000 to 15,000 listeners to understand that democratic equality meant economic equality. On March 28 King came to Memphis again, as he had promised, to lead a march through downtown Memphis. King's nonviolent tactics were confounded, however, when a group of black teenagers began breaking windows and looting stores during the march. In reaction to the rioting, Loeb placed a curfew on the city and called for the National Guard.

Memphis's chamber of commerce and the Downtown Association stepped forward and proposed that the city adopt a program to provide training and jobs for the city's unemployed, most of whom were black. The national coverage of the strike was hurting business and tarnishing the city's reputation. Simultaneously, Loeb requested a federal injunction forbidding another march led by King. But neither the efforts to ameliorate the problem nor Loeb's inflexible actions mattered, because on April 4, 1968, King was killed on the balcony of the Lorraine Hotel at 7 o'clock in the evening. The strike was settled shortly after King's assassination, but the crisis put the city of Memphis in the national spotlight, and it was characterized much as Birmingham had been four years earlier. *Time* magazine, for example, explained that King's assassination was a result of a minor labor dispute in "the decaying Mississippi River town of Memphis."[41] Such a depiction was painful to the citizens of Memphis, but city leaders must have realized that it was true, because the chamber of commerce immediately began trying to refurbish the city's image and began working with black leaders. Memphis slowly began to develop a powerful African American political force, finally electing an African American mayor in 1991. Such political changes helped to reshape the way the predominantly white business community responded to the demands of the African American community.

In the 1970s urban renewal swept through downtown Memphis, leaving pockets of the city in ruins. In 1972 a *Press-Scimitar* reporter wrote, "Downtown Memphis is in the middle stages of major surgery, and while the life signs are encouraging, many viewers of the operation are startled by the large amount of 'tissue' removed from the patient. The tissue in this case is brick mortar and beam—removed because of cancerous condition. The operation is called urban renewal."[42] In the end many Memphis residents came to believe that the cancer was, in fact, the urban renewal program. More than 1,300 acres of the downtown district were bulldozed; significant buildings were razed; and many African American and elderly Memphis residents were forced out of their homes as a result the city's aggressive urban renewal efforts.

By 1973 even the conservative *Commercial Appeal* realized that urban renewal was not going to be the salvation of the downtown district. "Main Street grows dingier and the wrecking ball swings harder," stated one article, "as planners continue to sit in hand-wringing sessions that seem to generate and spread infectious pessimism."[43] The shabby appearance of the area, unsafe streets, a lack of quality merchandise, inadequate and expensive parking, inefficient public transportation, and a lack of interesting restaurants are cited in the article as the main reasons for the deterioration of downtown. Even Memphis's grandest hotel, the Peabody, had closed, and Beale Street—the home of the blues—which was the city's most significant landmark, was boarded up.

Memphis began the process of rebuilding its city center in 1976. A public initiative was set in motion in order to resuscitate the downtown area. A pedestrian mall along Main Street, called the Mid-American Mall, was constructed to be a downtown destination; however, it was not particularly successful and ultimately became a pathway that connected various downtown attractions. In 1977 the City of Memphis and Shelby County chartered one of the first downtown redevelopment agencies and business improvement districts in the country. The Memphis Center City Commission served as the official agency for the revitalization effort, facilitating the relationship between private business and government.

Many of Memphis's downtown movie theaters—the Princess, Loew's State, the Majestic, and the Strand—were razed as part of the Memphis Housing Authority's urban renewal program. The Orpheum Theatre (called the Malco from 1940 to 1975) was not demolished, but was suffering all the same. Situated in an area of downtown that the *Commercial Appeal* called "the one section of town that may never recover from its financial slump," the Malco appeared to have a grim future.[44] M. A. Lightman had purchased the theater in 1939 and created MALCO (M. A. Lightman Corporation). The downtown theater had served as the corporation's flagship theater and the site of the company's corporate office. Malco Theatres had taken good care of the theater through the years; it continued to bring in patrons, and the building stayed in fairly good condition, even in the mid-1960s, when other downtown movie palaces were already in decline or closed. In 1965 the movie *Goldfinger* (Guy Hamilton, 1964) brought 100,000 people to the Malco during the first week of its exhibition. Nevertheless, a downtown theater with 2,700 seats was not a profitable venture in an area that had been ravaged by urban renewal. When a Malco cashier was killed in a robbery at the theater in 1972, the stigma of danger that the downtown area bore was magnified even more.

The promise of the population boom east of downtown Memphis led Malco Theatres to build a new flagship theater and home offices in east Memphis. Before the corporation decided to vacate their downtown theater, they looked for a buyer. The City of Memphis offered to purchase the theater for $100,000 in August 1976, but that price included only the auditorium, a piano, and an organ. In order to purchase the office space and the ground-floor commercial shops as well, the city would

11. Many picture palaces, like the Orpheum (then called the Malco), tried to keep their doors open during the 1970s by exhibiting soft-porn movies like *The Bod Squad*. Orpheum Theatre, Memphis, Tennessee.

have to pay an additional $175,000. Malco Theatres denied the city's bid on the theater alone, and city officials declined to bid on the additional facilities, believing that the $275,000 cost was too much of a financial risk for the city. Memphis's chief administrative officer stated in a *Press-Scimitar* report, "Our problem is that we don't feel the price of the building with potential utilization costs, such as maintenance and restoration, is viable for the city."[45]

The Jehovah's Witnesses then became prospective buyers. The religious organization envisioned the 2,700-seat theater as an appropriate venue for their biweekly regional meetings. However, the prospect of a religious organization's purchasing the theater posed serious problems for downtown Memphis, because of zoning laws. A nonprofit, tax-exempt group called the Memphis Development Foundation was formed in 1976. Their goal to revitalize downtown Memphis hinged on the Beale Street Landing plan, which involved purchasing and renovating warehouses in the area and transforming them into apartments, stores, and restaurants. They envisioned the Malco as the cornerstone of a downtown historic district. But even without the theater as their foundation, the Beale Street Landing project would have been foiled if the Jehovah's Witnesses purchased the Malco, because no alcohol is permitted within 1,500 feet of a religious building. Such a condition would have meant disaster for restaurants and bars included in the revitalization of Beale Street. The fate of the theater as a public venue and the revitalization of downtown Memphis went hand in hand, and both were on the brink of collapsing a new downtown dream.

Biloxi and the Saenger Theatre

Situated in a small city of 55,000 people, Biloxi's Saenger Theatre is not as opulent or as grand as theaters in larger cities, but Biloxi residents have just as much passion for their theater as people do in Tampa or Atlanta. Biloxi is not a typical small southern town, as it has a cosmopolitan flair similar to neighboring New Orleans. Since it is located next to the Gulf of Mexico, its history is different from the landlocked Mississippi cities more associated with the deep South. Biloxi's location on the northern shores of the Gulf of Mexico has helped to shape its unique image. In the nineteenth century the city's economic base depended on lumber mills. In the twentieth century the shipping, seafood, and tour-

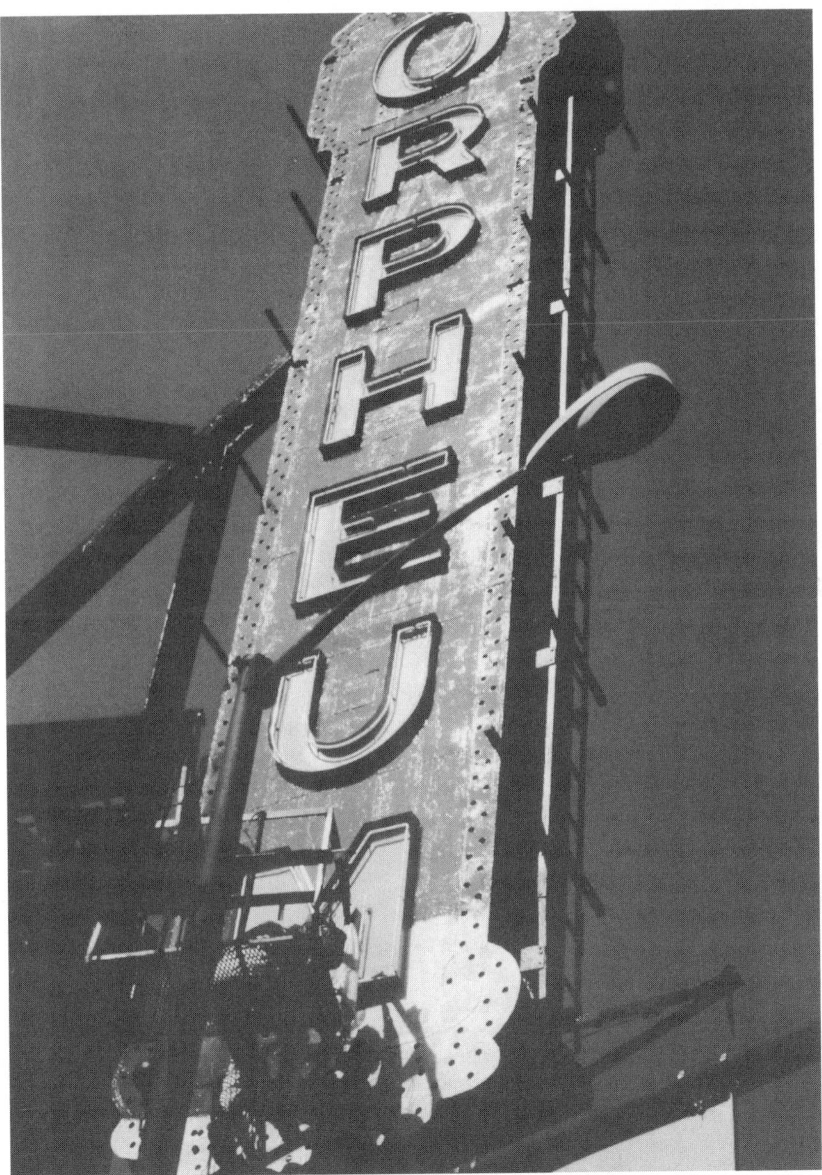

12. The worn and faded marquees such as this one at the Orpheum are usually one of the first renovation projects to be undertaken. When marquees are restored, they signal to the community that the theater is becoming vital once again. Orpheum Theatre, Memphis, Tennessee.

ist industries as well as Keesler Air Force Base brought people from all over the world to the small Gulf city. Biloxi was under Spanish, English, and French dominion until it became part of the Mississippi Territory in 1811. Like New Orleans, some sixty miles to the west, Biloxi celebrates its French heritage with its own annual Mardi Gras celebration. All of these influences have helped to make the city of Biloxi a more urbane place than one might expect of a small Mississippi city.

Biloxi's race relations between blacks and whites may not have been as strained as in many other southern cities, but Biloxi has had its struggles. Biloxi and the adjacent town of Gulfport did not experience racial conflict at a downtown lunch counter, theater, or library. Instead, the racial violence erupted as a result of a desire to integrate the city's beaches. In October 1959 four African Americans presented a petition to the Gulfport board of supervisors, requesting that blacks have "the unrestrained use of the beach" and asking that the police stop denying blacks from using the beach.[46] The board of supervisors did not act upon the petition, and Joseph Austin, one of the petitioners, was suspended from his job as Gulfport's director of the Colored Division of Recreation. Within a few days a burning cross appeared on Austin's front lawn, followed by another burning cross at the beach, on the water's edge.[47]

The following April, on a Sunday afternoon, two groups of African Americans enacted a "wade-in" on Biloxi's all-white beach. The first group of forty to fifty protesters assembled on the beach in front of the Biloxi-MacArthur Hotel, and some of the demonstrators went swimming. A few groups of whites were alerted that African Americans were going to attempt to integrate the beach, and they came to the beach armed with pool sticks, clubs, and other instruments. The whites gathered around the demonstrators and then chased them away from the beach. A few minutes later, thirty more protesters went to the beach in front of the Biloxi Hospital, and once again whites carrying clubs chased them away from the beach. Apparently, the demonstration touched off violence that did not erupt until six or seven hours later, when crowds of young white men began assaulting blacks who happened to pass by them. Although no one was killed, twelve blacks were injured; six of them were shot, and six of them were beaten with clubs. One white person was also shot. The chief of police called a curfew, and officers escorted African Americans who had been at work safely back to their homes.

Felix Dunn, president of the NAACP, explained that the demonstrators were not trying to integrate the beach; they were merely trying to use it. The *Daily Herald* reported that Dunn said, "Integration would have occurred on the beach if the Negroes had been conversing or picnicking with the white people." Dunn also explained that blacks were not actually interested in using the beach, but "if they are paying for it, they have a right to use it."[48] There were, in fact, no more racial confrontations, and blacks gradually began using the beaches of Gulfport and Biloxi without antagonism from whites.

Although the Saenger Theatre was a segregated theater with a separate entrance and balcony for African Americans when it opened in January 1929, there seems to be no public memory or record of any demonstrations to integrate the theater. A photograph of the theater on opening day reveals a crowd of both black and white patrons standing outside the theater; while African Americans were segregated to the balcony inside the theater, the crowd outside was not divided by race. Gwen Gollotte, who has been instrumental in preserving the Saenger Theatre, believes that the theater was already integrated when she began attending in 1945. She explained to me that Biloxi is such an ethnically diverse city that it did not seem to have the same mind-set as other Mississippi cities. Lee Hood, the director of the Saenger, explained that Biloxi was integrated quietly and much sooner than the rest of the state.

Although the racial conflicts that divided other southern cities did not seem to have as large an impact on Biloxi, the decline of the downtown area took place just the same. Racial rioting and demonstrations may not have marked the city center as a dangerous place, but the trend toward suburbanization and parking limitations helped destroy the vitality of the downtown area. The lack of parking places in the small downtown district led developers to build the first regional shopping center in 1963. Edgewater Plaza, situated between Gulfport and Biloxi, was an air-conditioned mall with 3,000 parking spaces. In 1971 demolition crews dynamited the forty-seven-year-old Edgewater Gulf Hotel to make way for forty more stores at the Edgewater Plaza.[49] In the years that followed, suburban shopping centers were built all along the Gulf Coast, further diminishing the status of downtown Biloxi.

But shopping malls were not nearly as dangerous to the city center as the powerful forces that washed ashore in the form of Hurricane Camille on August 17, 1969. Biloxi's downtown, which is only blocks from the shoreline, faced a twenty-foot storm surge and top wind speeds of more than 230 miles per hour. Hundreds of people died; nearly

10,000 were injured; and property losses were estimated to run into the hundreds of millions of dollars. While Biloxi's unique architectural heritage had suffered great damage in the hurricanes of 1947 and 1965, the destruction of Camille was nearly inestimable. Many homes and landmarks from the antebellum period were destroyed either by the tremendous winds or by flood damage.

Biloxi used its urban renewal funds to rebuild its downtown district in the aftermath of Camille. In an attempt to revitalize the area, the city transformed the near-vacant area into a business district called "Vieux Marché." The "Old Market" consists of a four-block area of mixed architectural styles. Today there are only a few stores open in the Vieux Marché, but the area is hardly vacant. Medical offices, a large hospital, the Biloxi Library and Museum, the Mardi Gras Museum, the Magnolia Hotel, the well-known restaurant Mary Mahoney's, and a few coffee shops keep the downtown district alive. And of course, only a few blocks away, Biloxi's newest attraction, the casinos, tower over the quaint downtown area.

The Saenger Theatre is one of the anchors of the Vieux Marché area. Opened in 1929, the theater was an important landmark and entertainment site for people around the Gulf Coast area for many years. Never as opulent or expansive as picture palaces built in larger cities, the Saenger suffered all the more when ABC Interstate Theaters in the 1950s and 1960s attempted to keep pace with the modernization of the film industry by lowering the domed ceiling, replacing the original damask silk walls with acoustical materials, and painting the proscenium arch a dark brown. Still, the theater managed to stay in business and continued to show films through the early 1970s.

But in 1974 disaster struck again, in the form of a fire. The Saenger, which has suffered more than its share of disasters, was left in near ruins as a result of the fire and the subsequent water damage. Because one-screen theaters were hardly profitable enterprises at the time, and because the damage was so extensive, ABC Theaters closed the doors of the Saenger and sold the building to the City of Biloxi in 1975 for $10. Though it seemed like a small sum for a building that had cost more than $200,000 to build forty-six years earlier, the fact that the building had sustained so much damage caused the city to consider tearing it down. It seemed that the small downtown area would suffer one more calamity, this time as a result of human action, rather than a natural disaster.

John Eberson, the architect who designed the Tampa Theatre, had vacationed in Florida for several winters before he was commissioned to draw the plans for Tampa's premier picture palace. Eberson noted that his winter holidays helped him to conceive of the theater's design. "I was impressed with the colorful scenes which greeted me at Miami, Palm Beach, and Tampa," Eberson explained. "Visions of Italian gardens, Spanish patios, Persian shrines and French formal gardens flashed through my mind, and at once I directed my energies to carrying out these ideas."[50] While Eberson's imagination far outmatched the realities of Tampa in the early 1920s, his perceptions are a reminder that even though Tampa is geographically in the South, its history differs from much of the antebellum South.

Tampa has been influenced by several factors that have shaped its unique character. Like Biloxi, it is situated near the Gulf of Mexico in a state that has for nearly a century enjoyed the profits of tourism. One of the effects of the tourist industry on Tampa has been an influx of people from other parts of the country. Many tourists who have vacationed in the area through the years and were attracted to the weather and the moderate cost of living eventually moved to Tampa and its outlying areas. Like many Floridians, many of the residents of Tampa have fairly shallow local roots, bringing to the city an inflow of diverse practices and ideas. Yet this diversity also brings with it a lack of connectedness and tradition. Perhaps the cigar industry is one exception. Cigar factories put the city on the map in the 1920s and brought thousands of immigrants from Cuba and Italy to Tampa. These cigar-factory owners and workers helped to create a Latin culture and heritage that still resonates throughout the city at the beginning of the twenty-first century.

Like many other cities, however, Tampa has a past of discriminating against African Americans. Efforts to integrate the city in the 1960s had more in common with the relatively smooth transition in Biloxi than with the troubles in Birmingham, but there were still plenty of obstacles. Although the Latin community was also discriminated against by Anglos, Latinos generally were not prohibited from eating at white lunch counters, swimming in public pools, or attending public parks. In fact, the Latin community often participated in the discrimination against blacks in Tampa—selling Spanish and Cuban food to the city's blacks, for example, only by way of a separate pick-up window.

On February 29, 1960, Clarence Fort, a twenty-one-year-old barber and president of the NAACP Youth Council, led a group of approximately sixty young people to the lunch counter at Woolworth's. There, they were allowed to have a peaceful sit-in, though the management refused to serve them food at the counter. The protest was mediated by Tampa's Biracial Committee, a group of black and white community leaders that had been appointed by Tampa's mayor, Julian Lane, in 1959.[51] A series of protests followed, until, seven months after the initial protest at Woolworth's, the committee negotiated an agreement with the NAACP and the Merchants Association that eliminated segregated eating policies at downtown stores. Following the change in lunch-counter policies, Tampa's Biracial Committee helped to desegregate municipal facilities, including the Florida State Theatres, a corporation that owned the Tampa Theatre.

Clarence Fort, in a 1978 interview, attributed the ease of Tampa's desegregation to the police protection that the city offered to the protesters. "That's the key difference between the other cities and Tampa," Fort explained. "They didn't let a soul get near us. The second day they were down with us, in fact they directed traffic. And they stood behind the lunch counter, so no one else could even get there."[52] The lack of turmoil in Tampa was also due, in part, to an agreement between the Biracial Committee and the local media not to give publicity to the city's attempts to integrate. There were very few objections to integration because people who would have protested against the integration efforts did not know about them until it was already completed.

Fear of economic stagnation was a major factor in the decision of Tampa's white leaders to fully cooperate in the city's integration. In a 1978 interview Lane admitted that bad race relations were bad for Tampa's economy. "We just felt it was the right thing to do, and it would help us to create a good impression upon industry. Tampa had slowed down considerably," Lane explained, "and we just knew we had to expand."[53] When downtown merchants realized that Tampa's lunch counters were not being financially drained as a result of their integration, other downtown restaurant owners integrated their businesses as well. Historian Steven Lawson contends that Tampa's Biracial Committee owed much to the nature of black leadership, which blended "militancy with restraint." The committee's moderate approach of negotiation enabled Tampa to quietly abandon segregation in public buildings and facilities, such as beaches, swimming pools, parks, movie theaters, and most hotels. Nevertheless, their work was not complete, as Lawson notes: "Although from 1960 through 1967, the civil rights movement stormed the legal barricades of segregation, it had only begun to attack the unofficial remnants of racism still embedded in economic, social, and political institutions."[54]

Florida State Theatres presented one of the biggest roadblocks to the integration of downtown Tampa, prior to the Civil Rights Act of 1964. Tampa's Biracial Committee attempted to reach the Jacksonville-based company for a month to discuss the possibility of integrating their facilities, but the company's officials did not return the phone calls until several successful peaceful demonstrations occurred in front of their theaters. Integration took place after a successful meeting between officials of Florida State Theatres and members of the Biracial Committee. "What the blacks wanted," Lane remembered, "was just to be able to say, 'I can go there.'"[55]

The Tampa Theatre, the premier theater in the city, never had a separate balcony, stairway, and entrance for African American patrons. No blacks, except for a maid and a porter, were permitted inside the theater until Tampa's Biracial Committee encouraged Florida State Theatres officials to integrate their movie theaters. Roweena Brady, an African American teacher, activist, and lifetime Tampa resident, lived five blocks from the Tampa Theatre when she was growing up in the late 1930s and 1940s. She remembered the exterior of the Tampa Theatre, but explained that she never considered going inside, because she knew she was not welcome. "You just didn't go to the Tampa Theatre," Brady recalled. "We never said, 'Mom, can we go down to the Tampa Theatre?' We never said, 'Is it OK to go to the movies there this afternoon?'" Although Brady was aware that she was not welcome at the theater, it was not entirely removed from her consciousness. "We would go downtown, and we would pass by this place called the 'Tampa Theatre.' The best part of passing by the theater was that cool air that came out of it. It was air-conditioned," Brady said. "We wondered why in the world we couldn't have a show like that. It was so cool. We didn't know how it was inside because we were never allowed to go in, but we always felt that cool air."

Even though Tampa's black community had their own theaters, longtime Tampa resident Darryl Miles remembers that the Lincoln Theater was not as nice as the white theaters that he was not allowed to attend when he was a child. "My mother told us that black people—of course, she said 'colored' then—could only go to the Lincoln Theater," Miles explained. "It was dirty. It had a balcony and you could see some of those big rats running across the bottom of the screen." Brady had similar memories of the Lincoln Theater. "Rats and bugs used to be all around the theater," Brady recalled. "While we were looking at the movie, you might hear somebody scream, 'Whew!' because they saw a rat."

By the time Miles was ten, however, blacks in Tampa began attending the other theaters. "I guess my mother told us that we could start going to the other movie theaters downtown. I remember thinking that the Tampa Theatre was much nicer than the Lincoln," Miles said. "The seats were larger; the theater was larger; and I didn't know what mezzanines were, so I thought the theater had two balconies." Brady, on the other hand, explained that after integration she chose not to attend the theater. "I had no interest in going down there. They didn't want me before. Why should I go now?" she said. When she finally attended the theater to escort students on a field trip, she found the theater disappointing. "When I took the children, I thought to myself, 'You mean to tell me this is what they have been keeping me out of all these years? I don't believe it!'" she said. "You know, like it was some kind of king's palace."

A retired Tampa Theatre employee, Maggie Radin, who worked at the Tampa Theatre as it was integrated, remembered that the manager told her that there would be "no colored people at the Tampa Theatre." "I started to laugh under my breath," Radin said. "I thought that he was behind the times. He was going to see a lot of changes. And it wasn't too long after that the coloreds started going to the theater." In fact, by the early 1970s, African Americans who resided near the downtown area became the primary patrons of the theater.

As in other cities, the economic vitality of Tampa's downtown was drastically affected by the middle-class flight to the suburbs. It is a familiar story. The migration of commercial enterprises to the suburbs and the severe parking limitations downtown (because it had been developed before the explosion of the automobile industry) left the center of the city economically drained. The Tampa Theatre, with its 1,500 seats, suffered from the lack of ticket buyers. Florida State Theatres changed the theater's programming to B movies so that they could put off the inevitability of closing their doors for good. Lee Duncan, the man responsible for saving the Tampa Theatre, explained that when ticket sales plummeted, the theater owners changed their marketing strategies. "It changed from a regular theater to an ethnic theater. When I say 'ethnic,'

I mean a black theater," Duncan explained. "There was no one going to the theater anyway, so they showed films that dealt with the ethnic background of people, and when word got out, they started coming to the theater." By 1970, Tampa's white middle-class population rarely thought about going downtown to see a movie at the Tampa Theatre. "People stayed away; they went to other theaters," Radin explained. "The pictures they were getting weren't that great either. They built a new theater out on Hillsborough [Avenue], so that's where the whites went to the movies."

Gary Radcliffe, who worked at the Tampa Theatre during the early 1970s, recalls that the theater management's decision to change programming seemed feasible. "I guess you need customers to stay open, but unfortunately a lot of customers were coming in the back door. You would have forty kids coming in the back doors, and seventy-year-old ushers working retirement jobs trying to keep them out. It was an impossible situation," he said. "Once they got inside, the vandalism was rampant. It was not a pretty sight." Stained-glass signs, rest-room signs, and light fixtures were broken because young patrons hung on them and ripped them from the walls. "So one week I took every remaining light fixture off the wall. We locked everything in the organ chambers, and we built a solid wall, so they couldn't get upstairs, and then we chained the balcony doors."

A 1973 newspaper article lamented the demise of the Tampa Theatre by noting the shift to a predominantly black audience who watched films such as *Shaft, Shaft's Return,* and *Ghetto Freaks.* "Things have changed. You have to realize this," the theater's manager explained in the article. "It is happening all over the United States. More blacks are frequenting downtown."[56] "There is still some fun to be had in the Tampa Theatre today, but it is of a less genteel nature," the article explained. "The fun for the audience now often comes when a black man on screen is doing violence to a white man, for the old Tampa [Theatre] now has a different complexion."[57] The racist opinions expressed in the article dramatically depicted the belief of some whites that the movie palace had somehow been tainted by the presence of African Americans. Although the article was written about the Tampa Theatre, it illuminates a broader portrait of the southern movie palace. Once premier picture palaces were integrated, their prestige was corrupted in the eyes of some white middle-class people who had once attended them regularly.

The presence of African Americans at the theaters marked the end of a venerable era of social entertainment for some people with racist perceptions. And the fact is, when blacks were the primary patrons of the Tampa Theatre (and other movie palaces like it) in the early 1970s, the theaters were not as they had once been. While some white audiences probably did stay away because of their prejudice and fear, other reasons kept people at bay as well. Because suburban theaters were taking ticket sales away from the downtown theaters, there was little money to care for the aging buildings, and many of them were in poor condition. Martial-arts, black exploitation, and borderline pornographic movies did not help to attract a middle-class audience—black or white. But perhaps the most significant reason for the decline of the movie palace was location. The middle class had simply lost interest in or were frightened of going downtown.

After five years of dwindling ticket sales, the Tampa Theatre owners finally gave up on the old movie palace. In 1974 they wanted to close the theater and demolish the building because they did not want to pay taxes on it. It seemed that the nearly fifty-year-old theater was destined to become a parking lot in a nearly empty downtown. But the preservation movement was beginning to spread across the country, and Lee Duncan, a longtime Tampa Theatre patron, Tampa city councilman, and a business owner, had heard that people in other cities were embarking on efforts to save old theaters. It was possible, he surmised, that he could persuade the theater's owners to donate the structure to the city, but first he would have to convince both the owners and the city that it was the right thing to do.

Conclusion

The likely demise of each of these movie palaces was a result of several factors. Civil rights protests that ultimately led to the desegregation of the theaters and other public facilities in downtown districts ensured African Americans the right to complete access to public space; however, this newfound freedom helped to drive away many white middle-class residents who perceived downtown districts as dangerous places and who were already looking toward the suburban malls as viable alternatives to the diminishing shopping and entertainment offered in downtown districts. Urban renewal, which promised to bring back the vitality of city centers, often did just the opposite. Significant landmarks were torn down, and city blocks were often left in rubble because building projects were not realized. The downtown theaters suffered because they lacked enough patrons to fill their thousands of seats. Less expensive but substandard film programming offered little motivation for the middle class to go downtown when they could easily buy tickets for more popular films at theaters closer to their homes. The theaters were also suffering from old age and a lack of repair. The remaining theaters that had once been opulent showplaces in the center of vital downtown areas were now white elephants in the middle of dying cities.

CHAPTER 3

Rescuing the Past from the Wrecking Ball

Michael Putnam's book *Silent Screens: The Decline and Transformation of the American Movie Theater* chronicles, primarily by photographs, the disappearance of the small-town and neighborhood movie theater.[1] Putnam's lovely black-and-white photographs of empty theaters in towns and cities are lonely pictures of quiet, nearly empty streets in towns and cities across the United States. As I look at his photos of abandoned theaters, I mostly notice the blank marquees and the deserted sidewalks in front of the theaters. They are nostalgic, melancholy photos, to be sure. But it is the section entitled "Demolitions Noted" that is perhaps the most dramatic. It is a four-page list of demolished theaters in towns and cities from Aberdeen, North Carolina, to Zapata, Texas. As I looked at the list of theater after theater that had been torn down, their names printed in white on black pages, it seemed like a memorial, similar to the names of soldiers inscribed on a war monument. The register of the leveled venues, along with the photographs, suggests that the theaters were carelessly forgotten, given up without a struggle, when they were no longer useful to the people who had once loved and inhabited them.

And while I cannot deny that such abandonment has often been the case, the many hours that I have spent researching this book have shown me that there are people in cities across the South who have not turned their backs on their downtown theaters. Some—like Joe Patten in Atlanta, Cecil Whitmire in Birmingham, and Monte Moses in Durham—have devoted literally decades of their lives to saving, preserving, and maintaining their theaters. There are many others too, who have defied logic and maneuvered around all of the financial difficulties and regulations that have stood in their way. They have spent thousands and thousands of hours working and volunteering their time because they have cared passionately about their picture palaces. And so, while Putnam's book offers a plaintive record of the ending of an era, this chapter tells an alternative, more hopeful story, chronicling some of the fervent efforts that saved theaters from destruction.

Although dedicated people confronted many obstacles in the effort to save each one of them, this chapter focuses primarily on the efforts to save the Tampa Theatre, the Fox Theatre, the Carolina Theatre, and the Alabama Theatre. At the center of this chapter are a variety of desires and motivations that drove the popular and political battles: a nostalgia for an urban center in the face of suburbanized life; the hope that the palaces could be anchors for revitalizing stagnant downtowns; the belief that movie palace architecture is culturally significant; the judgment that the social history of moviegoing is historically important; the wish to create a museum of sorts for longtime city residents who had fond memories of spending their leisure time at the theaters; and, less obvious, a veiled desire to rescue the theaters from their new urban audiences. In order to begin to understand the desire to reclaim old buildings and attach a symbolic historic significance to them, it is important to understand the philosophies that have motivated the evolving trends in preservation in the United States during the last 150 years.

A Brief History of America's Preservation Philosophies

When Benjamin Franklin's house was razed in 1812, no one voiced public regret about the decision. Patriotic and public shrines in the form of preserved structures would not take root in America for forty-one years after Franklin's house was destroyed and seventy-seven years after the states formed into a union. Mid-nineteenth-century Americans, self-conscious of their roots and anxious about their cultural destiny, made several unsuccessful attempts at preservation in Massachusetts in the 1840s; however, the first efficacious nationwide preservation organization was formed in 1853.

George Washington's heirs offered to sell a decaying and farmed-out Mount Vernon to the state or the federal government, but neither the state nor the federal government was interested in paying $200,000 for a dilapidated plantation house and its surrounding land. Greatly disturbed by the stalemate, a thirty-seven-year-old woman named Ann Pamela Cunningham wrote a scolding letter addressed to "The Ladies of the South" in the Charleston *Mercury* in 1853.[2] The letter was reprinted nationwide, and, soon after, Cunningham inspired and organized the Mount Vernon Ladies Association. By 1858, the association raised enough money to buy Mount Vernon. They continue to govern the property today.

At first, the American preservationists seemed inspired primarily by patriotism. Late-nineteenth-century and early-twentieth-century preservationists were interested in homes of great men or buildings of great events. Preservationists restored the home of Paul Revere, for example, so visitors might be instilled with the patriotic virtues of an American revolutionary.[3] While the preservation pioneers saved some important structures, their focus was narrow, and since no other groups either were interested or had the power to preserve other genres of antiquated buildings, many potential sites for making and marking American heritage disappeared.

The 1876 Philadelphia Centennial Exposition helped to shift the nation's preservation perspective by introducing Americans to both the exotica of far-off lands like Japan and Turkey and the arts and artifacts of the colonial period. Besides celebrating 100 years of political and military history, the exposition displayed representations of colonial culture. The Connecticut pavilion constructed a colonial homestead, exhibiting early examples of Connecticut furniture and hostesses in period costumes.[4] The daily life of America's recent past appeared nearly as exotic as Turkish artifacts. The exposition sparked a flicker of interest in the domestic past's habits and artifacts of everyday life. For the next quarter of a century, admiration for nearly all things colonial flourished; however, this interest did not always lead to preservation as we think of it today. Sometimes colonial buildings were stripped of their interiors, which were then placed in museums such as the Philadelphia Museum of Art and the American Wing of the Metropolitan Museum in New York City.

Nevertheless, this activity marked a second phase of the preservation movement. It was a shift away from a concern with the associative value of the architecture and a turn toward the significance of the architecture itself. This move toward preserving architecture because of its relevance as an art form is explicit in William Appleton's 1910 statement of purpose for the Society for the Preservation of New England Antiquities. The organization, Appleton asserted, would save structures from the seventeenth, eighteenth, and early nineteenth centuries that were "architecturally beautiful or unique or have special historical significance."[5]

American preservation took a spectacular swerve in 1926, when John D. Rockefeller restored a large area of a colonial village in Williamsburg, Virginia. Rather than attempting to restore one structure, Rockefeller preserved nearly an entire town. Representing a narrow vision synthesizing patriotism and preservation, Rockefeller's Williamsburg embodied what would become part of a national debate about preservation. His effort aimed at preserving the structures that had housed the elite and powerful, but it did not include the slave cabins and the outhouses of Williamsburg. "Historic Williamsburg" envisioned a recovered past by preserving great public monuments and mansions and became the model for safeguarding America's national heritage. As Americans remembered their country's past by preserving the buildings of the powerful and the wealthy, they implicitly established a preservation ethic that left a wide range of architecture as fair game for destruction.

The Historic American Buildings Survey, established in the 1930s, inventoried the country's architectural lineage before 1830. By the early 1960s nearly a quarter of the buildings on the survey had been demolished, as well as countless others that were built after 1830. The rampant destruction was partly a result of federal programs that were established to improve the quality of urban life.[6] The post–World War II national imperative toward funding for roads, schools, housing, and factories and a series of bills providing public funds and aid to the private sector fulfilled the needs for new construction and led to the destruction of existing structures. Billions of dollars paved over America's past in the name of urban renewal. Only a tiny fraction of those funds was spent on preservation.

In reaction to the weed-like growth of new construction after World War II, the National Trust for Historic Preservation was established in 1949. But it was not until the 1966 publication of *With Heritage So Rich* that the federal government began championing the preservation movement. The influential text—complete with powerful rhetoric, a preface by Lady Bird Johnson, and photographs of old buildings being demolished—helped to inspire the National Historic Preservation Act. The National Park Service's partnership with the National Trust for Historic Preservation led to the empowerment of state preservation organizations and to rehabilitation tax benefits.[7] Rather suddenly, a country with comparatively little architectural history to preserve—at least Eurocentric architectural history—had one of the most comprehensive preservation policies in the world.

As with Rockefeller's preservation efforts, most of the support, leadership, and finances for the National Trust came from a cultural elite who had money, time, influence, and concern for their own architectural past. Like the patriotic preservationists before them, they had a narrow focus. They wished to preserve what they saw as architecturally important or culturally rich. In doing so, they effectively gave definition to the concept of a national heritage. The politics of culture and Eurocentric insecurities had long blinded this American cultural elite and impeded their vision of history and preservation. Buildings that were not somehow associated with the preservationists' heritage or their interests were not considered worthy of preservation, leaving them vulnerable to deterioration or destruction. It was not until the mid-1970s, nearly thirty years after the National Trust had been founded, that the elitist practices of preservation came into question.

In a 1975 opinion column in the *New York Times,* the urban sociologist Herbert Gans, an outsider to the preservation movement, attacked New York's architectural preservation commission for rewriting New York's architectural history. Gans argued that the commission preserved an elite portion of New York's past by preserving only mansions and buildings designed by famous architects. He lamented that the commission allowed popular architecture to disappear. Ada Louise Huxtable, the architectural critic for the *Times,* a member of the editorial board, and a supporter of preservation institutions, disagreed with Gans. In her published reply she claimed that the buildings the commission had preserved were an irreplaceable part of civilization. "Money frequently made superb examples of the art of architecture possible," Huxtable argued, "and there were, fortunately, great architects to design and build great buildings." She also contended that in addition to the monumental buildings that she judged essential to public life, the commission had designated 11,000 vernacular buildings in twenty-six historic districts.

Gans's rebuttal, which appeared in abbreviated form as a letter to the editor, pleaded for a broader approach to ordinary buildings as part of public history. He claimed that it was suitable for the elite to preserve their buildings when they used their own funds, but once public money was involved in preservation, then all pasts must be deemed worthy. Gans noted that of the landmark designations, 105 of 113 were by major architects, and most were not accessible to the public. Ninety-one of the buildings were located in Manhattan, and seventeen of the twenty-six historic districts were built as affluent neighborhoods. Gans wanted a preserved social history that represented all of the neighborhoods of New York City, rather than just the Upper East Side or Greenwich Village. He did not believe that only beautiful buildings should be preserved, nor did he believe that an aesthetic judgment should be made.

Huxtable, on the other hand, wanted to preserve "culture," which, from her point of view, was exemplified by the aesthetic qualities of great buildings designed by well-known architects and built and inhabited by New York's elite. Her notion of "vernacular" was the unusual Upper East Side townhouse built by a lesser-known architect. Her argument follows the trajectory developed early in preservation's second wave. Like Appleton, Huxtable believed preservation should benefit only highbrow architectural structures.

More than a quarter of a century later, philosophical debates about preservation practice continue; today, however, racial and class equality is not considered an unusual philosophical foundation for preservationists. While the architectural preservation movement continues to struggle over what is the most important for Americans to remember and how to remember it, buildings and places that are significant to ethnic and minority populations are becoming more frequent sites of preservation. In New York City, for example, a tenement building that housed immigrants in the early decades of the twentieth century is slowly being renovated room by room. The Tenement Museum, located at 97 Orchard Street in the Lower East Side, depicts the daily life of struggling immigrants. The museum is currently working on educational programs focusing on class-based bias and is preparing a sweatshop exhibition, which will be linked to current practices in the garment industry. And while women, American Indians, African Americans, and other minority groups continue to press for the inclusion of their interpretations of historic sites and the preservation of sites that they deem historically significant, places such as the Women's Rights National Historical Park in Seneca Falls, New York, and the Manzanar National Historic Site in California, an internment camp for Japanese Americans in World War II, are noteworthy examples of a new wave of historic preservation.

The Tenement Museum, a member of the International Coalition of Historic Site Museums of Conscience, promotes a view that historic sites should engage citizenship rather than participating in customary passive history-telling. The coalition—which includes members from Russia, South Africa, the Czech Republic, Senegal, and the U.S. National Park Service—declared in 1999: "We view stimulating dialogue on pressing social issues and promoting humanitarian and democratic values as our primary function."[8] The coalition's belief that history can be put to use to promote social change is a radical revision of the original patriotic philosophy of preservation. How long that preservation philosophy and its practices will continue to be modified is an open question. As Americans' view of what counts as history and the purpose of history continues to transform, the preservation of old buildings and their histories will persist, but the philosophical underpinnings that ensure their preservation will undoubtedly continue to undergo revision.

In order to understand the practices and politics of rescuing movie palaces during the 1970s and 1980s, we must take a few steps back from the current trends in preservation. Preservation in the 1970s was a partial reaction both to the tremendous growth of new construction following World War II and to the effects of urban renewal in the 1960s. Preservationists were not wrestling with issues of diversity and representation, they were simply hoping to save old buildings that they believed were architecturally and culturally important. By examining the philosophies and the rhetoric of those who desired to save downtown theaters from destruction, we can begin to understand not only how preservation was valued but also the anxieties and desires of various communities during the period. "What a self-defined group or a nation seeks to preserve, and to represent to others," writes Prys Gruffudd, "allows us to understand something of what a particular imagined community thinks it is."[9] In other words, by examining the rhetoric and the methods that preservationists used to go about saving the movie palaces in question, we can have a better comprehension of the meaning of preservation in the 1970s. We can better understand the significance of the theaters, the downtown districts where they were situated, and what they symbolized to the people who, one way or the other, contributed to their preservation.

Saving the Tampa Theatre

Wearing a black T-shirt that reads "Tampa Theatre Volunteer," I stand by the theater's massive auditorium doors, holding a flashlight. It is 7:30 in the evening, and the a cappella group Sweet Honey in the Rock will not begin their performance for another thirty minutes. Still, at least two dozen fans are already in the lobby, some of them holding glasses of wine. Two African American women, dressed in satin suits, pose for a photograph in front of an ornate gold table. An elegantly dressed gentleman and a tall, thin woman in a crepe pantsuit walk over to me and ask me where their seats are located. Within a few minutes, more volunteer ushers join me in the back of the theater, as the lobby and the auditorium begin to fill with the voices and laughter of a primarily African American audience. Camera flashes momentarily break the twilight of the theater, as amateur photographers aim to document the evening's festivities. The other ushers and I work quickly for the next twenty minutes, escorting hundreds of people to their seats.

At eight o'clock, six black women assemble on stage. Standing in the back of the theater, I watch and listen to the hundreds of African Americans and Anglos applauding enthusiastically for Sweet Honey in the Rock. As I stand at the back of the theater, I think about the theater patrons who filled these seats in the decades before the theater was integrated. Would they have been horrified to see their theater filled with black and white hands clapping for a group of women who have committed their professional lives to racial equality? After Bernice Reagon Johnson introduces herself and the rest of the women, she tells the audience that they are happy to be performing in such a beautiful old theater, and the audience applauds warmly. As I, too, applaud for the theater that has come to mean so much to me, it occurs to me that I am one of the few people in the audience who are considering the fact that racial prejudice most likely helped to save this grand place.

A half-century ago this concert would have been inconceivable to both the black and white residents of Tampa. No one would have thought African Americans would even be allowed in the Tampa Theatre, much less to watch shows side by side with white patrons. And while the climate of the theater changed after it was integrated, the theater was still, in reality, treated as a segregated space, because the theater was increasingly shunned by many of its past patrons. In the 1960s, as Tampa's black residents began to populate the auditorium, the once-esteemed movie palace became known as the city's "ethnic" theater and fell into disrepair. Had it not been for the preservation movement, which was gaining momentum during the 1970s in cities across the country, the Tampa Theatre's doors might have been permanently closed. In part, the theater was rescued because some of Tampa's leading citizens were anxious about their movie palace falling into the hands of African Americans. Ironically, it was the prejudices of these elite and their desire to reconstruct their image of Tampa's once-lively and predominantly white downtown that now enabled this group of politically charged singers to be performing here.

Economic interest was the official motivation for preserving the Tampa Theatre. While the theater was originally built in the spirit of the economic boom in the 1920s, the crusade to preserve it was generated in the spirit of reviving an increasingly deserted and commercially disintegrating downtown. After five years of declining attendance and deteriorating conditions, it became clear to a few of Tampa's prominent citizens that the Tampa Theatre needed to be rescued. At the request of Tampa Mayor Lloyd Copeland, Lee Duncan, who was a Tampa city councilman, and Raymond Mesler, the executive director of the city's Arts Council, researched the possibility of the Jacksonville-based ABC Florida State Theatres' donating the theater to the City of Tampa. "There was not enough attendance, so the owners wanted to close it up and tear it down," Duncan explained, "because they didn't want to pay taxes on it."

After Duncan heard that the theater might be demolished, he almost single-handedly began a campaign to save it. In 1974 he met with Raymond Mesler to discuss the ways that the city could use the theater if it was saved. For the next two years Duncan also began corresponding with directors of recently preserved theaters around the country. He met with the Tampa Theatre's owners' attorney, Lamar Sera, to propose a possible donation of the theater to the city. "I sat down, and I talked to Lamar, and I said, 'Your company made nothing but money; why can't you donate it to the City of Tampa?'" Duncan remembered. "He said, 'We can't do that,' and I said, 'It's a good write-off and it's for the city.'" After a period of more than a year, Sera told Duncan that there was a good possibility that the theater could be donated if the city would have the theater properly appraised. Duncan did so, and then he began negotiating the price of the theater with the owners during the summer months of 1975. They agreed to sell the theater building to the City of Tampa for one dollar.[10]

The Tampa city council drafted a resolution in April 1975, designating a committee to seek the donation of the theater to the city. The resolution stated that the Tampa Theatre was a beautiful structure and that it was in the best interest of all citizens in Tampa that it be preserved as a vibrant part of the city. A letter from a Massachusetts planning consultant explained more specifically that the theater's renovation would contribute to the redevelopment of Tampa's downtown. Clearly, economic revitalization was crucial to the city's interest in the theater, and in 1975 downtown Tampa was in desperate need of redevelopment.

For some of the city council members, government officials, and citizens, acquiring and refurbishing the theater meant the possibility of a return to the past—to a time when downtown Tampa was the vibrant and middle-class center of the city. As many Tampa residents had heard or remembered, the building of the theater was the crowning jewel of the prosperous downtown district in the 1920s. Restoring it to its original condition seemed like an important first step in rejuvenating the downtown area. Tampa's new mayor, Bill Poe, said that the theater takeover plan would serve as a "catalyst for investments by businesses in downtown redevelopment projects" and that the rejection of the plan would "produce a negative psychological effect on the ability of government to produce redevelopment."[11] An editorial in the *Tampa Tribune* expressed hopes that renovating the Tampa Theatre would aid in revitalizing the sluggish downtown area. "It should, if properly promoted and managed, generate activity. Get people participating in a downtown," the editorial maintains, "other than a place to work—and Tampa can begin to achieve what other cities have in reversing their decaying downtowns."[12]

In the mid-1970s downtown Tampa had an identity crisis, of sorts. The suburbs had taken away its commercial draw, even as it was still evolving as a central business district. Part of the attraction of a city-owned Tampa Theatre was the notion that it could draw people back to the area. C. L. Miller, a planning consultant, in a letter to Mayor Poe, stated that if the theater were turned into "a real people activity center," it could attract people to the area both during the day and in the evening. "The prospect of the Tampa Theatre once again bringing 1,000 to 1,500 people into the heart of the downtown core every evening is an exciting one. The combination of the mid-day and the evening programs can and should have an annual attendance of the order of 1,000,000 people."[13]

Some of Tampa's citizens became interested in the city's attempt to save and preserve the theater as well. A letter to the editor of the *Tampa Tribune* cited several reasons for preserving the theater: a preserved Tampa Theatre would recall the prosperous Florida boom of the 1920s; it was designed by an important, internationally renowned architect; other cities had rescued similar movie palaces and had transformed them into beautiful community assets; and, finally, restoring the past of Tampa would set the stage for the future of the city.[14] The letter concisely illustrates several of the factors that have motivated American historic preservation through the years. For one, saving an old building can effectively symbolize a prosperous past. Secondly, the letter reinforces the notion that it is important to commemorate a well-known architect. It also supports the belief that preserving the past can have a positive economic influence in an area that is in need of revitalization. Finally, the letter exemplifies economic preoccupation with the future, even in consideration of the past. Referring to Pittsburgh's restoration of its movie palace into a symphony hall, the writers state, "By restoring the past, they have also provided a showcase for the future, a wise investment that has paid double dividends."[15]

Those interested in saving old public structures generally juggle both the past and the future simultaneously when they attempt to convince others that preservation is a sound idea. "The past in the United States has been turned toward interests of the future," notes Robin Winks. "That which we preserve must be relevant to some future point. The past must be usable."[16] While nostalgia is surely an important factor in the efforts to save old theaters, the immensity of the structures requires millions of dollars in restoration; therefore, the buildings must have a potential for profitable public use in the future. The rhetoric of those who hope to save an old building can be characterized as time-traveling, because it requires highlighting the cultural significance of the past and at the same time creating a viable yet unknown portrait of the future.

Reports in the local press also expressed concerns that the theater was being denigrated by the presence of African American patrons. It may be that part of the motivation for the city to take over the theater was to change the complexion of the audience. Judging by the tone of a 1973 article, there must have been some general acceptance that the theater was worse off because of its black audience. "For so many years, the Tampa [Theatre], excepting black porter George Richardson was lily white," the article explained. "There was not even a separate 'colored' entrance, nor a 'colored' section in the balcony, like those found in many southern movie houses." While the article laments the physical demise of the theater, there is also a sense of alarm at the state of the theater's programming in the early 1970s. "During the last year or so, the film selection has run to black-oriented movies," the article states, "like *Shaft, Shaft's Big Score,* and *Ghetto Freaks.*" In the article, the Tampa Theatre manager, Bob Harris, denies that he is catering only to blacks. "*General interest* movies play there," Harris explains in the article (my emphasis). "But it's getting more and more difficult to lure suburbanites back downtown for an evening's entertainment in the old-time pleasure house."

A personal letter to Duncan from Mrs. H. L. Culbreath mentions that the Tampa Theatre is "outstanding" and that it was being reduced to "shambles." "Surely, The Palace could be kept open in its place," Culbreath wrote in her letter, "rather than having this beautiful interior ruined beyond repair."[17] Culbreath seems to be suggesting that the Palace Theatre, which was also located in downtown Tampa and which was a less architecturally and socially significant theater, would be better suited for the martial arts and black exploitation films that were playing at the Tampa Theatre. Culbreath also seemed to be implying that the young, primarily African American patrons who were attending the Tampa Theatre could just as easily move over to the Palace, where their presence would not matter as much because the theater did not have historic significance to Culbreath or other Tampa residents who had regularly attended the Tampa Theatre. She concludes her letter by saying, "The Tampa Theatre was so much a part of Tampa, and our lives. I'm sure there will be support for this project."[18]

The Tampa Theatre was important to some people who had lived in Tampa for many years, and part of the desire to save the theater was the fear of losing one of Tampa's social and cultural monuments. And while no one I talked to would readily admit that part of the motivation to rescue the theater was the desire to rid the theater of its African American audience, there seemed to be an underlying disdain for the image of blacks populating the theater auditorium. Duncan explained to me that the reason the Arts Council did not want responsibility for the theater was that it was a tainted space. "The Arts Council made a statement that you would never get the smell of popcorn and collard greens out of the theater. Do you know who eats collard greens?" Duncan asked me. "Us crackers and black people. Collard greens would always smell up the lobby. That was their theory."

There was another reason that some doubted the wisdom of accepting the donation of the theater. The theater's stage is much more modest in size than most movie palaces' stages because the theater was built on a small parcel of land as a result of costly real estate prices during the 1920s Florida boom. In addition, the theater was built specifically for motion pictures and was never intended to be a performing-arts hall. It would have been nearly impossible to expand the stage because the backstage exterior wall shoulders up against Florida Avenue, a major downtown street. If the stage were expanded in the other direction, it would have been necessary to remove some 200 seats. Thus, it was generally understood that the theater could never be suitable as a live performing-arts hall. Most renovated movie palaces become profitable performing-arts centers, but those who were envisioning the Tampa Theatre as a cultural venue for downtown Tampa had to provide other possibilities. In addition, its usefulness as a movie theater was in question because if the city accepted the theater, there was an agreement that the theater would be prohibited from showing 35-millimeter films. Arts workshops, art shows in the lobby, senior citizen performing-arts groups, slide shows, puppet shows, and 16-millimeter films were some proposed activities that could take place in the theater—none of which seemed like moneymaking activities that would help pay for the theater's upkeep.

Even when the price was only one dollar, the decision to buy the theater was not an easy one for some members of Tampa's city council. In January 1976, after Duncan had been working for two years to have the theater donated to the city, the council voted 4 to 3 to turn down the donation offer. "I thought everything was working smoothly. I brought it before the city council and authorized the council to accept the theater for a dollar," Duncan professed. "We got everyone to agree on everything completely. Then we had four votes against it." The council majority officially rejected the donation offer because they were uncertain how popular the Tampa Theatre would be with the many residents who had grown unaccustomed to going downtown. They were also understandably concerned with the renovation costs of the building, and they were worried about a renovated Tampa Theatre's relationship with the $4 million cultural complex that the city was in the process of building.

Duncan explained that he knew he could again bring up the resolution to the city council when he thought it was appropriate. When a new member joined the council, he brought it to them again, and this time he had the four votes he needed. On April 30, 1976, more than two years after he began the crusade to save the theater, the City of Tampa bought the theater for the cost of one dollar.

When Duncan began investigating and then initiating the proper legal procedures for saving the Tampa Theatre in 1974, he publicly argued that saving the picture palace was crucial because of its cultural heritage for the citizens of Tampa, its potential as a mainstay in downtown Tampa's rejuvenation, and its architectural significance. Yet now, many years after Duncan saved the theater, he speaks less of his public agenda and more of his memories of going there with his wife during the late 1930s and early 1940s. Duncan told me about their date nights before they married. Finishing his workday at another movie theater, Duncan would rush to Ann's house, and then they would drive together to a drive-in restaurant for a limeade and a hamburger. Then they would go to the Tampa Theatre. "My wife and I always sat in the one place. The ushers never worried about seating us because they knew where we were going to sit," Duncan remembered. "As soon as you go inside, you turn left, right next to the wall by the mirror—the first two seats. In 1991, when they dedicated the auditorium in my name, that's where we sat."

As I listened to Duncan reminisce, I did not doubt that his public agenda for preserving the theater was sincere, but I realized that saving the Tampa Theatre was also important to him because it was a building that contained many desirable memories from when he was a young man. The rescued and renovated theater is a pleasurable and meaningful monument for Duncan, who can access parts of his personal past when he is there. It also helps him to measure the distances he has traveled. In a way the theater serves a similar function as the photograph of a small sharecropper house that sits on a table in his insurance office. It is a picture of the house Duncan lived in when he was a child. Duncan's wife explained that they keep the photograph as a way to measure the lives they have lived. "We like to keep that," she told me as she showed me the photograph, "so we can say—'we've come a long way, baby.'"

The People's Effort to Save the Fox Theatre

The rescue of the Fox Theatre in Atlanta was notably different from the effort to save the Tampa Theatre, because it received a great deal of legislative support and attention from the press. While Lee Duncan was a primary rescuer of the Tampa Theatre, many citizens of Atlanta rallied to stop Southern Bell from tearing down their old theater. The fact that the theater was threatened by a corporation generated great support for the theater. Southern Bell was characterized as a villain, and the Fox Theatre was portrayed as a victim. This clear-cut dichotomy enabled the city's citizens to come together and support the theater's preservation.

The Fox Theatre opened its doors on Christmas Day in 1929, only two months after the stock-market crash that ushered in the Great Depression. The building, originally named the Yaarab Temple, was built for the Ancient Arabic Order of Nobles of the Mystic Shrine for the purpose of accommodating Shriner functions and performances. The conception of the Shrine mosque began in January 1916. Its Islamic, Egyptian, Turkish, and Arabic architecture, minarets, towers, domes, arches, and mystical "Arabian Nights" atmosphere and decor were in keeping with the fantastic design of movie palaces, though the auditorium was not originally designed for moving pictures.

In 1928, twelve years after it was designed, the Yaarab Temple's board of trustees announced that they had signed a contract with the Fox Theatres Corporation. The Shriners leased the enormous auditorium to the Fox organization; the contract ensured that the building would finally be completed after the twelve-year waiting period. George Fox explained, "We will give Atlanta whatever it wants in the way of entertainment. If Atlanta wants Roxy presentations, they will be produced in the same elaborate fashion that characterizes them in New York. If it is vaudeville and high type pictures that are desired by the Atlanta public, we will give them the best. Our purpose is to present the highest class of entertainment in the splendid new theater and to satisfy Atlanta patrons in every particular."[19] The auditorium, which was built to look as if it is situated between two Moorish palaces, was frequently compared to the famous Roxy Theatre and Radio City Music Hall in New York City. It maintained its status as the "Showplace of the Southeast" for many decades despite periodic financial problems. By 1932, for example, the Fox Theatre was closed because of unpaid taxes. In 1935 Mosque Incorporated bought the Fox and continued to own the theater until 1975.

Today the Fox Theatre is once again a major venue in the Southeast, regularly receiving national recognition. Walking through the theater today, one can hardly believe that in the early 1970s the movie palace had fallen on hard times, was in a state of disrepair, and even was closed in December 1974. When corporate associates of Southern Bell Telephone began looking for a new regional headquarters and began negotiating the purchase of the Fox Theatre and adjacent land parcels with Mosque shareholders, it is likely that they anticipated a fairly smooth transaction. Much of the theater's magnificence was dulled; three other Atlanta theaters had been recently demolished with little protest; and there seemed to be scant public interest in the huge building. Once Southern Bell completed the negotiations and finally obtained the theater, the corporation planned to raze the theater in order to construct a major office building on the site and use the adjacent parcels of land for parking and future expansion.

Yet Southern Bell was in for a great surprise, because as soon as Atlanta preservationists learned of the potential transaction, groups against the demolition of the Fox Theatre were swiftly formed, and public outcry was dramatic and uproarious. Southern Bell's first obstacle was the fact that the theater had already been marked in 1973 as one of forty-six buildings and ten districts in Atlanta that were part of a public policy stance favoring historic preservation. As a result of the policy, the theater was placed on the National Register of Historic Places on May 17, 1974. Atlanta Landmarks Incorporated, a nonprofit corporation, was founded in July 1974, in response to the potential demolition of the theater. Its founders had increasing concerns about the recent demolition of historically and architecturally significant buildings in Atlanta, and they determined that the Fox Theatre should not be added to the growing list of lost buildings. Even though the group had formed in response to the potential razing of the theater, Atlanta Landmarks stated that its broader mission was to preserve, restore, and maintain buildings, monuments, and sites that were perceived as having historic and cultural significance to the city of Atlanta and the state of Georgia.

Atlanta Landmarks believed that the theater should be saved because it had great architectural and cultural value; it was well loved by many people who resided in Atlanta and Georgia; and the theater, if saved, could become an inspiration and working example for the preservation of other historic buildings in Atlanta. "What better model could be selected than a building whose many attributes clearly could fulfill the practical need that our emerging international city has for major entertainment facilities!" the group stated in "A Proposal to Save the Fabulous Fox Theatre." They further noted, "And at such a bargain: here was the chance to preserve a perfectly exquisite theater building and acquire more than three acres of prime real estate on Peachtree Street for around one-third of what it would cost just to construct a replica of the Theatre alone—even if that was possible."[20]

Both the general public and politicians began taking steps to save the theater in the summer of 1974. The Historic Preservation Section of the Office of Planning and Budget commissioned an economic feasibility study for the Fox Theatre in the late summer, and the citizens' group "Save the Fox" presented 150,000 petition signatures opposing the demolition of the theater to Atlanta's mayor, Maynard Jackson. Many telephone calls and letters went out to the press; more than 2,500 people assembled at the Fox Theatre for a public hearing held by the Georgia Senate Committee on Tourism. A resolution opposing the demolition, passed by Atlanta's city council, urged the mayor to cooperate with efforts to save the theater because it was a significant architectural structure and events had occurred within the theater that represented cultural, economic, and social history that was important to the country.

As a result of these various pressures, Jackson announced that he would withhold the issuance of a demolition permit, an action that brought representatives of both Southern Bell and Mosque immediately to the mayor's office. On September 10, 1974, Jackson and members of both Southern Bell and Mosque announced that there would be an eight-month moratorium on issuing the demolition permit so that any interested parties with a plan to save the Fox could come forward and purchase the properties for $4.25 million—the value of the Bell-Mosque transaction. Shortly after the moratorium was announced, representatives of Atlanta Landmarks and Southern Bell met in order to begin discussing a feasible plan for saving the theater from destruction.

While the moratorium was seen as a huge victory, the money required to save the Fox was tremendous, and the eight-month period of time was not long. The Georgia legislature stepped in with a resolution in March 1975, requesting that the shareholders of Mosque and the management of Southern Bell postpone the May 1, 1975, deadline set for the acquisition of the theater so that sufficient time could be provided for the necessary planning and financing by those who were interested in the preservation and continued use of the theater. The resolution stated that the Fox Theatre should be preserved for the benefit and enjoyment of Georgians because it was one of the most "outstanding architectural achievements of its kind in the United States" and because it is considered "by people everywhere to be a landmark of the City of Atlanta and one of the most glamorous buildings in the State of Georgia."[21]

In August 1974 the Historic Preservation Section of the Office of Planning and Budget secured $11,000 in state historic preservation funds to commission a feasibility study to be used to convince corporate leaders and private citizens of the theater's viability. Unlike the Tampa Theatre, with its small auditorium and stage, the Fox Theatre has a massive auditorium, with 4,700 seats. In the era of the multiplex, it was not economically possible to use the theater as a movie house, so the auditorium would have to be used in other ways. The firm of Hammer, Siler, George Associates studied the economic reuse potentials of the theater by examining the reuse of other historic picture palaces, evaluating the Atlanta entertainment market, and projecting the financial prospects of the theater. It concluded that the Fox Theatre could serve as a symbol of Atlanta's past and complement its growth and spirit as a national and international city.

The study determined that there were four major theater restorations that set significant precedents for the Fox Theatre: Powell Symphony Hall in St. Louis, Heinz Hall in Pittsburgh, the Orchestra Halls in Detroit, and the Ohio Theatre in Columbus. All of these restored movie palaces had been transformed into profitable live-performance theaters. The study also found that there was a conspicuous void for a facility that provided the combination of acoustics, stage arrangements, seating capacity, and aesthetics that the Fox Theatre could fill. While both the Civic Center and the Memorial Arts Center's Symphony Hall were named as comparable facilities in the report, they were both booked to virtual capacity during prime times of the year. With a projected population of 2.8 million people in Atlanta in 1985, the study stated that the Fox Theatre would be needed even more in the coming years. The study concluded that, while competent management would be crucial, the theater could be self-sustaining with revenues that included direct event profits, concessions, and rents from retail stores and office space. Finally, the report suggested that the Fox Theatre could serve as a major tourist attraction, be a significant convention resource in the center of the city, and strengthen the inner city of Atlanta.[22]

Joe Patten, one of the founding members of Atlanta Landmarks, explained that as negotiations between Southern Bell and Atlanta Landmarks proceeded, Southern Bell became quite cooperative. "Southern Bell didn't like the attitude people were taking—'Save the Fox' written on their telephone bills—it wasn't going over well with the community. Everything was in our favor for saving the Fox," Patten told me as we sat in his 3,000-square-foot apartment that sprawls over a five-level labyrinth above the stage door of the Fox Theatre. "The television people and the newspaper people—there were people from New York and California. Movie actors—Helen Hayes was involved. There was a lot of turmoil that Southern Bell wanted to get out from under. They turned out to be one of our best friends after it was all over with. The president of Atlanta Landmarks is a retired executive vice president of Southern Bell."

As I interviewed Patten in his meticulous, beautifully appointed apartment inside the Fox Theatre, where he has lived for the last twenty-two years, I could not help but be in awe of (and a little bit distracted by) his many family heirlooms and antiques. Surely, I thought, this home would be the absolute envy of Atlanta; though most people, I suspect, have no idea that this apartment even exists. During the interview, Patten, who sports a "Fox" belt buckle nearly the size of a block of cheese, quite modestly explained to me his deep involvement with the theater, which started nearly forty years ago with his interest in restoring the theater's pipe organ. Patten's technical abilities and tenacity enabled him to fix, rebuild, and maintain the organ, the electrical systems, the plumbing, the air-conditioning, and the heating. He was instrumental in forming Atlanta Landmarks, and obviously it was his passion and vision that, in part, saved the Fox Theatre from destruction.

Atlanta Landmarks took the position with Southern Bell that it would be impossible to raise the more than $4 million they wanted, and that saving the theater would not require the purchase of the adjacent land parcels that were part of the original agreement between Mosque and Southern Bell. Although Southern Bell hoped to stay within the terms of the moratorium, they agreed to work with Atlanta Landmark's position, and over the next few months they structured a plan that essentially meant that Atlanta Landmarks would acquire adjacent parcels of land within the Fox Theatre block that were equal in value and acreage to the theater site and then exchange the land parcels for the theater. Southern Bell would obtain the land parcels and a site for its new building, and Atlanta Landmarks would finally have the Fox Theatre. Patten explained that Atlanta Landmarks took options on all of the land that Southern Bell had not picked up during the negotiations. "The way we got the options is I took almost every nickel I had in my savings, and Bob Foreman took a lot out of his, and we were able to take options on the land on this block, and then we utilized those options to trade for property that Southern Bell wanted," Patten told me. "By doing that and having a negotiating point of view of saving the Fox, we were able to do this with the cooperation of the owners."

It was a fine compromise except for the fact that Atlanta Landmarks still had to find $1.8 million for the purchase of the theater. It took several months to devise a plan to generate a sum of nearly $2 million to buy the theater. "We had five banks we dealt with; we really didn't have any money," Patten explained. "Southern Bell put the pressure on the banks in town and told them to give us a chance, which they did. Five banks loaned us $1.8 million interest-free for the first year. After that it was five percent interest, so we paid interest only in quarters. We were getting donations coming in, and we had a three-year period to do something."

The five banks agreed to lend Atlanta Landmarks the money provided that the shareholders of Mosque would guarantee the principal and Bell would agree to cover any unpaid interest in the event that Atlanta Landmarks defaulted. The due date for the principal amount was established as June 20, 1978. That meant that if Atlanta Landmarks defaulted in the principal amount or an increment of the interest, the Fox would be given back to the Mosque shareholders, and they would tear it down. On June 25, 1975, Atlanta Landmarks acquired the title to the Fox Theatre building, and while their strategies for saving the theater were overwhelmingly successful, the real work had just begun, as they had to generate the nearly $2 million in a period of three very short years.

Patten remembers that on June 25, 1975, he finally had official access to the entire building and was prepared for the theater to begin operating. "I had been involved with it [the theater] since 1963. In all that time I had made a thorough study of everything pertaining to the building:

electric, plumbing, air-conditioning, heating. I knew how to operate all of it; I learned how so if the day came that the people who were running the theater were gone, I'd be able to do it," Patten remembers. "I had to put $3000 for a deposit on the electrical to the power company. I talked them down to $1000. We started cleaning it up with volunteers, and money started coming in from all sorts of sources." Atlanta Landmarks had begun searching for a competent management team even before they had acquired the theater.

Patten explained that in October 1975 Linda Ronstadt was the "saved" Fox Theatre's first live performer. The concert was a sellout performance. Other sellout performances by such well-known musicians as Paul Simon, Fleetwood Mac, Aerosmith, and the Atlanta Rhythm Section followed during the last few months of 1975. On July 7, 8, and 9, 1976, Lynyrd Skynyrd performed at the Fox and donated $5,000 to the theater, which, Patten is quick to point out, was a lot of money in the mid-1970s.

As well as the theater was doing, during the first year it was still touch-and-go, but the theater had a tremendous support system that included the national media. In March 1976 the *Washington Post* wrote, "The Fox is making money again, but not enough so that the Atlanta Landmarks group can meet the first $135,000 interest payment next June 25. What is at stake here, we believe, is not just an Atlanta landmark, but a national landmark—perhaps even a part of America's soul."[23] Yet, as a result of a competent management team, an excellent concert promoter, the rental of the auditorium and other parts of the theater, tax exemptions, and the dedication and hard work of Patten and the other members of Atlanta Landmarks, the nonprofit corporation was able not only to repay the $1.8 million within the three-year period, but also to generate a profit each of those three years, which enabled them to work on and upgrade the theater and its technical equipment.[24]

Today Joe Patten is trying to lessen his activities a bit. He has had three spinal fusions and is a diabetic, though he explained that he does not let that get in his way. "I am trying to slow down; I used to run all the air-conditioning, heating, and plumbing. We had no money and no other people to do it," Patten remembered. "The renovation department had Rick Flynn, and he and I ran all these things and did everything. Now there are fourteen people doing it and not getting as much done as we did. I restored the pipe organ to begin with, and now I have a crew that maintains it, so I don't have to do that anymore." Yet Patten explained to me that after he reads the paper and has breakfast, he still goes downstairs at 10:30 every day to work in the theater. While there are obviously many people who are dedicated to the Fox Theatre, I do not believe that it could be the outstanding facility it is today—perhaps it would not exist at all—without Joe Patten. As I have conducted my research, I have come to the conclusion that, while it takes more than one person to save an old movie palace, there has to be at least one individual who is as doggedly determined and single-minded as Joe Patten for the theater to enjoy a second life in the spotlight.

The Determined Duke Professor and his Loyal Following

When Steve Martin, the director of the Carolina Theatre, guided me through the theater, pointing out the significant rooms, I took only mild interest in the Connie Moses Ballroom. It is a long, empty, and somewhat plain room that looked as if it would be a useful space for gathering together a group of 75 or 100 people. I knew that I would be meeting Monte Moses later that day, and I assumed that Connie was his wife. Probably like a lot of people, I am not overly curious when I encounter a building or room named after a person I do not know, even though I strongly believe that it is the human element that fills a physical space and makes it interesting and important. Nonetheless, until I spoke with Connie's husband, Monte, and her friend Pepper Fluke, I could not understand the significance of the room. Only after I learned of Connie Moses's contributions to the theater, could I return to the room and see it as a memorial to a woman who invested so much of her creative spirit in the Carolina Theatre.

Just as the Tampa Theatre has Lee Duncan and the Fox Theatre has Joe Patten, the Carolina Theatre has Montrose (Monte) Moses and his wife, Constance (Connie), to thank for saving it from the wrecking ball. Of course, many others were crucial in saving the theater, but it was the vision of the Moseses that enabled the Carolina Theatre to flourish in its rebirth. Monte and Connie moved to Durham from New York in 1959, when Monte, a cell biologist, was hired by Duke University. Connie, who died in 1985, was a singer and an actress who quickly became involved in theater around the Chapel Hill–Raleigh–Durham area. Monte explained that, in their early years in Durham, he kept his "nose to the grindstone," doing research and teaching at the university, until he and Connie began seeing some of Durham's old homes and buildings being torn down.

The Moseses joined the Durham Historic Preservation Society, which was a newly formed group in the mid-1960s. The city of Durham, meanwhile, was, according to Moses, noticing that the downtown had all but been abandoned. "The city rolled up its sleeves and said, 'We have got to stop this flight to the malls, and what we'll do is gussy up downtown and make it look better, and maybe we can get some businesses back,'" Moses remembered. By the late 1960s, Durham, like many cities across the country, turned some of its downtown streets into one-way streets. And, as in many cities, the one-way streets in Durham merely exacerbated the problems that the downtown was experiencing.

Moses remembers that the next phase of Durham's attempt at saving the downtown was the idea to build a center—which included an office building, a convention center, and a hotel. "The irony of this for us," Moses said, "was the fact that the owner of a wonderful old hotel called the Washington Duke asked the city for some tax relief while he reconstructed things and upgraded the hotel. The city refused. So he said, 'O.K.,' and he announced that he was going to tear it down." Moses explained that Connie and he watched the implosion of the building on television. "We had connections with it [the hotel] because Connie had done *Showboat* in a production in the ballroom of the hotel, and I had been sort of involved backstage," Moses told me. "We thought, 'This is outrageous,' and it began to get our blood pressure up, so we got even more involved with the Historic Preservation Society."

As outside consultants were creating plans with city officials and discussing the potential of the downtown Civic Center, the Carolina Theatre's existence became threatened, because the area around the theater was run down, and the theater itself was a symbol for the decay of the area, as it was showing B movies and attracting mostly people who were using it as a place to spend time indoors. Moses explained that the city fathers did not support the theater very much. "They saw the theater as simply a place where bums hung out, and some used it as a residence. The theater was trying to show films, but people came in to get warm; they would sit through all of the showings of a film," Moses remembered. "They tried to show *Equus,* and the hangers-on and freeloaders were incensed that they had to sit through this kind of movie." Monte and Connie heard that the theater might be torn down, and the vision of the Washington Duke Hotel being imploded remained with them. "I couldn't sit still, so I opened up my mouth," Moses said laughingly. "And that was a mistake, because whoever shoots off his mouth first is the one who usually gets hooked into it."

Moses and Connie began telling their friends about the potential demise of the theater and found that many of them were willing to get involved. "I started with friends, and friends brought on other people. It wasn't difficult," Moses said. "We went through it [the theater], and we said, 'This is not hard to put back into business.' You don't have to make a great renovation, just to keep it going." Moses explained that while there was a good bit of enthusiasm from attorneys and business people in the community, they met with a great deal of skepticism as well. Through the efforts of Moses and the Historic Preservation Society and the Department of Archives and History, the theater (then named the Durham Auditorium) was declared a historic site. With such a declaration, the Historic Preservation Society was able to begin the process of saving it and, over time, restoring it.

A group of local citizens, an outgrowth of the Preservation Society, began coordinating their efforts in order to find a new purpose for the theater, researching the possibility of local musical and theater groups using the theater. Their eleven-month investigation uncovered the fact that local groups could in no way defray the running costs of the theater, and they realized that they would have to find an alternative use for the theater. Still the nearly one-year process helped to create a cohesive group of dedicated citizens who ultimately became the Carolina Cinema Corporation, a nonprofit group that ran the theater for more than a decade.

The Carolina Cinema Corporation decided that the best thing that they could do with the theater was show movies. Moses explained how they came up with the idea for using the theater for film exhibition:

> The answer was right in front of us, because there was a movie house downtown called the Rialto. It was just a crummy little backstreet theater, one you would expect would show dirty pictures. But there was a woman in the community named Maggie Dent, and she was quite a remarkable person. She loved two things: cats and movies. She knew films backward and forward. She had run a film series, and she decided that she would put her money down and do what she always had wanted to do—which was run a film house.

> She cleaned it up and got the word out in the community. There were so many immigrants from the North and from big cities where art and movies are just a necessary part of life. She got the word out, and it caught on, and it was going very well, and she could have kept it going, but the city came along and said, 'I'm sorry, but the footprint that the theater occupies is one that we want to clear in order to build a forty-story high-rise.' They had to close it down, and she went out of business. [The high-rise never materialized.] We thought that she was the perfect manager, so we talked with her. And she got excited about the idea.

The Carolina Cinema Corporation believed it could support itself by regularly exhibiting old and new films of artistic, educational, cultural, and historic merit, and it would also make the theater available to performing groups from the community on an occasional basis.[25] Remembering Maggie Dent's Rialto Theatre, the Carolina Cinema Corporation's prospectus for a new use for the theater stated, "The films she showed were unusual. They were made because they had something to say, or were of artistic merit. They were not made to please the mass consumption market, although, as is apt to be the case with creative excellence, they often did. They helped to make our lives in Durham fuller."[26] While the Carolina Cinema Corporation suggested that regular exhibition of the art films would enrich the cultural lives of Durham residents, the proposal also emphasized their hope that an active, fully occupied theater could bring people back to the downtown area. The prospectus explained that the board of directors of the nonprofit group was aware that a civic center was being planned and that the theater would not compromise such an addition to the downtown. "In fact," the prospectus explains, "the revitalization could complement these propositions. It could very well be the first step to bringing a supportive public back to the area, and facilitate the realization of other efforts to make downtown a cultural center and a focal point of community pride."[27]

The nonprofit corporation took their plan to the city council and its finance committee. Over the course of seven separate meetings with the council, the city finally agreed on May 31, 1978, to rent the theater to the Carolina Cinema Corporation for one dollar per year, for three years or more. Because the corporation's research demonstrated that the theater would be an asset to the city only if it exhibited films, the city agreed to buy all of the film equipment that was already in the theater. The Carolina Cinema Corporation agreed to assume routine maintenance and pay the city $250 a month to defray possible major maintenance costs. The corporation also agreed to make monthly financial reports and build a $20,000 cushion for operating capital, with any surplus being deposited into a fund maintained by the city for improving and restoring the theater.

Once Durham's city council agreed to lease the theater, the Carolina Cinema Corporation arranged for a $10,000 loan from the Central Carolina Bank. Thirty cosigners, each liable for $400, underwrote the note. "We were terribly proud of the fact that not one of the co-signers took more than ten minutes deciding to sign it," the board of directors of the Carolina Cinema Corporation wrote in 1978, "and that better than half of them volunteered without ever being asked. And some were folks we didn't know at all, who'd only read about our plan in the papers."[28]

While the documents were not officially drawn until July 1, 1978, the Carolina Theatre reopened as an art house two weeks after the agreement with the city council, on June 14, 1978. Dent was convinced that the theater needed to open immediately, as the spring and summer months had proven to be much stronger for box-office revenues in Durham than fall and winter. Because the city council had taken longer than expected to come to their final decision about the theater, and timing was crucial, volunteers and members of the Carolina Cinema Corporation had only days to get the theater ready for its reopening. Pepper Fluke, who has played an integral role in the comeback of the Carolina Theatre and who is a longtime friend of the Moseses, remembers that Connie recruited a Boy Scout troop to wash all of the auditorium chairs. "She got a bunch of us to come in, and she said, 'Everybody bring your acrylic paint that is either white or beige, the lightest colors, no colors, just light colors.' And she dumped all this paint into a big fifty-gallon drum, and we painted the whole building, the lobby and the walls, with this totally costless paint."

A large amount of monk's cloth, a beige fabric, was donated to the theater for the purpose of draping the fabric on the auditorium walls to absorb noise. Fluke remembers that there were four sewing machines going all day until three in the morning, so that the fabric could be hung in time for the reopening. Fluke recalls that Connie told the volunteers that since they could not afford new carpeting, they were going to paint the old carpet red. This was the last task before they opened. They literally backed out of the building painting the carpet red. "It was rolled on, and it dried, and it was there until it was torn up," Moses explained. "There was ingenuity all the way along the line—we really got it cleaned up, and it was a funky, great theater with an ornate feeling."

While millions of dollars would be spent renovating the theater in the 1990s, the cost for preparing the theater to be reopened in 1978 was $200. For more than a decade the Carolina Theatre and the Carolina Cinema Corporation would cherish their successes and experience plenty of failures, but the theater developed and then maintained a reputation as the Research Triangle's premier art house.

Moses, who continued his research, writing, and teaching at Duke University, also remained the president of the Carolina Cinema Corporation for more than ten years. When I asked him how he managed to hold both of these positions and have a family as well, Moses answered, "It is amazing that I got any papers published, but I did. I love both of them. Anyway, it wasn't just me; I'm the one that is talking, but there were so many other people, many of whom hung on for a long time. I stepped in when I was needed, or when I wanted to—simply because I had had it up to here with academia. It was good to get my hands dirty, and sit and try to talk about something that needed to be done." Moses remembers that his daughters did not see much of him during that time period. "I remember one Christmas Eve there was a telephone call, and a very distressed manager at the theater said, 'I hate to tell you this, but we've got a good house, and the heat has gone off.' So I picked up a few special tools that I had, and I went down. It didn't take very long," Moses remembered. "An hour or so; the heat came on, and I went back [home]."

Both Moses and Fluke told me that it was without a doubt the creativity and personality of Connie Moses that drew people to the theater. "The place was alive, but the thing that really kept it alive was Connie's contribution," Moses explained. "In the beginning—when I made some statement like, 'Over my dead body will they take a wrecking ball to it'—she said, 'If you're going to do that, I want a piece of it; I want the ballroom.' I said, 'What ballroom?' She said, 'That balcony. I'm going to turn it into a little ballroom.'"

Over the course of five years from 1980 to 1985, Connie Moses worked on the project of turning one of the balconies into a ballroom. She convinced her friends and acquaintances to donate furnishings from their attics, and she enlisted two window decorators at the Salvation Army to help her. Moses remembers that merchants gave Connie anything she wanted from their shelves. With help from volunteers, Connie cleaned, scraped, and painted. "The result was the most amazing two tones of sort of earth-pink; not two shades but about four or five. She did all of the molding and just fixed up the whole room," Moses recalls. "She painted the floor, which I think was cement, and brought the whole thing into the most charming, semi-Victorian, kooky room with gilded chairs with red velvet seats. She managed to find people who would refinish them for not very much [money] because they liked the idea. And it became the ballroom."

The renovated ballroom provided the Carolina Theatre with a significant source of income, because it was used as a rental space for community groups. Moses remembers that people would stop by the ballroom after work to have a drink and sit and talk with friends. Small jazz and classical music groups performed in the ballroom as well. Moses remembers that Connie had an enormous following of admiring people who also came to appreciate the ballroom. "Whatever faults you could find about the theater, there was that room, and her spirit which brought it about." Fluke recalls that Connie had a vision to sing a jazz concert with a couple of her musician friends in the ballroom. Her performance took place on March 31, 1985. Connie died on April 28, 1985. "The day before she did that concert, they took two liters of fluid off her lungs; she hardly had enough lung capacity," Fluke explained, "but she could belt her songs just as well." Moses remembers that Connie's favorite jazz pianist and his bass player accompanied her. "They did a bunch of her favorite songs," he said. "It was really lovely."

While the Moseses worked diligently and with a loving, creative spirit to save the Carolina Theatre from being demolished, that same diligence and spirit transformed the theater as much as it preserved it. In other words, what the Moseses managed to do was to create a new space in an old building. They marked the space, and in many ways the theater was a product of their vision and imagination. Their signature added a new layer to the history of the building. During the years that the Moseses and the Carolina Cinema Corporation ran the theater, walking through the doors of the theater meant that one encountered not only the traces of the past, but also the ingenuity and creativity of the present. In some ways *not* having the financial resources to entirely renovate and rehabilitate the theater enabled the people who were passionate about the space to have the freedom to create the theater's meaning without the confines of the past.

The Carolina Theatre has now once again been transformed, as it has been entirely renovated, and it is presently a state-of-the-art performing-arts hall and theater. And although I have been in the theater only as it is presently, I have a nostalgia for the theater that the Moseses envisioned and then set about creating, perhaps because during that period there was still the possibility of surprise, mystery, and spontaneity within the space of the theater. Whatever the reason, it is as important a part of the theater's history as any other era and should not be imagined or dismissed as just a quirky, transitional period in the life of the theater.

At all of the theaters that I have researched, there were one or two people who clearly stood out as the most influential in terms of creating strategies and providing the vision and the salesmanship that were needed for saving the theaters. These individuals naturally linked their efforts to save the theater with the broader interests of the community, but there are more personal reasons for their nearly heroic efforts. For Lee Duncan the rescued theater functions, in part, a bit like a photo album. By being able to return to it in its preserved state, Duncan and his wife can reminisce about their years of courtship and early marriage. Duncan saved part of Tampa's cultural heritage, but he preserved part of his own history as well.

It is obvious that Joe Patten's identity is strongly connected with the Fox Theater; he even lives inside the theater. I believe that it was the mechanical complexity of the theater that originally drew Patten to the theater and led him to be a powerful agent in its rescue. First drawn to the theater's organ, Patten rebuilt it and then started exploring and conquering the intricacies of the air-conditioning and heating systems, the electricity, and the plumbing. While it cannot be disputed that Patten appreciates the aesthetics of the old building, through the years the theater has served as his personal technological landscape that he first inventoried and then set about taming.

The Carolina Theatre, for Connie and Monte Moses, was, I believe, a way for them to express a personal artistic statement. While it was clear that they were concerned about the destruction of old buildings in Durham, their interest in the theater went beyond preservation. In its less-than-perfect condition, they saw its potential as a site for self-expression. Because the building was not considered particularly valuable to city officials, they were given the creative license to create a social space—a playground, if you will—where they could express their artistic and theatrical imaginations. I imagine that the theater became an extension of the Moseses' home; they could entertain their friends and acquaintances in a huge building that they designed themselves. The financial constraints that prevented the Moseses from refurbishing the theater entirely did not hinder their pleasure, for those constraints enabled them to utilize their creativity even more. As is often the case in revitalization efforts, the earliest stage of preservation for the Carolina Theatre was its most creative and perhaps most distinctive era because they lacked the capital to create a perfectly renovated theater. Like Patten and Duncan, the Moseses were able to save a part of Durham's heritage and satisfy their creative urges.

I contend that in order for a building to be rescued, there must be a desire to serve the community, but that desire must be accompanied by personal longing that the structure can somehow satisfy. In fact, I did not come to this conclusion when I was interviewing Duncan, Patten, or Moses. It was not until I reached the Alabama Theatre and interviewed Cecil Whitmire that I realized there must be at least one individual whose personal identity is so significantly tied to the theater that he or she will commit nearly superhuman efforts to ensure its well-being.

Selling a Vision

More than anyone else I interviewed, Cecil Whitmire has made it his personal mission to create the conditions for the comeback of his movie palace, the Alabama Theatre in Birmingham. A hardware salesman for forty years and a general manager and vice president of a wholesale hardware house, Whitmire had no theater business experience when he became president of Birmingham Landmarks Incorporated in 1987. But he is a consummate salesman, and his persuasive charm and tenaciousness have created the conditions for the Alabama Theatre to be the most lovely theater of the ones that I have studied. By the time I left Birmingham, I felt that I should be giving him money for the theater. In 1987 Whitmire managed to raise $190,000 in sixty days, so that Birmingham Landmarks could purchase the theater. Recalling the day that he bought the theater, Whitmire said, "I was as shocked as anybody. We signed all the papers, and I was walking back to the theater to put them in the office, and I opened the door to walk across the stage to go to the office, and I looked out at the theater and thought, 'I'm like that dog that's chased the truck—I have caught me a truck—what in the world will I do with it?'"

Although he bought the theater in 1987, Whitmire had been maintaining it for six years. It had been closed during that time period, but Whitmire and a few other people in Birmingham kept the theater from deteriorating completely by running motors, turning the lights on, greasing and oiling mechanical parts, and polishing brass. When I asked him why he had bothered to do that, he told me that he simply had a passion for theaters. "They represent a very short period of time of our overall heritage. Thirteen years—they built these theaters," contended Whitmire. "During that period of time they were a very, very important part of our heritage, our growing up, and our entertainment."

Between 1987 and 1998 Whitmire raised $4.5 million for the purpose of installing new air-conditioning, new heat, new carpet, and a new roof. What is incredible about the donation of that sum of money (in a city of fewer than a million people) is that it went to projects that did not change the aesthetic appearance of the theater. It was not until 1998 and another half million dollars in donations that the aesthetic restoration took place. I asked him how he managed to raise so much cash for the purpose of restoring an old building. He shrugged his shoulders and said, "I'm a salesman. A lot of people say I'm still selling the Alabama Theatre; it's an easy sell. So I say, 'The Alabama Theatre needs your help. Will you dig down, and in a lot of cases, dig down deep, and give us the money we need?'" When I asked him if he ever gets tired of raising money, he replied, "Certainly. It's like kissing up to the world!" But he contends that people do not turn the other way when they see him coming because the theater is proof that he has spent the money well. Whitmire explained how he goes about raising money for the theater:

> Everybody that walks in the theater is a potential donor. I stand out front of the theater every time we have an event, no matter how cold it is—and it was cold last night—I stood there until the show started. There is an inside joke. If you are working for me as a volunteer, and you ask other volunteers, 'Where's Cecil?' [they will say,] 'He's outside trolling for rich people.' That's essentially what I am doing. I'm out there shaking hands, hugging, kissing, everything I can do to make me well-known enough so that when I come to you, you'll know who I am. People don't give money to buildings; they give money to people, and I have to be well-known enough that you know who I am; you know what I'm all about, and what the theater is all about.

13. The current state of the Lyric Theatre's interior. Decades of neglect have taken a toll on the "lady in waiting," but its dilapidated condition is not a deterrent to Cecil Whitmire's vision for the theater. Mark Neumann, Documentary Works, Tampa, Florida.

If you have been to the Alabama Theatre, you know that what Whitmire has done with it is extraordinary. You would be certain, as I was for a while, that a man who is past retirement age and has created such a successful and beautifully restored theater would be satisfied with his accomplishments and would be nearly ready to stop working so hard and pass on his responsibilities. But if you talked to Whitmire long enough for him to stop boasting about the success of the Alabama Theatre, the conversation would inevitably turn to the Lyric Theatre across the street that has been closed since 1958. And if you listened to him explain that it is his "lady in waiting" and if he only had $5.5 million for its renovation, then downtown Birmingham would have the kind of entertainment density it deserves, you might begin to wonder about him. But then if he decided to take you over to the theater that has been closed for nearly half of a century, and you saw it, you would know that Cecil Whitmire simply cannot stop selling.

You would *see* a place that looks more like a remnant of a building that was bombed in World War II, but you would *hear* Whitmire saying, "Where you are standing, just think: Will Rogers, Groucho Marx, Jack Benny, and Fred Allen stood right here. I can feel the energy still in this building from these people. A lady from the Birmingham newspaper said, 'I can't see anything except an old dirty building,' and I said, 'Don't ever get into the restoration business, because you've got to have vision.'" And as you stand on the stage looking out toward the auditorium where there is nothing but rubble, and you know that it is an auditorium only because you are aware that you are in a theater, and Whitmire points to a space amongst the debris and says, "Up here is going to be our golden horseshoe, our grand tier; I am not sure what we are going to call it, but these are *great* seats"—then you would be certain that Whitmire has vision and that the man was born to sell his vision to whoever will listen to him.

It is not a coincidence that the Alabama Theatre, located on a quiet downtown street with no restaurants or clubs nearby, is booked 300 nights a year and has been financially in the black for six years. Whitmire contends that he has worked so hard because he has a passion for the Alabama Theatre, and I do not doubt that this is the truth. Yet I believe that like the Moseses, who used the Carolina Theatre to express their creativity, Whitmire uses the Alabama Theatre as a vehicle for his desire to sell. Ultimately, Whitmire is marketing himself, as his identity is so closely intertwined with the Alabama Theatre that the man and the building are nearly interchangeable.

Conclusion

Preventing an old downtown movie theater from being demolished takes passion, patience, creativity, and a good bit of strategic know-how. During the mid-1970s the Tampa Theatre, the Fox Theatre, and the Carolina Theatre were saved from the wrecking ball as a result of similar influential rhetoric. The notion that saving and restoring a movie theater could help begin the process of revitalizing a downtown area would have been considered more than strange in the 1950s. By the mid-1970s, however, this idea was one of the most powerful arguments for saving the movie palaces. Imagining 1,000 or more people once again filling a downtown area, as they had done decades earlier, was fairly persuasive for many city officials. Because the movie palace had great sentimental value for many longtime city residents, it was conceivable that they could be lured back to the center of the city—a place that they had begun vacating some two decades earlier. All three theaters were envisioned as the first step in downtown rejuvenation. Because these buildings had great public sentimental value, they seemed like the logical first step in creating interest in the downtown area.

While it is true that perhaps a bank or a courthouse might have been equally or more architecturally significant than the movie palace and could have easily been the first rebuilding block for the downtown district, the movie palace has more emotional appeal and cultural value to the general public. Thousands upon thousands of people had regularly frequented them in the past, and the memory of their social interactions, the pleasure of moviegoing, and the fantastic designs and architecture made them care about keeping these theaters safe from destruction. Of course, Michael Putnam's photographs remind us that many theaters in the United States were not given a second chance and were turned to rubble with not much more than a second thought. One might argue that many of those theaters were not grand enough to save, and perhaps that is the case.

The idea of saving the movie palace in order to save the downtown was not the only argument that preservationists enlisted. The notion that a preserved picture palace could help to safeguard the cultural heritage of the city was also influential. The culture that a preserved picture palace could protect was twofold. First, and most obvious, the theater met the traditional preservationist criterion of architectural significance. While the design of the movie palace was never regarded as a pure architectural form, the fantastic mixture of styles (particularly at the Tampa Theatre and the Fox Theatre— the Carolina Theatre is rather staid in comparison) did create an adventurous, mysterious, out-of-the-ordinary space that is more magical than the films that were shown on their screens.

Yet the architectural significance accorded to the theaters during the efforts to save them in the 1970s was different from their original populist category in the 1920s. The movie palace in the 1920s, notes Charlotte Herzog, still contained traces of the huckster elements of vaudeville. The pseudo-elegance of their designs projected an ambience of "tastefully tacky or refined vulgarity," which was intended to appeal to an emerging semiclassless audience.[29] While most of the patrons of the movie palace did not perceive the theaters as gaudy, critics did. The Marshall Field and Company monthly magazine, for example, claimed that the movie palaces had been "built and decorated with perhaps more extravagance than taste because the great mass of people are hungry for beauty, for color, in a form they can assimilate and comprehend."[30] Samuel "Roxy" Rothapfel justified the extravagant design by explaining that the architectural style was a training ground for the masses who were not sufficiently disciplined to understand the subtleties of high-class design. Tampa Theatre's director, John Bell, believes that all of the movie palace architects were "given the same set of marching orders and that was to overwhelm the audience. And so it didn't really matter whether it was architecturally pure," Bell explained. "The architectural critics of the day were aghast that an architect would take such liberties and throw all of this stuff together."

The 1920s movie palace design was regarded by critics as clownish; just garish enough to wow the aesthetically uneducated, the picture palaces were perceived as a first step in aesthetic training for the masses. Yet during the efforts to save the theaters and designate them as historic buildings, their architecture was no longer considered populist, but rather was elevated to high architecture. When the City of Tampa Architectural Review Commission recommended that the Tampa Theatre be designated a City of Tampa Landmark, the commission explained in its report that the theater was architecturally significant because it is "an excellent example of the Mediterranean Revival Style" and offers "an excellent, intact example of the elements of that style in which architects drew upon the organic and vernacular vocabulary of Spain, Italy and North Africa."[31] Although the Fox Theatre was not originally designed as a movie palace, its architecture is similar, but even more dramatic and garish than the design of most movie palaces. Yet, like the Tampa Theatre, it too was elevated to high architecture in the efforts to prevent it from being destroyed. The Georgia state legislature resolution stated that the theater was "one of the most outstanding architectural achievements of its kind in the United States, possessed of magnificent proportions, outstanding architectural detail and ornamentation, extraordinary organ, mechanical equipment, and acoustics."[32]

In part, the theaters' architectural redesignation was helpful for the rhetorical purpose of protecting them from destruction. But such redesignation also demonstrates how cultural categories can be transformed over time. Lawrence Levine argues that accessibility is a key to cultural categories, explaining that popular art is transformed into high art when it becomes or is rendered inaccessible to the types of people who appreciated it earlier.[33] The half-century that had passed between the construction of the palaces and the protection of them was enough time for their design to become architecturally significant. More examples and analysis of the effects of time on cultural categories and preservation will be discussed in the next chapter, but for now it is enough to say that while the theaters' designs did not change through time, the perceptions of those designs did change, and those perceptions helped to protect the theaters from destruction.

It would have also been almost economically infeasible to re-create such theaters in most of the cities where they are located. Saving the theaters meant that this part of architectural history would not be erased from memory and that city residents and tourists could not only go to see the theaters, but could also use the theaters in the same spirit that they were originally intended. In other words, the architectural heritage is preserved, but people are not limited to peeking into roped-off rooms. They can use the buildings as original patrons did, sitting in a theater seat and being entertained by either live performances or movies.

The second aspect of cultural heritage that was being protected by preserving the theaters was the history of moviegoing. While this would once have been a laughable notion—that movies and moviegoing could be equated with culture—by the mid-1970s Hollywood and the entire movie industry had enough history under its belt to make this a viable argument. Besides, it was not simply the memory of the movies shown at the movie palaces that was being protected. It was also the mostly middle-class social interaction of moviegoing that was being constructed as cultural heritage. The Atlanta city council's human resources committee stated that the mayor of Atlanta should provide support and cooperation in the efforts to protect the Fox Theatre in part because events that had occurred there had made a significant contribution to "the broad cultural, economic and social history of the Nation, and from which an understanding and appreciation of the larger patterns of American heritage may be gained."

Similarly, the designation report from the Tampa Architectural Review Commission in the effort to make the Tampa Theatre a City of Tampa Landmark stated that the theater, "with its mighty Wurlitzer organ, is a reminder of that time when motion pictures were a central part of most people's social lives."[34] By the mid-1970s, and even more so today with the popularity of video and DVD rental and home entertainment centers, moviegoing had become a more private entertainment than it was prior to World War II. The memory of the movie palace as a center of social life created a nostalgia that helped save these movie palaces. In the face of privatized, unspectacular cinematic viewing, the memory of the thousands of people seated together to watch the same film in an ornate public space helped to create an emotional appeal that encouraged activism.

African Americans, naturally, did not have the same kind of nostalgia for the theaters, so it is not surprising they did not actively involve themselves in the efforts to save the theaters. And, in some cases, patrons who had once frequented the movie palaces were unhappy with the fact that African Americans and the indigent were the primary customers at the theaters. That distaste also helped to lead to the support for preserving some of the theaters, so that the theaters could be reclaimed by the white middle class.

The rhetoric for saving the movie palaces centered on theaters' serving as catalysts for downtown revitalization, bringing people back downtown, preserving significant architecture, and preserving the cultural heritage of the white middle class. In fact, nearly thirty years later, each of the picture palaces discussed in this book has been a cornerstone for downtown revitalization and has brought people back downtown to varying degrees of success. And while it is clear that the rhetoric used to

14. Hard work and a substantial amount of money will be necessary for this organ to play again at the Lyric Theatre. Mark Neumann, Documentary Works, Tampa, Florida.

save the theaters was effective, I believe that the movie palaces were primarily saved because of the colossal efforts of individuals like Lee Duncan, Joe Patten, and Monte and Connie Moses.

When Whitmire told me, "People don't give money to buildings; they give money to people," I began to better understand why there were no people in Michael Putnam's lonely photographs of abandoned theaters. A building cannot save itself. There must be at least one individual willing to protect it from destruction who can formulate the appropriate rhetoric about its cultural value, its architectural significance, and its importance to redevelopment. And while I do not doubt that each individual who has saved a movie palace believes nearly all the rhetoric that they help to generate, I believe that in the end the building must also have a deep and personal meaning for its rescuer to make such a commitment to it. Originally designed to encourage the fantasies of its patrons and to stimulate desire, the movie palaces, it seems, continue to do so, even in a state of near ruin. When all that is before rescuers is faded grandeur, they can fulfill some of their own fantasies as they set about re-creating the material and social space of the theater.

CHAPTER 4

Creating the Illusion of a Material Past

A movie palace is not a historic museum. A restored movie palace does not rope off its rooms to visitors, nor does it require visitors to stand at a respectable distance from the valuable antiques that help to complement its atmosphere. A restored theater does not freeze its space in the peculiar manner of many historic homes of famous people. The curators of the famous Stowe home in Hartford, Connecticut, for example, imaginatively place a complete meal on the dining-room table and position pots and pans in the kitchen to look as if they were used to prepare the food sitting on the table. While the shellacked cuisine and culinary equipment is authentic to the period of the house, the peopleless but lived-in appearance of the house somehow reminds me of a crime scene—as if the Stowe family simply disappeared without explanation.

The absence of people, the lack of vitality, is an essential difference between the frozen past of the historic museum and the usable past of the preserved movie palace. While both kinds of historic buildings take care to present the past, the level of the public's interaction with the past is quite different. The museum past demands that people observe from afar what has come before them, so that they do not change or alter the tableau presented to them. The usable past creates a space where people are often encouraged to interact with the past, even though it is usually understood that this necessarily alters the historical tableau, as the past can never remain the same when it mingles with the present.

The curators of the Stowe house can take great care to place a mirror and brush set at a precise angle on a dressing-room table because, at the end of the day, the objects are almost certain to be in the same precise position as they were at the museum's opening hour, for the simple reason that visitors must stand politely behind a rope and observe all that they can from the bedroom doorway. The rope prohibits them from touching, rearranging, damaging, or stealing any of the carefully positioned artifacts in the house. When the tour guides leave the premises after the museum closes, the material representation of the famous family remains in paralysis, as it will until the curators shift and replace objects, so to complement the next season that will fall upon Hartford.

While I am certain that the curators of the Stowe house and other such museums encounter plenty of difficulties in presenting the material life of historically famous people to the public, the obstacles that they face cannot compare to the task of restoring and maintaining a historic building that people *use*. At the movie palace, patrons walk on the mosaic-tiled floors, sit on the mohair-covered chairs, and touch 300-year-old tapestries with little supervision. Food and drinks are regularly consumed in rooms displaying restored artifacts. And while movie palace patrons are most often appreciative of their surroundings, accidents and theft do occur. At the historic museum they happen also, but the effects of shellacked cuisine that is dropped on an antique carpet, for example, cannot compare to the damage of spilled wine on a theater carpet. And while this is only a small illustration, it helps to demonstrate and introduce one of the complications of the practice of movie palace preservation and renovation. Attempting to freeze a moment in time within a building that people use with few constraints is simply more difficult than in a museum where people are carefully monitored.

The fact that the space of the restored movie palace and the artifacts displayed within it are more accessible to the public than the historic museum results in different tactics by their respective craftsmen, but the attempt to preserve a distinct time period within almost any building creates some common and curious temporal juggling and changes in perception for both preservationists and visitors. For one, those who attempt to preserve or restore any old building must first drastically manipulate time by dragging the building back to a distinct time in the past, and once this has been accomplished to their satisfaction, they then attempt to permanently immobilize time, so that the building will not once again carelessly slip into a more contemporary period. Visitors of a restored or historic building naturally have less concern for the process of time alteration, but nonetheless they are aware that they have entered a space that represents a different era than their own. They are thus prompted and enabled to look more carefully and differently at a building and its surrounding than they perhaps otherwise would. More attention is paid to time and its passing in a preserved space than in a contemporary site, in part because the less-familiar surroundings jar the normal perception of time.

Yet the presentation of everyday objects, such as a drinking fountain or a toilet, in a historic site also shift perception because the functions of such objects are familiar, but their aesthetics are antiquated. Therefore, the present and the past intermingle, for the present is never forsaken in a historic building; rather, it is always judged against the backdrop of the past. As the geographer David Lowenthal has often contended, we cannot help but view and understand the past by way of our present-day sensibilities. "Historians justly deplore making things past uncannily like (or wholly unlike) things present," Lowenthal explains. "Yet most inheritors, much of the time, must see the past in such an anachronistic fashion. We cannot avoid misconstruing other times and earlier ways in terms similar or opposite to our own."[1]

To better understand how a preserved building and the artifacts within it shift the perceptual experience of time, it is helpful to compare the effects of preservation to that of a photograph. In other words, while the technologies are different, the consequences of preservation and photography are quite similar, for both allow observers to see what would otherwise be invisible to them. If we can imagine the act of preservation as a function similar to that of photography, we can begin to see how both immobilize and arrest the temporal field. Walter Benjamin, in his famous essay "The Work of Art in the Age of Mechanical Reproduction," suggests that the camera changes the way that we see by introducing us to an unconscious optics. Benjamin explains that the photograph does not make familiar images more precise; rather, the image provides an entirely new formation of the subject. "Our taverns and our metropolitan streets, our offices and furnished rooms, our railroad stations and our factories appeared to have us locked up hopelessly," Benjamin explains. "Then came the film and burst this prison-world asunder by the dynamite of the tenth of a second, so that now, in the midst of its far-flung ruins and debris, we calmly and adventurously go traveling. With the closeup, space expands; with slow motion, movement is extended."[2]

In a similar way the technology of preservation allows us to view both time and space in a different way than our daily life affords us. With the aid of the "frame" of preservation, we pay closer attention to the details of how time passes. Preservation, like the camera, interrupts, reduces, and isolates the way that we navigate space and time, allowing us to "calmly and adventurously" travel to the past. However, once the photographer has arrested time, the work is finished—meaning that time and space within the image are stagnant once and for all. The preservationist, on the other hand, must remain vigilant, for preserved matter resists stillness and will inevitably transform once again.

And while both the historic museum and the restored movie palace may create similar frames of perception, there is another difference between them. When I stand in the Stowe house, I am aware that both the objects and the rooms are, or at least should be, the focus of my attention. I have come to the house and paid admission expressly to view and consider these artifacts. The preserved space of the movie theater, however, is generally not the only object of my attention, because usually I go there to see something else—a film, a concert, a theatrical performance, or maybe a Broadway show. It may be that I consider my surroundings and their historic value only while waiting for the show to begin or while standing in the rest-room line at intermission.

Because restored movie palaces are public and accessible historic spaces that require people to use them in order to stay financially healthy and because they often serve as only a backdrop for the entertainment on their stages, the practice of preserving the past is particularly complicated for preservationists. In this chapter we will see the difficulties that the Fox Theatre preservation staff confronts. Their frustrations are a result of attempting to halt material erosion caused by both human and natural causes in a building that is not perceived to be a museum by much of the public or even the theater's management. However, preserving artifacts from present-day wear and tear is only one of the complications of restoration work. I have discovered that the complication of interpreting the past while simultaneously accommodating present-day sensibilities also weighs heavily on preservationists and theater directors as they go about restoring downtown movie palaces.

The Illusion of an Authentic Past

Recently I went to the Tampa Theatre to see the film *The Widow of Saint Pierre* (Patrice Leconte, 2001). As I sat in the auditorium with my husband and friends, waiting for the film to begin, we talked about the history of the theater. While I answered my friends' questions about the theater, I gazed upon the statues that adorn the proscenium area, as I often do when I am at the theater. They seem like old friends, reassuring me in their familiar poses. The following day, I viewed a videotape that Jack Casey, the theater's original restoration manager, had given me. It is a short tape that briefly documents part of the restoration that Casey and others did to the theater in 1981 and 1982. The tape depicts the work he and his crew managed to do at the theater with a limited amount of time, experience, and financial resources.

As is typical of restoration documentation, the tape showed a series of "before" and "after" shots. I was not surprised, of course, to see the flaked paint of the proscenium that was darkened and dull in the "before" shots. But when Casey began to narrate the process that his crew used to restore seventeen damaged statues, I was stunned as a shot of one of the statues before it was repaired came into focus. Burns from cigarettes scarred the statue's face; two holes had been carved into its lips so that a cigarette could be shoved into its mouth; and a swastika and obscenities were scratched into its cheeks and forehead. I was incensed to see the deliberate damage. Thankfully, Casey's crew had been able to repair the defaced statue and sixteen others that had suffered similar insults, along with missing heads and broken arms and hands.

I realized as I viewed the videotape that I had been subconsciously assuming that the statues I routinely admire at the Tampa Theatre have been standing untouched in the theater's niches and alcoves since 1926. While it sounds foolish that I would presume any element of a preserved theater would not need restoration, I realized, in that moment, the power and illusion of restoration and preservation. Crews labor for months and years to bring a theater back in time, creating a semblance of a place that has not been touched by human hands since the theater's opening day.

Preservation work can be compared to period-piece set designers who construct an impressive-looking past for contemporary audiences. In other words, rather than uncovering the past, preservationists create an illusion of a credible material past. Jeff Greene, the most reputable preservationist I interviewed, admitted that his work is illusionary, as he has built his reputation on creating a sense of the past for contemporary sensibilities. As I conducted my research, I discovered that most of the preservationists I talked to understood that they were illusionists, yet one of the most significant issues they wanted to discuss with me is the importance of authenticity in preservation work. In varying degrees, all of the preservationists and many of the theater directors I interviewed believed that a well-preserved theater is one that is restored as authentically as possible.

Authenticity, or how closely the renovation is imagined to mirror the material past of the picture palace, is usually the most crucial standard by which preservation work is judged. At the same time, preservation work is usually understood by preservationists as an illusion of the past. The idea that an illusion could be authentic puzzled me until my second trip to the Saenger Theatre. As I pressed Lee Hood, the theater's director, to explain why she felt scientific paint analysis was an important step in the preservation process, she finally unscrambled the puzzle. "It's all an illusion, Janna. It's a magical illusion from the time you walk in the door," she said. "If we just did a modern version of the building, it would not have the nostalgia and that special feeling of going back in time. Maintaining as much of the past and being as authentic as possible helps maintain the illusion for the audience." Hood believes that such scientific techniques as paint analysis create the best kind of restoration because they help to produce an illusion for the audience. In other words, science helps to create the best fantasy by creating the illusion of an authentic past.

Restoration craftsmen and theater directors generally believe that the best preservation work mirrors what can be known of a theater's material past. With the aid of historic documents such as theater blueprints, early-twentieth-century newspaper articles, black-and-white photographs, written statements by the original theater architects, paint analysis, and documentation and analysis of paint patterns, preservationists can often learn a great deal about a theater's original decorative scheme. Using such historical and scientific information, preservation craftsmen can then interpret some of the original aims of theater architects and craftsmen. While restoration work cannot uncover or re-create a "real" past, many theater preservationists use scientific processes and historical documentation to help them create an interpretive semblance of the past. They use snippets of the past (like paint chips) as clues in order to construct something new that looks old.

Unfortunately, however, it is often the case that the material past has all but disappeared because of deterioration, remodeling, repainting, and damage by fire or water. When there is not even a trace of the past to be found, their work becomes a guessing game. At that point preservationists must use their past experience, intuition, and aesthetic talents. It seems that the most-respected preservationists rely on both the tools of science and their own artistry. In other words, both science and intuition guide the preservation process. Yet those who restore old theaters must also have an intuitive sense for present-day sensibilities. Aesthetic adjustments (such as color schemes) are made to suit contemporary perceptions because ultimately an old movie palace is for people who live in the present. Thus, preservation work is an interpretation of what can be known about the past in order to create a semblance of it, all the while keeping in mind the tastes and perceptions of modern-day people.

Really bad restorations and really good restorations are fairly easy for preservationists to evaluate. The bad ones, according to the people I interviewed, pay no heed to the past; the good ones do. Yet, like the often perplexing aesthetic criteria of the art world, the standards by which preservation work is evaluated tend to be abstract, because the evaluative criteria are based on how well an illusion is created. Because illusion-making is an abstract process, preservationists and their work are often judged by more concrete criteria, such as their use of scientific paint analysis and historic documentation and their reputations and credibility in the preservation field. Ultimately, such standards are used to ascertain the degree of illusory authenticity that a preservationist's work achieves.

Battling the Present to Save the Past for the Future at the Fox Theatre

"Lara, do you have any idea where that exit sign could be?" Howard Massing, a member of the Fox's preservation staff, asks.

"No. What exit sign?" Lara replies.

"You know," Howard says, "the replacement sign. I don't know where it's gone to. It's not on the ground. There's no pieces. There's nothing."

Lara groans. "Are you kidding me? The replacement sign is gone?"

15. The Fox Theatre's proscenium and auditorium. The light fixtures hanging in front of the proscenium were part of the theater's original plan but were not installed until the theater was restored. Michael Portman, Atlanta, Georgia.

"Somebody thinks they've got a historic souvenir," Howard says. "Little do they know . . ."

I have just walked into the preservation offices at the Fox, and already I have stumbled upon a small but interesting crisis.

"What happened?" I ask them. "What exit sign are you talking about?"

Lara Mathes, a preservation intern at the Fox, tells me that at a recent Hank Williams Jr. concert the music was so loud that the sub-woofers vibrated the green glass right out of the original exit sign's metal frame. Regulations require that all exit signs be illuminated during a show, so while they were waiting for the glass to be replaced, they scanned the original sign, in order to create a stencil, and then painted the stencil bronze. Then they taped a piece of green gel, a substance used to change the color of stage lights, on the back of a stencil and hung it where the original one had been. Now it seems that someone has stolen the temporary replacement sign, thinking that they were taking a piece of the historic Fox home with them.

The staff at the theater are accustomed to this kind of thievery. The most common theft, they explain to me, is the taking of glass teardrops that hang from the many antique floor lamps situated around the theater. It happens so frequently that they keep a large bucket of replacement teardrops. After each show, one of the preservation staff takes an inventory of the stolen teardrops, places new teardrops on the lamps, and then files a report. So many teardrops have been stolen that Lara and Dawn Chapman, another preservation intern, imagine that it is very unlikely that any of the original teardrops remain. "Maybe there's one or two, somewhere in the theater," Dawn says with a tone of resignation, "but the odds of it are, well, very slim."

As I listen to Lara, Dawn, and Howard discuss the many careless and intentional acts of damage that have harmed both original and replicated artifacts in the theater, I sense that there is a terrible irony in the good work that they do. The preservation staff's diligence has maintained much of the theater's original artifacts and atmosphere, and as a result the historic building feels like a sunken ship full of treasures. Because the preservation staff has worked so hard to maintain the building's mystery, some patrons cannot pass up the temptation of stuffing a relic of the Fox in their purse or pocket before they leave the theater.

The Fox Theatre is one of the most heavily attended restored movie palaces in the United States, and it enjoys the status of being one of the most successful live performing-arts facilities in the country. It also has been added to the National Register of Historic Places and has been designated a Landmark Museum Building and a National Historic Landmark, which is the highest historical designation for private properties in the United States. The theater's restoration has achieved national acclaim with the help of one of the largest movie palace preservation departments in the country. The well-preserved theater is held in high esteem by the public because of the building's fantastic design and because of its popular programming. Middlebrow and well-known shows and concerts fill the auditorium more than 200 nights a year.

Because of its popularity, the large amount of traffic within the theater places a great strain on the material condition of the building. Since the Fox enjoys so much financial success, however, the theater management is able to comfortably fund the building's restoration and preservation. Thus, although both programmers and renovators who work for the theater realize that they are dependent upon one another's efforts, there is an inherent tension between those who work to preserve the theater's past and those who work to secure its future. Ed Neiss, the Fox's general manager since 1981, for example, contends that Atlanta Landmarks focused too much on the theater's past at the expense of its future:

> It was a preservation perspective and not a business perspective. It was a national landmark; it stayed a historic museum, but no one thought of it as a working museum. How was it going to operate? Succeed? What was the purpose for it being saved is what I think needs to be looked at. If it was saved just for a caretaker to open the doors and let people take pictures, then I'm not sure it should have been saved just for that purpose. It needed to be saved to be a resource for the community and to operate the way it was meant to operate. Otherwise, why do it? It's not Buckingham Palace; it's Hollywood kitsch and there is something to be said for that.

While Atlanta Landmarks managed to raise $1.8 million, the nonprofit corporation did not raise enough money for the theater's restoration and operation. As an example of their lack of foresight, Neiss cites the fact that Atlanta Landmarks did not purchase any land adjacent to the theater so that the Fox could have its own parking lot. However, he also contends that business and restoration have often worked in harmony since the acquisition. Within the last twenty years, $14 million has been spent on renovation and restoration of the building, yet the theater has been closed to the public only once, in 1985, to install replicas of the original seating on the main floor and to convert the orchestra pit. In March 2000, when all of the seat backs on the main floor needed to be re-covered, the upholsterers worked from eleven o'clock at night until seven in the morning. Neiss explained that restoration work done around programmed events is both difficult and expensive, but necessary in order to ensure profits and to maintain and restore the building.

On the other hand, Atlanta Landmarks has contended that the proper balance between the theater's preservation and its marketing has been neglected. In 1986, for example, the board of trustees drafted a document entitled "Thoughts on a Policy for Preservation." The document argued that the use and operation of the theater should support Atlanta Landmarks' ultimate goal: permanent preservation. The board suggested that the theater's general manager be given monetary incentive for his efforts to protect and preserve the Fox, just as he is rewarded for the financial success of the theater. The board also recommended that each employee be informed of the preservation policy of the theater. "Every effort should be made by the management to instill in each employee a sense of pride," the document reads, "not only in the operation of the Fox but its preservation."[3] The document recommends that security personnel should be positioned throughout the public portions of the theater and that sales activities should not take precedence over the preservation of the building: "Theatre furniture should not be moved to promote sales activities; if a particular sales activity cannot be carried on without the moving of theatre furniture, then such activity should not be allowed—because our venerable furniture will not stand, and must not be subjected to, constant movement."[4]

While Atlanta Landmarks outlined what they believed to be a suitable plan for the protection and preservation of the Fox in 1986, the tension between the theater's profit-making operations and the need to care for the theater's vulnerable artifacts and materials continues to be a concern for the theater's preservationists. According to the preservation staff the most damage is not caused by patrons, but rather by production company crews and contractors who set up and dismantle the ballrooms that are rented by private parties.

The "jewel drop incident" is one of the most dramatic examples of damage to the theater by a production company that has occurred within the last several years. The jewel drop is an original (Shriner) decorative curtain that hangs from the proscenium arch. The curtain's focal point is a grand mosque. Moorish riders on horseback and others on foot seem to be approaching the magical mosque. Hand-sewn jewels on the curtain create the illusion of stars in the sky and of gems adorning the costumes worn by the Moorish characters as well as the horses' saddles. Few people, in fact, have actually seen the jewel drop in its lowered position because the curtain, which is approximately eighty feet wide by sixty feet long, is quite heavy and extremely fragile. While the jewel drop was in its raised position, the curtain was damaged by the production company of the New York show *The Scarlet Pimpernel.* Dawn and Lara speculate that while the crew was moving equipment, something got caught on the jewel drop. Near the bottom of the curtain, a hole measuring approximately twelve feet long by six feet tall was discovered by a Fox staff member before the production company left the theater. The production company did not report the damage to anyone at the Fox.

According to Lara and Dawn, the decision was made by administrators not to bill the production company for the damage that they had done. The entire curtain, which was dismantled into three separate panels and packed in crates, was sent to I. Weiss curtain manufacturers in New York for repair and restoration. Working with Biltmore's textile conservator, Patricia Ewer, the I. Weiss craftsmen repaired the damage, vacuumed the front and back, replaced and restitched the curtain's jewels, put a fire-retardant liner on the back of the curtain, and ran aircraft cable between the liner and the curtain to support the extreme weight of the tassels.[5] I. Weiss repaired and restored the curtain for $35,000, which included the cost of shipping the curtain to and from New York. The added support and the lining will enable the curtain to be used more frequently, which means people will actually be able to see the real jewel drop rather than a photograph of it. The increased use, however, will also create the possibility of more damage to the curtain, which would cost $300,000 to replicate.

While production companies do not usually cause such formidable harm, they do routinely damage the theater or steal from it. Cast members of the recent shows *Fosse* and *Annie,* for example, spray painted stencils and signed their names on an original painted bronze elevator

16. The Fox Theatre's magnificent jewel drop, which was damaged by a touring production company. The eighty-by-sixty-foot curtain was repaired and restored for a cost of $35,000. Michael Portman, Atlanta, Georgia

door that had no other markings on it. Lara believes that the second production company did it because they saw the first production company's stencil and thought that the Fox allowed companies to stencil the elevator. But neither Dawn nor Lara could understand what motivated the first production company to stencil the bronze door. "It is not something like 'Johnny was here,' and you don't know who did it. They were proud," Dawn explained. "I mean they were like, 'WE ARE FOSSE!'" Another production company took a settee from the theater and used it in their production and then tried to load the settee on their truck when the show was finished. Other production companies routinely steal the framed posters hanging on dressing-room walls.

Although the production companies cause quite a bit of harm to the theater, the preservation staff and the theater suffer the most from the contracted workers who load and unload objects in the ballroom. Chip Miller, a restoration craftsman at the Fox, believes that the work he does is regularly confounded by contracted workers (such as caterers) who load and unload objects with little regard for walls, floors, fixtures, or furnishings. Even though contracted employees are briefed about taking care of the building, the damage they routinely cause suggests that they are neither adequately trained nor particularly concerned about the historic nature of the building. Similarly, the contracted housekeeping staff has a substantial turnover of employees, which means it is impossible to train them to take care of the building and its furnishings appropriately. Furthermore, the chemicals used by a contract cleaning firm are not approved for conservation.

But what is worse, Miller and most of the preservation staff contend, is that even Fox employees do not receive training in the appropriate care of the theater's collections. Miller explained:

> There is no time spent with a new hire and no time spent refreshing existing employees on the cultural significance of the building and its collections. That is one way we are recognized: we are a museum building so we encompass collections. We encompass a collection of light fixtures, furniture; we have a collection of photographs; and we have a collection of lantern slides. We have other collections we can coddle and take care of that aren't subject to use by anybody but those who are familiar with and trained with conservation, but it's tough to do that with the floor lamp in the lower men's lounge, for example.

Rick Flynn, a former restoration project manager, expressed his frustration with Fox employees in a letter written to Fox management in 1986. "Two weeks ago I saw one of our staff walk into the Grand Salon with a six foot table over his head," the letter reads. "He slammed it into the door frame and broke the painted surface as he passed, and as I was about to point out the damage to him, he walked through a door on the opposite side of the room and did exactly the same damage again." Little has changed since Flynn wrote the letter detailing his frustrations with the staff's carelessness.

The preservation staff today believes that the problems stem from the fact that employees do not receive training, not because they are careless. "We don't have any training program for maintenance or housekeeping staff, at all," Dawn said. For example, Dawn explained that when the preservation staff moves a chair, they pick it up by the seat. When maintenance staff moves a chair, they tug on the arms or lift it by the back. "It's not because they think it is a bad piece of furniture or they want to mess it up," she said. "They just don't know that you are supposed to pick it up by the seat because that is the most structurally sound part of the chair. They just don't know." Howard agreed, stating that one of the staff members that he works with has been employed at the theater for 15 years and has never been trained in the proper techniques for handling and maintaining the furniture collections. Yet he also added that, while education would make a huge difference, "if staff thinks that this is just a job to go to eight hours a day and someone will be right behind them fixing everything that they break, then they are never going to stop, no matter how well they are trained. I'm all for education, but I just don't know how to get people to appreciate where they work."

Dawn suggested that if there were training, it should include a lesson in the theater's history. If staff knew, for example, some of the history of the theater and what elements of the theater were original to it, and they were aware that a particular chair, for example, was placed in a certain position in a certain room in 1929, then perhaps Fox employees would be more reluctant to spray Windex on the chair's stenciling or move it at their whim. While Howard, Dawn, Lara, and I were discussing the lack of training and the problems that it causes, Michelle, an archivist, came out of her office and added, "I think part of it, too, is that people on the housekeeping staff are making peanuts. If you are making nothing and you aren't appreciated, why would you appreciate pieces of furniture?"

Howard agreed, stating that low wages created bad attitudes that prevented Fox employees from caring about the building that they work in.

Clearly, the preservation staff advocates a training program for Fox employees, and it would seem that such a program could be implemented without too much trouble. However, it is important to remember that the ideas and voices of the preservation staff are often contrary to the beliefs and perhaps larger voice of the operation side of the facility. Trained in preservation and hyper-focused on conserving the theater's collections, they work together in a separate office that is geographically and ideologically distanced from the operation side of the theater. While they appreciate the fact that the theater's profits fund their preservation efforts, they pay little attention to fiscal realities. Several times as we were talking, I would ask Lara or Dawn how much profit a particular show brought to the theater during its run there. They never knew, and Lara finally confessed that she never thought about the theater in terms of money or profits. As they were telling me about the frustrations of being a preservationist at the theater, they recounted a statement from Ed Neiss, the theater's director, that shed a direct light on the ideological differences between the operational side of the theater and the preservationists. Lara told me that he came to a meeting of the archives committee. "He's funny. At the meeting," Lara said, "he said, 'I don't care what is going to happen in 100 years. I'll be dead.'" For a preservation staff that has a 500-year vision for the theater's collection, such a mind-set as Neiss's is inconceivable.

Clearly the Fox Theatre is shaped by two competing realities: the reality of taking care of the past by caring for the theater's collections and the reality of running a successful business, so that the theater can continue to prosper. Miller explained that, because the building is used so much, employees are often in a hurry to get their work done before the theater doors are opened for a performance. "When one tries to inform another staff member that perhaps what they're doing isn't the best thing, it's sometimes difficult to communicate that," Miller said. "Particularly in the face of 'I have to get this thing back together, or apart, or some task that involves historic fabric, and I have to get it completed by the time the doors open for the volunteer ushers at 6:15.' We are chronically short staffed, and it's made all the worse by a lack of any sort of formal education about what really matters and what doesn't."

On the other hand, Roxanne Smith, the director of sales and marketing at the Fox, contends that vendors and contracted companies receive an information kit that has a complete list of positively worded do's and don'ts that outline how to care for the building. Smith, who books private events in the theater's ballrooms and the main auditorium, gives vendors with a reputation for carelessness a contract that addresses the building's historic fragility. Such vendors agree in writing that they must pay for any damages that the company's employees cause. The companies with the worst reputations must pay a damage deposit. Smith understands that the building must be treated gently and believes that she is doing her best to prevent any unnecessary damage to the building. "It's plaster everywhere, and it's easily damaged and chipped, and it's hard to repair. The columns in the Egyptian Ballroom are hollow, so it's not hard to do some real damage," Smith said. "It's an ongoing friendly war [with the restoration department], and an ongoing balancing trick: how to keep the business coming in the building to make the money to restore it. Yet [the business] is constantly eroding the building because there is so much of it."

Problems with contracted workers are only part of the battle. Miller is also troubled by the fact that the increasing numbers of people who use the theater accelerate the human erosion caused to the building. As more and more people put strain on original doorknobs or lock sets, for example, they become worn out and must finally be replaced. When Steve Tillander, another restoration craftsman, took me on a tour of the theater, he pointed out several artifacts that have suffered as a result of the natural effect of time and the less natural effect of human carelessness and thievery. The original brass ticket chopper, which was used to cut tickets into small pieces so that people would not attempt to use them again for a different movie, originally had embossed butterflies as part of its design. Today, as a result of people leaning on the ticket chopper through the years, butterflies can be distinguished on only one part of it.

At times, however, it is not the inevitable wear from patrons that causes damage to the theater. While the entire preservation staff assured me that patrons do much less damage to the theater than production crews, contracted workers, and Fox employees, ticket buyers do steal and cause harm to the theater. In the Ladies' Lounge, Tillander pointed out intricately designed lamps that hang from the wall. He told me that there is only one original lamp and the rest are replicas. "Ladies come in and screw them off and snatch them with the wires still attached and stuff them in their purses and take them away," he told me. "We were down to one, so we had it replicated." Dawn and Lara shuddered when they recalled the Chinese New Year concert sponsored by the trendy rock station 99X. After the concert, Fox staff discovered seats that were literally pulled out of the concrete block that keeps them secure. During a recent country concert featuring Martina McBride, a young man attempted to leap onto an original light fixture and swing from it. Two original tables were crushed; one table's leg was dismantled; and a chunk of the other table's apron was missing.

The preservation staff noted that they find little damage to the theater after ballets, operas, and Broadway shows, but rock and country concerts are definitely trouble because people drink too much, and they do not pay attention to what they are doing. Howard explained that many times patrons have been drinking before they come to the theater and continue to consume alcohol once they are at the Fox. "At one of the rock shows, a kid was in the basement kicking one of the bathroom doors," Howard told me. "Somebody went and got a cop, and the cop said, 'Look, don't kick the door again, or I'll have to arrest you.' And the guy said, 'OK.' And then he kicked the door again and got arrested." The entire preservation staff concluded that trying to educate the public about the theater's historic significance and the importance of caring for it is a lost cause. But they are quick to remind me that the public is not the biggest problem. "It's the behind-the-scenes that cause the most damage," Dawn said.

The harm caused by production crews, contract workers, employees, and patrons jeopardizes the individual pieces that form the original collections at the theater. For the preservation staff, which is consumed with preserving each original element of the theater, it seems that they are constantly confronting an uphill battle. The watchdogs of the theater's artifacts, the preservationists are personally affronted by each act of abuse and the operation staff's lack of interest in the theater's collections. But what weighs more heavily on their minds is the fact that if the damage continues at its present rate, the theater's historic significance and uniqueness will eventually disappear. "You are going to get to a break point where for some reason it doesn't seem special anymore. Enough of the good old stuff is gone that the experience is no longer complete," Miller explained. "I can see that being the case, at the rate deferred maintenance is piling up. It's going to get worn and torn so hard, that there's going to have to be a wholesale replacement, instead of appropriate conservation, and that is going to be a problem."

Craftsmen like Tillander and Miller, who are trained to keep a constant vigil over the theater's fragile artifacts, advocate conservation and care, but Lila King, a preservation assistant who was not trained in preservation, questions the rationale behind the incessant guardianship. She particularly dislikes documenting and cataloging everything she does in the theater. In fact, she has stopped keeping a personal journal as a result of the persistent documentation that she must do in her job. "We write down every single thing we do. It's made me—in my life outside of work—not want to do that at all," King explained. "I don't want to have any record. It seems tedious and somehow stifling to write down everything you do and say and make. I can't do it." King also questions the rationale of trying to maintain the theater's condition as it was in 1929:

> I'm always thinking of the 1929 version of the building and the 2000 version of the building and why we want to take it back to the 1929 version and what parts of that idea are necessary for today and what parts we can leave behind. Making sure we have 1929 door handles instead of 1989 door handles—it's being around that environment where everything is so technical that it makes me sort of wander back to the side where I think: instead of doing all of this, we should think more philosophically about it and try and make the theater work in the community the same way it worked in the community in 1929 or 1939 or 1949.

While King dislikes the technical details of preserving and maintaining the theater's artifacts, she actually does not object to preservation. What she wishes to preserve is the purpose of the theater; she wants to see the *idea* of the theater preserved. Of course, at one time the Fox was situated in the social center of Atlanta, and, like other downtown movie palaces, it was not only a place to see a relatively inexpensive movie but a place for social interaction for many different kinds of people who lived in Atlanta. Dawn and Lara believe that the expense and the genre of the current programming, mainly the Broadway shows that typically come to the Fox, prevent people from coming to the theater. They believe that families living in Atlanta's suburbs are the most typical patrons of such shows. Thus, while the theater maintains middlebrow entertainment as it did in its earliest years, middle- to upper-middle-class families who are not geographically or socially connected to the area where the theater is situated are the most frequent patrons.

The annual film series is the only time that the theater comes close to functioning in the same manner as it did in the past. During the summer months, a run of classic films and three or four new releases are exhibited at the Fox. With average ticket prices running five or six dollars, nearly anyone in Atlanta can afford to come to the theater. A cross section of teenagers, college students, city dwellers, suburbanites, and retirees all participate in the festival, creating a scenario that is similar to the theater's original role in Atlanta. However, as the operational staff members are quick to point out, it would be impossible to run a film series yearlong, because filling the theater's 4,700 seats is inconceivable, and the low prices are overwhelmingly unprofitable. King's desire to see the theater's role in the community preserved is a different kind of preservation, one I call "discursive preservation." But King's assertion that the Fox pays little attention to preserving the social history of the theater does seem accurate, for the preservation staff's total focus is on conserving the materiality of the theater.

Although the craftsmen and preservationists at the Fox are concerned with the building's historic atmosphere, the originality of the unobserved elements of the theater—such as heating, plumbing, and electrical systems—does not seem to fall within their realm of guardianship and protection. It is generally understood by both the theater's preservationists and those who work in programming and operations that the theater should stay close to how it was originally designed when it opened in 1929, but the technical elements of the theater are constantly being changed and upgraded. Len Tucker, the director of operations, explained that it is a real balancing act to keep the operations and restoration working together so that the theater can maintain its historic integrity. "We're trying to maintain what we had in 1929 and do everything possible in the building to restore it and keep it in its original form—that's the restoration department's task. On the operation side of the house, the shows that are coming in now are very elaborate, high tech, very demanding—and the theater wasn't designed to do those kinds of shows back in the beginning. For instance, when *Phantom of the Opera* came in, we spent three weeks just trying to modify the building."

In order for the elaborate Broadway show to be performed at the Fox, 2,000 amps of electrical power was added to the theater. Steel had to be added to the catwalk, in order that a chandelier could be hung from the ceiling, and a new device had to be added to the cable system in order to control the chandelier. Tucker, who has worked at the Fox for fifteen years, has seen many improvements and upgrades to the theater that were not originally part of its design. "When I first came here, we had a lot of weaknesses that caused us daily problems," he remembered. "A circuit that couldn't handle something—we were babying it along and trying to make it work. We had problems with the plumbing that was springing leaks every now and then, in places that had not been redone yet."

The system and operational upgrades enable bigger and better productions to be performed at the Fox, and they create better conditions for both workers and patrons, but such improvements do, in fact, change the original theater design. Such upgrades are not compatible with the theater's original system design, nor are they implemented so as to complement it. Fox's preservationists, however, if they consider technological renovation at all, do not consider the upgrades to be a corruption of the theater. As long as they do not infringe upon the building's historic aesthetics, they remain invisible to those most concerned with maintaining and restoring the building. Historic renovation and restoration at the Fox, then, are not treated holistically. Instead, the theater seems to be compartmentalized, with preservationists focusing only on the aesthetic and what is most visible to the public eye. And while the Fox's preservation philosophy nods to its opening in 1929 as an important reference point, there is an implicit understanding that it is the form, not the substance, that is being preserved and restored at the theater.

Preserving, restoring, and maintaining the Fox are difficult and complex tasks. Whenever the clock is partially immobilized by way of safeguarding material artifacts, there will be frustrations and complications, but in a building that people use, and at times abuse, those frustrations are multiplied enormously. The technology of preservation at the Fox seems to be for the purpose of holding on, of preventing matter of a past era from being permanently lost. Yet when I asked members of the preservation staff why their work is important, inevitably they had to pause for a moment to think through their answers. It seems that they are so riveted on the Herculean task of protecting the artifacts at the theater that the purpose behind their work is easily forgotten. Mary Catherine Martin, the restoration project manager, said that she feels strongly that the building represents a concrete realization of a high philosophical ideal and wants to preserve the efforts put forth to realize the building. "When I look at the period in history when this building came into being," Martin explained, "it blows my mind. They opened their doors seven weeks after the stock market crashed. People were committing suicide. They had no money for this. Can you imagine pulling this building together under those circumstances? I think it's extraordinary. As much as we're preserving history, we're preserving those efforts."

One of Lara and Dawn's concerns is that random decisions are made at the theater that lead to the breaking apart of collections. They believe that maintaining the theater's artifacts and keeping the collections intact will enable people in the future to have a better understanding of the original design of the theater because they will be able to analyze the design within its originative context. "Why did they choose that? Why did they choose this? What made them want to make the Ladies' Room Egyptian and the Men's Room Moorish?" Dawn explained. "If you have only three or four pieces, you can't accurately judge why these decisions were made. Some original pieces in a little white room—you lose the original historical context. The sum is much greater than the parts, in this case." While they admit that hardly any researchers have studied the theater or its collections, they believe that it is irresponsible to assume that no one will in the future, just because no one is now. Lara believes that the importance of their work will not be tangible in her lifetime. "I think it's great that people can come here and see what the theater looked like in 1929," she explained, "but I think we are contributing to a philosophy that runs counter to this idea of ephemerality that is so prevalent—you know, 'here today, gone tomorrow.'"

I cannot help but think that the preservationists at the Fox Theatre are a lonely bunch. In a city where new construction erupts from the ground like spring dandelions and the fresh bookstores, coffee shops, and restaurants in Buckhead presently hold the fascination of Atlanta's middle class, their task of steadfastly maintaining old furniture, lamps, and doorknobs in a 1929 building seems like a thankless job. But even within the theater, they face an uphill battle. While patrons enjoy the antiquated atmosphere that the preservation staff labors to keep intact, it is unlikely that many of them give much thought to the fact that they are turning an original doorknob or walking past an original lamp that has been meticulously restored. If a patron has had too much to drink, it is possible that he or she will even set about damaging an original piece. Careless production crews, hurried contracted workers, untrained Fox employees, and the profit-seeking operations side of the facility certainly are not consumed with saving the past. Yet it is unlikely that any of them would declare that they are against conserving the material of yesteryear; they just do not want history's relics to get in the way of the work that needs to be done in the present.

Trained in safeguarding the relics of history so that the past can be honored and future generations will be able to enjoy and interpret what has come before them, the preservationists at the Fox are like social workers in the inner city. There is too much to do and not enough support for what they are trying to accomplish. Their trained vision enables them to focus on both the past and the future, but perhaps it is at the expense of the present. The American philosopher Kenneth Burke, writing about the term "occupational psychosis," argued that any standpoint has both a focus and a blind spot. "Comprehensiveness can be discussed as superficiality, intensiveness as stricture, tolerance as uncertainty—and the poor pedestrian abilities of a fish are clearly explainable in terms of his excellence as a swimmer," Burke explained. "A way of seeing is also a way of not seeing—a focus upon object A involves a neglect of object B."[6] As guardians of the past, the theater's preservationists focus so much on the original matter of the theater, that the original purpose of the theater gets obscured. Movie palaces like the Fox Theatre were built for people to use; all buildings, in fact, are constructed for human beings. Too much focus on material authenticity and too much concentration on the past can turn such spaces into inaccessible places where people are considered, at best, an inconvenience and, at worst, gadflies.

I asked Lara if her work at the theater had worsened her view of humanity. "Oh no," she said with a laugh, "I used to wait tables." But several weeks after my trip to the Fox, I received an e-mail message from Lara, explaining that she had just finished taking digital images of theater seats that were damaged by audience members at a concert. Apparently, the two members of the rap group Outkast had encouraged the audience to "tear up the Fox," because they were offended by the number of security employees in place at the theater during the show. In her message she wrote, "What was that you asked me about how my opinion of the public is affected? Surely my response was too mild." Lara admitted that she accepts as inevitable the accidental wear and tear on the building, but that she could not accept the intentional and malicious damage that performers occasionally inflict or incite audience members to inflict. Indiscriminate accessibility, Lara explained, leads to such problems, though she objects to "aristocratic, elitist restrictions whereby only older, highly educated and well-to-do performers and patrons are welcome." Lara said she does find herself judging those who demonstrate their ignorance by inflicting damage on the building. Yet, while she knows that some people have a total lack of regard for their environment, many others do have a capacity for appreciating it.

Ironically, the success of the Fox Theatre has led to many headaches and much angst for the organization's preservationists. Obviously, the more the theater is used, the more the building suffers wear and tear. But, because the theater has experienced much recognition and financial achievement, preservationists such as Lara actually have the luxury to worry about issues of authenticity and maintaining the theater's collections. Preservation concerns at the Fox are far different from concerns at the other theaters I researched. When I attempted to engage Steve Martin, the director of the Carolina Theatre, in some of the same conversations as I had with the preservationists at the Fox, for example, he explained that because the building was city owned, the city was responsible for taking care of it. As for the theater's collections, Martin explained that the theater had only a few antique chairs and sconces to worry about.

Although the Carolina Theatre certainly did go through a vast restoration process, issues of authenticity were not center stage to the process. In fact, unlike any of the other theaters, the Carolina Theatre actually added on to the original building, creating three small cinemas for the exhibition of independent and foreign films. While the designs of the area around the cinemas' prosceniums mirror the blue and gold color scheme of the original Fletcher Auditorium, they are not at all intended to be intricate reproductions. Authentic restoration and preservation is so low on the agenda of the board members at the Carolina Theatre that when I asked John Ramsey, one of the board members, about preservation, he said, "Oh, no, I can't relate to that. I don't dwell on the past. Besides it doesn't mean much to people who are new to the area anyway." Thus, material preservation has not been first and foremost on the minds of those who make decisions at the Carolina Theatre, even though they have struggled to maintain the theater's discursive past.

To varying degrees, restoration and preservation are important to all of the theaters. While the Fox's concerns about maintaining an authentic material past exist on one side of a preservation spectrum, and, perhaps, the Carolina Theatre exists on the other side, the other theaters fall somewhere in between. In order to comprehend the various philosophies that surround material preservation and restoring and safeguarding the past, it is crucial to understand the philosophies and methods that were employed in initial restorations. In other words, how do preservationists and theater directors decide what is important as they initially attempt to coax their theaters back to the 1920s? Although the restorations of the Tampa Theatre and the Alabama Theatre were both successful (in that the buildings still look old but also restored), they were accomplished in decidedly different ways. The Tampa Theatre was restored over a longer period of time and was completed with less concern about authenticity than at the Alabama Theatre. A reverence for past craftsmanship and architectural standards played a part in most of the decisions at both theaters, but historic preservation is more complicated than a simple desire to restore history. As we have seen, returning to the past is influenced by both personal and economic factors, as well as a desire to save and restore a theater's history.

Recapturing Past Intentions at the Tampa Theatre

My naivete about the repaired statues at the Tampa Theatre demonstrates a significant point about renovated buildings. Upon entering a movie palace, people generally recognize and enjoy the fact that it feels old; of course, some may know about the building's history or have personal memories of it. But the restorative methods, practical decisions, and philosophies that shape the restoration process of such a building are not often shared with the public as part of their experience at the theater. Of course, there are two glaring exceptions to this generalization. When theater directors raise private funds for restoration work, they are quite eager to share their preservation visions with the public, particularly with potential donors. The other exception is when the restoration work is in process. During the restorative treatment, people using the building are quite aware that part of the building is being renovated. For example, the Tampa Theatre presently has scaffolding set up in the lobby, with a message explaining that paint samples are being taken from a column in the lobby in order to determine its original colors.

Most of the time, however, patrons enjoying a foreign film at the Tampa Theatre or delighting in a Broadway show at the Fox Theatre are not made aware of the behind-the-scenes preservation work in the buildings. I am not suggesting that directors and preservationists are attempting to keep their work a secret from the public. However, like the films and theatrical performances that take place on stage, preservation work helps to create and maintain an illusion. For the magic of the restored theater to work, the labor and philosophy of restoration should not stand in the forefront of the patron's theater experience.

When the illusion of preservation is maintained, patrons of restored buildings and cultural critics alike tend to read a renovated historic building as a finished text. Without the knowledge of the decisions and processes carried out by people doing preservation work, we can too easily forget that a historic building is a construction of the past made in the present. And, at the other extreme, we can too easily dismiss the historic building as complete artifice—a Disney World–like experience with no ties to history whatsoever. In other words, while the actual process of theater restoration tends to be hidden, it is significant, because if we come to better understand it, we will have a better sense of how and why an important aspect of America's cultural history is safeguarded. And, I should add, an explanation and analysis of how and why theater restoration projects are completed adds another chapter to the history of the many transitions that movie palaces have undergone since their beginnings in the 1920s.

The story of the Tampa Theatre's restoration is almost as compelling and as full of human drama as many of the films shown there. Once the city council voted to buy the Tampa Theatre for one dollar on April 30, 1976, a cleaning crew began to wash the dirty and neglected interior of the theater. Lee Duncan instructed the initial renovation crew that nothing was to be done with the paint, because no one was quite certain how to repaint the interior's surfaces. Duncan claimed that everything was gently cleaned because he wanted all of the colors to blend as they had originally, but Gary Radcliffe, who has worked at the theater since the 1970s, explained that the theater was cleaned with pressure hoses.

"Whatever dust and dirt there was just dripped down to the side and on the floor," Radcliffe remembered. "The orchestra pit was deep in black goop by the time they got through. You could see mud puddles. I mean actual mud when they started cleaning it." After the initial cleaning, the city installed new red seats, refurbished the ceiling, positioned the antiques (which had been placed in storage) around the theater, and replaced a missing stuffed peacock that was a John Eberson trademark. The Tampa Historical Society mended the antiquated tapestries that had originally hung on the theater walls. Less than a year after the city bought the theater, the Tampa Theatre was reopened, on January 22, 1977.

The image of the fire-hose housecleaning is a powerful one. Restoration is usually less dramatic than the baptism that the Tampa Theatre underwent, but preservation is a kind of purging nonetheless. Recently I went to the Criterion Theatre in Bar Harbor, Maine. It is an art deco neighborhood theater that was built in the late 1920s. Except for some technological upgrades, it appears that the theater today remains exactly as it was when it opened. The original proscenium drape is still hanging; the original seats and art deco decor are intact in the auditorium. All of it is shabby, to be sure, but it occurred to me that perhaps the theater owners were in no hurry to restore the theater because Bar Harbor is not attempting to create a new image for itself, since it has not experienced the painful upheavals of southern downtown districts. Perhaps the Criterion Theatre owners are in no hurry to restore it because they do not need to make any proclamations about the rebirth of Bar Harbor. The restoration of the Tampa Theatre, on the other hand, seemed, in part, to be an announcement to the city that the downtown was about to be born again.

Four years after the theater reopened, the restoration of the theater's paint and the rebuilding of the statues began. In 1981 Jack Casey received a phone call from city officials requesting that he come to their office to discuss the restoration of the Tampa Theatre. Casey explained that he had been writing Tampa Theatre restoration proposals to the city for three years prior to the phone call, but when the call came, he was in disbelief. Casey remembers that he was living in a shack in the woods as a poor starving artist. "Then I get a telephone call from the city, saying, 'Please come in and discuss the Tampa Theatre with us.' I thought to myself, 'My God in heaven, are they serious?'" Casey said shaking his head. "Six or seven weeks later, I'm sitting in a preconstruction meeting and going over the bid. I was thinking to myself, 'This is the funniest thing I've ever seen because I've been talking about this for so long, it doesn't seem real.'"

At the end of the 1970s, Casey, an abstract artist and sculptor, had decided he needed to make a living. He had heard about the possibility of restoring the theater, so he consulted with a friend who was a grant writer. "He taught me how to write letters back and forth. I'm dyslexic, so I have trouble concentrating," Casey told me. "I started writing letters to the Arts Council, and they forwarded them to the Department of Public Works, and then all of a sudden we were meeting and they were telling me that I was going to restore the building. One month I didn't know what was going to happen to me, and the next month the city is saying, 'You have a contract to do this.' So it was quite a learning experience for me." Casey fondly remembers the architect for the City of Tampa who led him through the process of creating a business.

Casey recalls that all the officials he worked with were quite helpful, except for "a guy from the government." "He wanted to know what minority groups had been hired and what they were going to be doing," Casey explained. "I had an Indian guy that was from the Midwest, but everybody else was just white men. He showed up at the job and wanted this Chippewa Indian to tell him where he had worked and what he had learned—to tell him his life story on this résumé. I told him, 'What? You want his life story on paper? He can't even write his name, for Pete's sake.' He would say to me, 'I'm sorry; it's an equal opportunity thing. It's federal money.' I just hated the guy."

I found Casey to be still quite passionate about the Tampa Theatre, and I discovered that he had done the restoration work at the theater with almost insurmountable odds stacked against him. It is true that Casey did not come to the restoration projects at the Tampa Theatre with a background in such work, and the educated eye can perceive that the repainted surfaces in the theater are not done with as much skill as a more trained craftsman might have accomplished. However, as we walked through the theater and Casey explained both the work he did and the personal battles he was facing at the time, I could not help but be impressed that he was able to do the work at the theater at all. His personal story cannot be interpreted by either the paint on the wall or the statues in the auditorium, yet it is an important one because it helps us to understand that the decisions that are made during restoration are not always about protecting the past; sometimes they are simply about people just trying to make it through the day.

As Casey and I stood near the stage in the theater's auditorium, he explained that during much of the restoration, he was battling many personal demons—some of which had a strong hold on him throughout the entire period he worked at the theater. For one, Casey was struggling with alcohol, and his crew, as he puts it, was "a bunch of alcoholics and drug addicts." In addition, Casey also had to overcome his fear of heights in order to work on the theater's walls. "The first two hours of the day my hands would sweat like crazy," Casey told me. "I could barely hang on to the scaffolding." Another obstacle for Casey was the fact that he has polio. "I was not yet a recovering alcoholic, and I was not yet able to come to grips with that, and I was purely amazed," Casey confessed, "that I could come here to work, put up a scaffolding with polio and a hangover and get up there and paint." For Casey, the Tampa Theatre restoration project represents a "personal crisis overcome." "What I am most proud of is that it was done at all," Casey admitted. "I think it was an amazing thing to accomplish this, thinking of what condition I was in personally. No one got hurt, and I don't think anyone felt like they were slighted by any rate of pay or anything like that, and everybody looks back on it fondly."

When Casey wrote his initial proposals for the theater's restoration, he imagined that he could retouch the original paint. But once he began the project, he quickly realized that his original ideas would not work. "When I got here, I realized how filthy the theater was. The paint was cracking so much that I had to find some way of stabilizing the surface to make it last," Casey remembered. "This meant putting masonry sealer on the paint, so all of the paint and the loose chips would stick down to the surface, and before the masonry sealer was completely dry, an exterior latex-base under-painting was put on, so it would bind permanently." When the Tampa Theatre was originally painted, free-hand painters mixed the paint on location. The only binder that was used in the paint at the time was rabbit-skin glue, which caused the eventual excessive cracking and chipping of the paint in the theater.

All the original photographs of the theater were printed in black and white, so they could not aid Casey in determining the theater's original colors. However, very little of the theater had been repainted in the years since it opened, so while dirt, chipping, and fading of the paint made it somewhat difficult to assess, Casey was able to determine a color chart that was fairly accurate. "In one or two cases there are some differences in the original color scheme," Casey admits, "but they are minor to me. There is a crest where the shields are divided into fours, and sometimes I would have the color mixed up between what was the upper half and what was the lower half, but that never bothered me too much."

Casey then began the painstaking process of photographing the entire theater, six square feet at a time, so that his painters could view the colors in a handheld slide viewer as they repainted the surface of the theater. Casey and the other painters lightly dry-brushed the paint onto the theater's surfaces. Once an area was finished, they would appraise it and put more color on the surface area, making sure that it wasn't "too garish, too strong, or too flat—just a gentle sparkle of color," Casey remembered.

As in all old theaters, the Tampa Theatre's proscenium is the focal point of the auditorium, and Casey explained that it was the first phase of the restoration. It also is the part of his work at the theater of which he is the most proud. He remembers that he was almost finished with the proscenium area when he realized from studying photographs of the theater that there were some original subtle color shifts that were missing from their work. "I started noticing it was not just umber on yellow ocher; it was shifts of color," Casey recalled. "I started noticing that the walls get darker green as you go up toward the balcony, and there are patterns up there of dark green and dark red-orange on the walls." The crew went back to work on the proscenium to re-create the color shifts that he had at first failed to perceive. "I really like the subtle shift and how we carefully modulated those colors, having it go from a subtle brightness toward the front and dark but rich color up in the back. I was happy we could do it consistently, and nothing was skipped over," Casey acknowledged.

The seventeen broken and scarred sculptures were an additional challenge. He remembers that vandals had carved profanity, initials, and holes into the faces of some of the statues and that head and arms were missing from a few of them as well. One of Casey's crew members, Dan Rahenkamp, made flexible molds of some of the permanently mounted statues and cast duplicate hands and heads to replace some of the statues' missing body parts. Casey explained, for example, that a statue of Mercury that sits above a balcony exit was missing its entire head. Rahenkamp cast a duplicate head from a statue situated across the auditorium and then positioned it on Mercury's body. When it was impossible to make molds, statue body parts were hand made in plasticine and then cast in silicone molding. In order to repair the sculptures' damaged faces, Rahenkamp applied a gelatin-like solution of plaster onto the heads and then gently sanded the surface. Once repairs were complete, they primed all of the statues with a masonry sealer, and then they sprayed them with an off-white vinyl base coat. Finally, they applied several layers of green and then umber transparent glaze.

In hindsight, Casey believes that the statues that are in close proximity to high-traffic areas should have been done in a more durable medium. "I've restored the sculpture in the basement, I don't know how many times," Casey confessed. "It's plaster of Paris, and people have a few drinks or just bump into it, and they end up taking a hand off. I've often thought if they could have afforded it, we could have cast it in fiberglass so it wouldn't be broken. It would have been the same color and the same shape, but it would have been more durable. But they wanted to keep it in the original material, so that's what we did."

Casey's Tampa Theatre restoration project was executed in several phases and required approximately seven and one-half years to complete. Casey explained that his crew worked around the theater's schedule, as the theater remained open throughout the restoration. During the proscenium project, Casey's crew had to take the scaffolding to the balcony, take out rows of seats, and set up ladder jacks on a forty-five-degree angled floor. "We would be fifty-five, fifty-six feet above the main floor, repainting and casting, and things like that," Casey recollected. "Then at three in the afternoon, we had to take down the scaffolding, fold up everything, recap our paints, put the scaffolding back down in the basement, put the seats back, crank them back down, and put them back in place, and then come back the next day and do it all over again."

Casey said that managing his crew was perhaps more challenging than hovering fifty-five feet above the auditorium floor. "I had to rule a crew of drunks and drug addicts so they would show up for work and come to work on time," Casey said shaking his head. "I had to give them reinforcement and tell them what great work they were doing, take everybody to lunch, keep everybody going, and be the cheerleader." Casey also had to prevent his crew from hurting themselves, since much of the restoration required them to work at potentially perilous heights. One of his crew members, for example, encased in a work cage, raised himself forty-five feet above the ground on a lift, a far greater height than was safe for the lift to be raised. Casey remembered that the latch stuck, and the lift would not come down.

> In the old days, the Florida State Fair had a monkey act in which they put a monkey in a race car and ran him through a loop; the monkey hated it. John [the crew member] was in that cage like the monkey in the car. He said, 'I know what I'll do, Jack. I'll jump out and jump onto the plaster cornice. It's only five feet away.' This is when I really earned my money because I had to be in charge of keeping these people from killing themselves. He was an old friend of mine, and I didn't want to see him get hurt. So I was frantically on the phone with the company trying to find out where the release valve was before he jumps, because he was convinced that was the way to do it. I found the release valve, pulled it, and thank God, the lift came straight down.

Although restoration at the Tampa Theatre is still not complete, Casey, who later became an oil painting conservator, is no longer involved with the project. In fact, the day I met him at the theater to talk about his work, another restoration craftsman, Jarrett Ellis, was nearly finished restoring the ceiling of the theater's entrance. Ellis, unlike Casey, came to the Tampa Theatre with twenty-five years of theater restoration training behind him. He worked at EverGreene Painting Studios for thirteen years and, as project manager for the company, was frequently in charge of theater and state capitol restoration projects around the country. Ellis's work is well respected in the theater business, and because his name is connected with EverGreene Studios, a $25-million-a-year restoration business, he comes to the theater with a high degree of credibility. Casey acknowledged that Ellis's restoration work on the theater's entrance was well executed and very clean, though he questioned his use of linseed oil as a glaze because he believes that it is a magnet for dirt and dust.

As I walked around the Tampa Theatre with Ellis, I asked him to evaluate Casey's original restoration work and what he would do differently. Ellis diplomatically explained that the painted surfaces in the theater do not have the qualities of a well-made cake:

> See all these big blues, heavy blue-green areas that are real muddy and not defined? It should be like a good cake. You know how you go to a nice bakery and get a four-dollar piece of cake? It's great, but

> you don't taste the sugar, the flour; you don't taste all the separate ingredients that make up the entity of the cake. You just taste the whole, and you know it's good. Here, that's what it is supposed to be. You are not supposed to be able to identify and feel and see blue, green, yellow; it's all supposed to blend and melt in and be a part of the feel. You don't want it to attack you. You shouldn't see all the individual colors; you should just get a feel for it. That's where I think I've been successful, in the sense that I understand this, plus I don't need to make my own personal statement.

Both Casey and Ellis explained that restoration work is an egoless craft. "You've got to get in and get out, like a thief in the night," Casey said. "I don't want people to come in and say, 'Look, it's Jack's theater.' I can't be interpretive or self-expressive in a restoration project; I have to use my objectivity, my science, my craftsmanship, and my aesthetics, with as little ego as possible, to make it work." Ellis, like Casey, explained that restoration craftsmen must try to re-create the original signature of the building, rather than leave their own signature. Often, much of the original signature has vanished as a result of being washed away or painted over. Ellis explained that part of his job and part of his success is that he spends a good deal of time searching for the original craftsmen's intentions by simply sitting in the building for hours at a time. "People will say, 'Go home! Get out of here!'" Ellis said with a laugh. "I'm not a real spiritual person, but I do get a feel for a building. I get a feel for what the intent was and how it was done. What did they want this place to look like? It's a thousand details that make up the big picture, and you need to have a feel for what it's supposed to be."

When a restoration project is finished, Ellis contended, no one should be able to determine just by looking at the building who did the work. He explained that one of the most difficult aspects of managing a crew of painters is supervising their painting "hand" and their ideas of how the project should be completed, because their mission is total replication. "So many times I have crew members that say, 'It would really look a lot better if we did it this way,' and I say, 'Yes, I agree, but we have to do it this way. We're getting paid to do what these other people saw and felt and work within those limitations.'" He acknowledged that sometimes it feels like a "slap in the face" because as a craftsman he has his own aesthetic opinions about how surfaces should be repainted, but those ideas cannot be articulated in his work.

When I asked Ellis why it was important to re-create the original craftsmen's work, he explained that it was a matter of trusting the intentions of the original artists. "Back in the twenties people didn't throw a million dollars around like they do today. They spent it with purpose; they labored; it was a labor of love; every detail was paid meticulous attention to," Ellis said. "It was a very exacting process that worked. They tried to create a certain feeling and environment, and that is why they were so successful." Yet Ellis admits that scientific precision is not as important as recapturing the original intent of the building. At times, he must confront architects and preservationists who feel that restoration work must be done exactly as it was done historically. One of the more frustrating elements of his job is his negotiations with preservation architects, who, he admits, have more credibility in the industry than he does. "I have to justify my existence to a certain extent. I am a painter—a lead painter, but still a painter; I'm still the worker. I'm getting paid to do what these other people [architects and preservationists] are seeing and feeling. I have to incorporate their ideas even though it's not in their blood like it's in my blood."

Ellis is essentially suggesting that high-quality restoration work does not have to be an exact science, and through many years of practice and an intuitive sense for old buildings, he is able to re-create the original intention of the building without exactly re-creating every brush stroke originally applied to a building's surface. Jan Abell, a preservation architect who had been involved with the restoration of the Tampa Theatre since the 1980s, acknowledged that most of the work done at the theater in both the past and the present has not been an exact science. She explained that such restoration would have required a vast amount of paint samples and microscopic analysis and would have cost three times as much to complete—with only slightly different results. Abell explained that the most difficult element of historic preservation in Florida is that the buildings are not very old, so people who originally used the buildings are still alive. "They all have memories, which may or may not be right, because we all probably don't remember what our bedroom wallpaper looked like," Abell claimed, "although I am convinced that I do."

Abell said that there are other human factors that make restoration in such buildings as the Tampa Theatre difficult. In addition to the people who believe that they still remember how the building looked before it began to deteriorate, often people who did early restoration work on the building are also still emotionally invested in the theater or may still work at the theater. While such people may have had the best intentions, generally they lacked training and the financial resources to do an adequate job. Ellis admitted that he is quite careful not to be critical of earlier renovation undertakings when he is working on a restoration project. As we walked through the building, he pointed to a few painted surfaces that he would like to see redone. As we looked at a painted beam in the theater, he explained to me that he knew this was not original paint because the color was flat, lifeless, and opaque, but then he said with caution, "For political reasons you don't knock it. You never know who painted it or what happened. It could be the executive director's most favorite thing." When Ellis, Abell, and I were in the theater's entrance looking at the ceiling, Abell pointed out a surface that Ellis had recently repainted and exclaimed that what had been done in the past was "multicolored baloney." Ellis cringed and told her not to criticize it because he happened to know that the person who had originally repainted it still worked at the theater. "Don't say anything about it," Ellis warned us. "A lot of time was spent on it; it was a labor of love."

Because public buildings like the Tampa Theatre have a passionate following, change, in the form of restoration work, may be resisted. People who have an emotional investment in the building are still alive, and in some cases, as Ellis points out, may still work in the building. Therefore, scientific processes such as paint analysis are the most rhetorically persuasive means of making restorative changes to a building. "People believe in science; they don't believe in art. That's what it boils down to," Abell admitted. "They think that if it was analyzed under a microscope, it must be right. That's much more convincing than if you explained to them how something would have been done artistically during that time and period. It is much harder to convince them that way and not offend them in the process."

Although Ellis did not use microscopic analysis in order to determine the color scheme for the entrance ceiling, he does firmly believe in documentation of the original work as a crucial point of departure. He admitted that he found it frustrating that no documentation was done during the original restoration at the Tampa Theatre. "All we have are stories," Ellis complained, "and those stories include hosing this whole place down with fire hoses." But documentation is extremely difficult and expensive work. During his restoration efforts at the Michigan state capitol, for example, documentation of the building's decorative scheme alone was a $0.5 million expense. When original paint is completely washed or chipped away and no original documentation exists, there is no way to precisely determine the original color scheme.

Ellis documented what he could of the ceiling, but he acknowledged that in certain areas of the theater's entrance, the surfaces had been completely scrubbed, and he could see nothing but "brown mud." Investigating the different layers of paint that remained on the ceiling, he was able to determine some regularities, but not a clear pattern. Eventually, the pattern came to him as he was driving home from the theater one evening. Ellis's work on the ceiling of the theater entrance transformed the area from an aesthetically lifeless area to a vibrant, inviting space. The colors are startlingly vivid compared to the rest of the painted surfaces in the theater, and some people were rather surprised by the bright colors at first. Even Abell confessed that she felt the final colors were brighter than she imagined when they started the project, but she admitted that she trusted Ellis's work.

I am neither an architect nor a restoration craftsman, so I cannot judge the ceiling or Ellis's work using educated criteria, but I do admit that I find the ceiling beautiful. As I assess why I feel that way, I realize that Ellis's diligent documentation procedures, his association with EverGreene Painting Studios, and his many years of working in the field influence the way that I feel. Knowledge of Ellis's intuitive approach to restoration also shapes my perception of his work. His seemingly instinctual feel for what the original craftsmen intended and his overall passion for old buildings affects what I see when I look at his work. In other words, Ellis seems to be both a methodical scientist, an intuitive artist, and a credible craftsman associated with a highly regarded preservation studio. If I had not interviewed either Ellis or Casey, perhaps I would simply have noticed that the new restoration work at the Tampa Theatre was a brighter color than the past work.

The city-owned Tampa Theatre has not had the financial resources to do the extensive and exact restoration work that has been done at the Fox Theatre, the Orpheum Theatre, or the Alabama Theatre. Ellis's work is, in fact, the most sophisticated effort since the theater was purchased by the city in 1976. Two years ago the Tampa Theatre implemented a preservation surcharge of seventy-five cents on each ticket sold. The money generated by the surcharge has enabled the theater not only to hire Ellis but also to begin to have more exacting standards for the theater's renovation.

The limited financial resources available in the past for renovation work have shaped the preservation philosophy at the theater. John Bell, the director of the theater, admits that the theater's renovation policies have not been extremely rigid about authentic restoration, but he does maintain parameters that he feels should not be encroached. He feels strongly that the colors of the theater, for example, should not deviate from the original palette, because the architect, John Eberson, intended for the atmosphere to replicate an old courtyard. Bell cites the Richmond Theatre (now renamed the Carpenter's Center for the Performing Arts), in Richmond, Virginia, as a grossly incompetent restoration. He explained that the Richmond Theatre was repainted in a yellow and green color scheme, and then a polyurethane high-gloss finish was applied to every surface in the theater. "The colors were wrong, even if you didn't know what they were supposed to be," Bell said, shaking his head. "I got this overwhelming sense of failure when I was in the building." Bell is extremely pleased, however, with the color of the Tampa Theatre's auditorium ceiling, which was originally created to look like a night sky. He is convinced that when the ceiling was repainted in 1977, the painters created an excellent effect. He explained that many restored atmospheric ceilings are light blue. "It doesn't really work because it never really gets dark," Bell maintains. "You know, when you look up at the sky at night, you don't see a blue sky; you see a black sky."

There are two reasons why Bell is not overly concerned with painstakingly authentic restoration. There are, of course, the financial burdens that such a process would entail, but beyond that Bell believes that microscopic paint analysis is unnecessary because the theater itself is an illusion, and a cornice forty feet above the audience's heads does not need to be the exact shade of the original color in order to maintain the magical atmosphere of the building. "Really what you are doing is painting a set for the audience," Bell explained. "The audience is within this theatrical set, so, if it's one little hue off, it doesn't matter that much."

Bell believes that the restorers at the Tampa Theatre should never forget about the architect of the Tampa Theatre. He claims that John Eberson was a master and an artist, and the theater should be closely restored to how it looked the day that Eberson completed his work. The restoration should be done with the mind-set of a conservator who restores fine oil paintings. "It's like restoring a work of art to the state in which the work of art was when he signed off on it," Bell declared. "If you were to restore it contrary to what he intended to do, it would be like taking the *Mona Lisa* and putting sunglasses on her."

Bell's preservation philosophy acknowledges the mastery of Eberson, and his high esteem for Eberson's creation steers his belief that strict attention must be paid to Eberson's intentions during renovation work. In this perspective the theater functions as a museum for the public, preserving the work of an artist in the final moment of a creative act. This kind of restoration philosophy attempts to arrest a moment in time; in this case the opening of the Tampa Theatre on October 15, 1926—a moment in time before any wear and tear or modifications to the building changed Eberson's original intentions. Bell explains that when people walk into the theater they experience "some weird sort of time travel" because the theater was built in 1926, and its restoration aims to bring the theater as close to its opening night as possible, for that was the theater's "most glorious moment."

The theater, however, was originally designed to look like a Mediterranean courtyard in the early eighteenth century, so any accurate restoration work done in the theater does not reproduce the atmosphere of an early-twentieth-century building. To complicate matters further, the theater has changed because of unavoidable improvements, such as electrical upgrades, handicap accessible areas, and the necessities created by modern demands of comfort in seating and sight lines. While Bell insists that the theater's opening night is an important reference point for its restoration, he, like Ellis, suggests that ultimately what is being restored or replicated is the idea of the theater on the opening night. He wishes to preserve the theater as Eberson, the "master," envisioned it, but he recognizes that we can know the building only in the present, as an edited panorama of the original Tampa Theatre.

Ultimately, it is impossible to conserve the substance of the theater, but the form and the original intent of the building can endure to a certain extent. Like the film images that flicker on the screen, much of the historic material within the Tampa Theatre is only a ghostly replication of what was once there. Nonetheless, the people who have been involved with the conservation and restoration efforts are guided by a high regard for the original philosophy, design, and craftsmanship of the theater. Admiration and nostalgia for early movie exhibition guide their work and their aim to restore the theater as closely as possible to its original state. In fact, it is simply impossible to stabilize the material

17. The Tampa Theatre lobby today. While preservationists acknowledge that the theater's opening night is an important reference point for restoration, additions such as the lobby's concession stand are rarely viewed as detrimental to the preservation plan. George Cott, Chroma Inc., Tampa, Florida.

past, as we have seen by the heroic but unavailing efforts of the Fox Theatre's preservationists. Perhaps the financial constraints faced by the preservationists at the Tampa Theatre have helped to shape their pragmatic view of historic restoration. It is their desire to recapture what they can of the past. Their work could be described as interpretive, for they are reverent toward what they perceive and what they interpret as the original aims of the architect and the craftsmen who designed the building.

Until I met with Casey in the spring of 2000, the only information I had about him was vaguely negative comments that I heard from Tampa Theatre employees. I was never able to pinpoint the reasons behind the ambiguous criticisms, except for the fact that some of the statues that his crew restored had not withstood the test of time. There seemed to be a feeling that he was a bit too heavy handed in his restoration work, but no one that I talked to articulated precisely what they meant.

Perhaps Ellis's work at the theater is regarded with more esteem than Casey's by those who are associated with the theater because his reverence toward the original craftsmen's intentions seems more pronounced than Casey's. Both preservation craftsmen claimed that it is important not to leave their personal and contemporary signature on a restored building, but Ellis's methodical documentation of the theater, his veneration for early-twentieth-century craftsmen, his extensive knowledge of old theaters, and his impressive pedigree enable him to protect the past against the encroaching present more effectively than Casey's less methodical approach to restoration. Casey managed to restore nearly the entire theater against overwhelming odds, but his work is not as well regarded as Ellis's (by those who work at the theater) because of his lack of formal training and his lack of knowledge about some standard preservation practices. In other words, the illusion of the past that Casey created does not seem to be as authentic as Ellis's. Perhaps Ellis's methodical diligence offers some reassurance that the Tampa Theatre's past will not completely disappear.

More or Less Exactly the Way It Was at the Alabama Theatre

I have not met anyone who is as fiercely dedicated to a theater as is Cecil Whitmire, the president of the board of directors of Birmingham Landmarks. His tireless promotion of the Alabama Theatre, along with his attention to nearly every detail within it, has served the theater and the city of Birmingham well. While all of the theaters in this book are exceptional in their unique ways, none can compare to the Alabama Theatre in terms of restoration aesthetics and precise attention to the original details of the theater. As you would suspect, this accomplishment did not happen by chance, for Whitmire does not leave any detail remotely related to the theater to fate.

In May 1987 Birmingham Landmarks assumed the ownership, the operations, and the $650,000 mortgage of the Alabama Theatre. Under the leadership of Whitmire, Birmingham Landmarks' initial goals in 1987 were to restore the physical plant of the theater, to begin operating it as a multiuse community performance facility, and to retire the mortgage by January 1, 1990. In 1989 Whitmire determined that replacing the original roof and plumbing, refurbishing 2,200 seats, replacing the main stage curtains and house drapes, installing new exit doors, repairing the ladies lounge, and retiring the balance of the mortgage were the priorities for the theater. Completing the restoration of the interior was considered to be a second phase of restoration, which, as it turned out, did not happen until 1998.

Whitmire remembered that in 1987 the plumbing did not work; the roof leaked; and the electrical system was far from being up to code. "We had four big boxes of fuses, and just to open the theater we would spend twenty minutes screwing in fuses," Whitmire said, shaking his head. "I would screw one in, and it would blow, and then I knew I definitely had another problem someplace." Raising the money to fix these unglamorous problems, Whitmire admitted, was difficult to do. From 1987 to 1998, $4.5 million was spent restoring the theater, but, as he said, none of it was for "anything that you could see."

"Where did you get the money to do all of that?" I asked Whitmire.

"I was the one who had to go out and ask you for the money," he explained.

"You got all of the money to do all of this stuff just by asking people? I asked incredulously.

"I did," he said, nodding his head. "Over the years the hardest thing to do was go to you and say, 'Miss Janna, I need 100,000 dollars.' 'What do you need 100,000 dollars for?' you would say. 'I need to rewire the theater; I need to replumb the theater.' If you are a rich lady, you want your name on whatever you spend money for. Well, it's hard to put your name on the commodes and the wiring and the plumbing and the roof, so that was a problem because the physical plant was falling apart from age."

Whitmire humbly admitted that the Alabama Theatre was an "easy sell" to older Birmingham residents, because many of them had powerful and nostalgic feelings for the theater. He also explained that it was difficult to raise all of the money, because the theater continued to look pretty good. Throughout the years, theater managers had taken good care of it. Although it was worn, the building's "bone structure" was still intact. "It was shabby; it looked dark and dingy and well worn, and the paint was chipping. It had what we call in the movie palace business 'faded grandeur.' It was like an old lady who had been a Miss America. As she gets older, you can still see that she used to be gorgeous. We were dark and dingy, but when we turned on all the pretty lights, then the old girl looked pretty good, and people thought, 'They don't need this or that.' So it was tough raising the money."

By 1992 Whitmire was making plans for the theater's interior restoration, even though he was six years away from having raised the money that would be required for the work to be completed. He traveled around the country during a two-year period, evaluating the restoration work at other theaters. The Alabama Theatre had similar problems as other picture palaces in downtown districts around the country—namely, cracked walls, water damage, layers of nicotine residue, and graffiti. By researching other theaters' restoration projects, he hoped to determine which restoration company would restore the painted surfaces, rather than merely decorate them, and which company would do work that would last. For example, Whitmire appraised another theater in Alabama, which had been restored by a nationally recognized restoration company, but the walls were already cracking and the paint was already peeling. That company was immediately crossed off his list.

In 1992 Whitmire and his board decided upon EverGreene Painting Studios. He explained that after seeing the "before, during, and after" stages of several of the theaters that they restored, including New York City's New Amsterdam Theatre and the murals in Radio City Music Hall, he was sure that it was the best company to restore the painted surfaces of the Alabama Theatre. It would be another five years after deciding to use EverGreene Studies before the goal of the interior restoration became close to a financial reality. When the Linn Henley Charitable Trust gave $150,000 to the Alabama Theatre in 1997, Whitmire was able to begin planning the restoration project for 1998.

Whitmire had ascertained that EverGreene Painting Studios did the best, most enduring restoration work in the country, but he also chose the company because of their reputation as restorers of painted surfaces, rather than decorators. In other words, he desired an authentic restoration for the Alabama Theatre. Whitmire recalled, "When Jeff [Greene] came in, he said, 'What do you want me to do?' I said, 'In 1927, Adolph Zukor said that in his opinion this theater was the showplace of the South. I want it fixed so if Adolph was able to come back today, he would say the same exact thing. I want it to look *exactly* like it did in 1927.' So that's what Jeff did."

It is difficult to pinpoint exactly why Whitmire wanted an authentic restoration at the Alabama Theatre, because there are probably many reasons. Movie palaces, Whitmire maintained, should have a look about them that produces a warm feeling when someone walks through the door. Theaters that have been "remodeled," he explained, look like they were done by people who did not know what they were doing:

> One of the ones that I think is the absolute worst—and I've told the people this to their face, so this is not something I'm saying behind their back—is the Saenger Theatre in Mobile [not to be confused with the Saenger Theatre in Biloxi]. It used to be owned by the University of South Alabama, and they didn't have the money to restore it, so they got somebody to donate paint, and students and maintenance people painted it. It used to be earth tones, darker tones—more elegant. Now the walls are painted bright white, bright red, and bright gold. It makes you feel like you have been swallowed by a circus calliope. You walk in, and it doesn't say anything to you except, "No one knew what to do with me, and now I look like crap."

Whitmire revealed that Garrison Keillor had had a strong impact on his restoration mission, since Keillor had impressed upon him that when the Alabama Theatre was restored, it should maintain its inviting feeling. Keillor told Whitmire that before the World Theatre in St. Paul, Minnesota, was restored, it embraced him and made him feel welcome, even though it was dark, the paint was peeling, and the plaster was falling. Keillor lamented that after the restoration of the World Theatre, the building was no longer appealing. "We talked about this in 1993," Whitmire recalled. "He said, 'When you restore your theater, don't lose that.' He told me that the welcoming feeling was the way the theater was meant to be, so I always remembered those words."

Perhaps a nostalgic impulse also steered his desire to return the Alabama Theatre to its original state. Though he lived in Knoxville, Tennessee, when he was a child, his parents were originally from Birmingham. When they visited relatives in Birmingham, Whitmire remembers that he would convince his father to "park him" at the Alabama Theatre so he could watch double features, cartoons, newsreels, and previews of coming attractions. Whitmire contends that he has a passion for all old theaters. "They were a very, very important part of our heritage, our growing up, our entertainment," Whitmire told me. "Everybody in this town dated here; they loved here; they got their first kiss here. This is just a very important part of our lives."

On the other hand, Whitmire is a shrewd businessman and downtown booster who has a vision for an arts district in downtown Birmingham. Because he was convinced that an authentic restoration would make the theater look its best, it is reasonable to assume that part of the reason he would want the theater to look exactly as it did in 1927 is that the better the theater looked, the more support it would generate from the public. More public support would assuredly generate more interest in the revitalization of the Lyric Theatre, which would, in Whitmire's estimation, eventually create more traffic downtown. In turn, entrepreneurs would begin opening restaurants, bars, coffee shops, and other services around the two theaters. The motivation behind restoring the Alabama Theatre to its 1927 grandeur, is, in other words, complex. Aesthetic criteria, nostalgic impulses, business savvy, and protecting a reputation as an accomplished and knowledgeable movie palace director surely helped to guide Whitmire's decision.

With the marching orders to make the theater look "exactly" as it did in 1927, or as close as humanly possible, the EverGreene crew began work in the winter of 1998. Terra Klugh had come to Birmingham in 1996 to document the theater for the Historic American Building Survey. Once the documentation was completed, she decided to stay at the theater because she wanted to participate in the restoration. Since 1996, as she explains it, she has "done every job in the theater that you can possibly do." Klugh and an EverGreene supervisor began cleaning the theater (except for the auditorium) one month before the rest of the crew began working. Using mostly water, Klugh began the tedious process of washing away the dirt that had accumulated for seventy-one years. A few mild cleaning solutions were used to tackle the layers of nicotine and popcorn oil, but no solutions containing strong chemicals were used, because they would have faded or distorted the original paint colors. Klugh admitted that the women's rest room was so imbued with nicotine that eventually they had to simply sand it and repaint it, matching the paint as closely as possible with the original color. In other areas, particularly where there was leafing, even water was not safe. Instead, the crew used dry-cleaning sponges, so as not to damage the leafing.

Once the cleaning was complete, the science of the preservation process began. Paint analysis, utilizing the scrape method, was employed. With a magnifying glass, members of the crew, like archaeologists in the field, examined the layers of paint, finally determining the colors of the base and the original paint. Some places that were not high-traffic areas had not been repainted over the years, making analysis easy. However, Klugh acknowledged that some areas were more difficult to analyze than she had imagined, because the theater was originally painted by many artists. "You could go to different places in the theater, and the color wasn't exactly the same, because they mixed their own paints," Klugh explained. "Every artist had a different hand, so sponge marks in one place were different than someplace else." The original plaster work was also done by a crew of plasterers; therefore, the plastered surfaces were varied throughout the theater. Because paint looks different when it is applied to various plaster work, restoration work was further complicated. "It was not always completely even," Klugh said. "We found that to be hard because we were trying to make it perfect, but that's not the way it was [originally] done."

Klugh explained that, whenever possible, restoration work should include the application of the original paint colors; the use of the original materials to restore decorative elements such as leafing; and the employment of original techniques, such as "scagliola," which is a method of pulling colored silk threads through plaster to emulate the look of marble. Contending that such efforts protect the historic integrity of a building, Klugh emphasized that it also maintains the high level of the original craftsmanship. Like Ellis at the Tampa Theatre, Klugh has great respect for the craftsmanship of the early twentieth century and believes that contemporary buildings are debased by prefabrication.

The last two months of the restoration required the Alabama Theatre

18. The Alabama Theatre's restored auditorium. The tremendous dome that towers above theater patrons needed an intensive cleaning but did not require painting during the restoration. Copyright 1994, M. Lewis Kennedy, Kennedy Studios, Birmingham, Alabama.

to close so that the crew could restore the auditorium. Scaffolding filling the entire space of the auditorium went up, and a deck was placed off of the balcony floor. Rolling towers were positioned so that the crew could reach the top of the dome and other sections of the ceiling. Whitmire explained that much of the ceiling and the topmost part of the auditorium only had to be cleaned. "If you bought a new car today and put it on blocks in the garage, if it never saw any rain, sun, and nobody touched it for seventy years," he conjectured, "what would be wrong with just cleaning it?" Though the upper reaches needed only cleaning, it was still a great deal of work. "There was seventy years of smoke and dust up there," Klugh remembered. "There was one section of banana leaves that goes all the way across that no one ever saw because they were covered with dirt. The shields up there were so dusty that we didn't know they were supposed to be shiny."

Klugh related that some of their discoveries during analysis led to some surprises and curious reactions from both the crew and other observers. For example, even the restoration crew was amazed by some of the bright, lively colors that were originally used. Because movie palaces like the Alabama Theatre were originally designed to be outrageous and eccentric, when the restoration crew restored the original colors in some areas of the theater, they seemed very loud for contemporary taste. Klugh remembers that when they analyzed the color under the organ chambers, they found a sea-green sponge color that was shockingly bright. They decided to keep the same color but mute it a bit to accommodate contemporary sensibilities. Because each level of the theater had originally been painted dissimilarly by different artists, the EverGreene crew chose to follow suit. Klugh remembers having to explain why the various levels of the theater looked different from one another when people politely inquired about the apparent inconsistencies.

The women's rest room and the box-office lobby were the most labor intensive elements of the Alabama Theatre restoration. The crew found nine coats of old cheap paint on the box-office lobby. All of it had to be removed, and it was a job that required hundreds of hours of extra effort for the crew. "All of it had to be taken off, which is something we hadn't planned on," Whitmire recollected. "I said [to Jeff Greene], 'Don't come to me halfway through and tell me you need another $100,000 because it's not there. I have in the bank exactly what it is going to take to do this theater.' I'm not sure he made any money, but I don't care. My job is to get the theater restored. His job is to take care of himself." But Whitmire assured me that if he had to do it over again, he would use EverGreene Painting Studios again, even if he had to wait years to fit into their schedule. "It looks newer than it did two years ago, but nothing has changed, and that is what I wanted," Whitmire said with satisfaction. "My entire board was dedicated to providing the city of Birmingham and the people that come here with integrity and an authentic restoration."

Impressed with his reputation for restoring movie palaces, I met with Jeff Greene at EverGreene Painting Studios in New York City. His Manhattan studios consist of two enormous floors in a building near Madison Square Garden. Greene began his career in 1978, by painting billboards in Times Square. Less than twenty-five years later, his company has restored approximately twenty-five capitol buildings, seventy-five theaters, and so many churches and courthouses that he has lost track of the number. EverGreene Painting Studios was responsible for the paint restoration of the murals in Radio City Music Hall, and they restored nearly all of the theaters in Times Square, including the New Amsterdam Theatre and the Music Box. EverGreene was also responsible for the paint restoration of the Library of Congress in Washington, D.C. EverGreene crews restore plaster and paint, create new murals and decorative painting for corporations such as Disney, and manufacture wallpaper. When I was there, I had an opportunity to see a mural that his artists were creating for Disney World in Tokyo. Essentially, Greene's studio has little competition in the United States or elsewhere, and Greene himself is considered the premier expert in paint restoration.

Greene acknowledged that he was impressed by Whitmire's astute business savvy, noting that he was well educated in theater history and that he understood the principles of architectural aesthetics. Greene also mentioned that Whitmire used the restoration at the Alabama Theatre as a way to generate interest in the theater, rather than viewing it as an obstacle to ticket sales. While this strategy helped to educate the public, it also meant the theater stayed open for much of the eight months of restoration work, which created difficult working conditions for the crew.

Greene expressed his opinion that Whitmire's desire to hold on to as much of the original theater as possible was misguided. "In hindsight, I probably would have done it a little bit differently," Greene said. "You know we had this mandate to maintain as much of the original fabric as possible and only replicate it where it was too far gone. It would have been more expedient and probably a better result if we had repainted more." Surprised that the leading restorer of theaters in the country would discount the desire for an authentic restoration, I pressed Greene to explain what he meant.

It seems that, unlike Ellis at the Tampa Theatre and Klugh at the Alabama Theatre, Greene does not have a reverence for the picture palace craftsmanship of the 1920s. He speculated that most of the artists who did the original work at the Alabama Theatre were scenic painters and that their work was really kind of "down and dirty." Their craftsmanship, he believes, was not "top-drawer." As a result of hundreds of theaters a year being built between 1926 and 1929, theater painters and plasterers were "plenty busy," essentially mass-producing theaters across the country. "Back then it was like writing your name," Greene said. "These painters did hundreds of theaters. They were good at it. They were fast at it." While he acknowledged that very few painters today have the "kind of chops" the original craftsmen did, Greene asserted that today's craftsmanship standards are higher. He pointed to the fact that it took as long to restore the paint finishes at the Alabama Theatre as it did to construct the entire theater in 1927. While Greene acknowledged that contemporary craftsmen do not have the collective knowledge or energy of the original artists who did such work every day, present-day artists have the advantage of high-load acrylic paints and the better techniques developed over the last thirty years.

As a result of the restoration, the Alabama Theatre, he claims, is presently "more or less exactly the way it was" when it opened its doors in 1927. The finishes in the theater now are the same finishes that were there the day the theater originally opened. Yet Greene believes that such highly authentic renovation projects do not necessarily add a substantial amount to the building's historic integrity. "We can do 100 percent museum-quality work, absolutely," he stated, "but theaters are not museums; they are functioning buildings. Nowadays, the decoration is in servitude to what happens on the stage. Often times it is appropriate to reinterpret the finishes based on a historic model."

Museum-quality restoration requires hundreds of hours of additional work for the restoration crew, without necessarily changing the end result—which is how people will use and move through the building. After working with hundreds of clients on hundreds of old buildings, Greene has come to believe that an interpretation of original work is often more useful than a curatorial mandate. Although he asserts that some restoration work does not need to be of museum quality, he was also careful to explain that he does not subscribe to decorative work, meaning that theater restoration needs to be grounded with a firm understanding of theater history and time-honored principles of aesthetics. Greene noted that Whitmire understood both of these factors, as is reflected in the theater's restoration. He simply questions the need for such a rigid subscription to authenticity.

Greene explained that restoration plans can also be complicated by the fact that aesthetic sensibilities have changed over time. Victorian aesthetics, for example, seem dark, cluttered, and claustrophobic compared to the light, airy sensibilities of modern design. Greene remembered an auditorium at the Art Institute of Chicago that was painted white in the 1940s and remained that way for more than fifty years. Paint analysis revealed that the room's original palette was composed of dark Victorian colors—dark green, red, and ochre. "The director of the museum said, 'I hate this. This is completely inappropriate for how we are going to be using this room now,'" Greene said. Although the decision makers at the Art Institute had initially intended to take the auditorium back to its original colors, they found them too dark and dreary. In cases such as this, Greene uses the Munsell Color System, which is a universal color system that enables clients to choose colors from the original family but in a different shade. The Munsell Color System allows for restoration that is historically accurate but that also accommodates the contemporary use of the building, modern lighting, and present-day taste.

Such adjustments exemplify Greene's belief that the historic-built environment should be restored, but because modern-day people use and move through the rooms, their sensibilities should be accommodated as long as the historic and aesthetic principles are not violated. "I can tell you, as many theaters as we have done," Greene stated, "there is a level of interpretation to all of them. I'm not talking about revisionist history—you know, changing it—but I think it has to look appropriate. The wonderful thing about these theaters is that they will continue to be used, and their beauty is that they are magnets for culture, and they can really hold a community together. They continue to have this life, and they have to be adaptable and continue to have vitality. They shouldn't be deadened by strict mandates of authenticity."

Greene's respect for buildings and the people who use them creates a view of the historic-built environment that pays homage to the past without sacrificing the needs and desires of the present. His moderate approach to restoration is not wholly guided by nostalgic impulses. He does not, for example, have total veneration for early-twentieth-century craftsmen, as do many of the preservationists that I have interviewed. Greene, however, is nostalgic for the time-honored principles of art and architecture that he contends have been forgotten by many contemporary designers:

> There are formalistic principles that have to do with the way that architecture is perceived. You know, like cool colors come forward. You have these designers—who knows where they get their education—but they don't understand how colors work architecturally. You go back and look at any books on my shelf and look at the principles that were discovered by the Romans and employed throughout the Renaissance. They were known by classic architects and modern ones too, such as art deco architects. People today aren't grounded in the history of architecture or the formalistic principles of painting. There are many designers out there who don't understand these things. It's about education, not money, because it doesn't cost any more money to do a job right or well—it might cost a bit more to do it well, actually, but good taste doesn't cost any more money than bad taste.

Greene stated that he did not wish to criticize; rather, he wished to educate and raise the overall standards of the industry. Still, it is clear that he has his own nostalgic impulses, like most people who work in the business of restoring the past. It is not too surprising that Greene's standards for preservation are different from Whitmire's. While both men have a stake in restoring architectural history, Greene must consider the economy of his work, and exact restoration requires more time and labor than a slightly less rigid renovation would require.

Whitmire, on the other hand, is in the theater business, and his profits are derived from the theater's rental and shows. Therefore, a museum-like restoration adds a particular aesthetic and historic value to the theater and enables certain bragging rights. For example, *In the Spotlight,* a quarterly newsletter for Alabama Theatre supporters, detailed the restoration during all of its stages. The reputation of EverGreene Painting Studios and the quality of the restoration were noted in most of the newsletters. During the final stages of the restoration, the newsletter explained that the transformation of the theater was perhaps more subtle than the public might have expected. "The startling look that you might expect is not there," a 1998 newsletter reads. "The paint job that is being done by EverGreene is so close to the original that we feel the restoration will be a huge success." Whitmire explained to me that he invented a new word for the restoration at the theater. "I coined a new word in 1998. We were making the Alabama Theatre 'beautifuler' because she was already beautiful. But I told Birmingham that we were going to make her 'beautifuler,' and that's what we did."

Although the Tampa Theatre and the Alabama Theatre were pulled back in time through different philosophies and different methods, the people who actually did the restoration work had similar impulses. First, it seems that most of them in varying degrees respected the original intentions of the designers and the craftsmanship that was employed within them. While Greene questioned the quality of the original artists' work, he respected the architectural principles that guided their efforts. Secondly, most of the preservationists who contributed to the restoration of the theaters accepted the fact that following the initial intentions is more practical and more likely than an exact restoration. No one believed that theater decoration—that is, repainting a theater without regard to historical accuracy—is appropriate. But it does not seem that most of the preservationists felt that an exact replica of the past was either possible or necessary.

What seems most significant to the preservationists at the Tampa Theatre and, to a lesser extent, at the Alabama Theatre is that the original work of the craftsmen and architects should be understood, analyzed, and then interpreted—without sacrificing the present in the process. In other words, preservationists like John Bell and Jeff Greene have a great respect for the past of the picture palace, including its vitality and liveliness. They want to preserve that vitality, which means that the restoration of the movie palace must accommodate the people who use the buildings in the present. They recognize that the science of restoration is for the purpose of creating an illusion—which has been, of course, what people have enjoyed about the movie palace all along.

Restoring the Saenger Theatre on a Shoestring Budget

If the Fox Theatre represents preservation in its strictest, grandest, and most well-funded sense, then the Saenger Theatre exemplifies the most humble form of preservation, for it is a modest, city-owned theater, in a small city that has struggled financially in the last few decades. While I am particularly fond of the theater, its director, Lee Hood, and the city of Biloxi, I have often imagined the Saenger Theatre to be the tattered stepsister of the other theaters that I have studied. And yet, while the theater itself cannot compare to other theaters in size or design, that does not mean that the building or its restoration is any less significant to many of the people of Biloxi.

The theater was purchased by the City of Biloxi in the 1970s, and efforts to restore it have taken place during the last twenty-five years, but it is only in the last few years that a master restoration plan has been created and work has begun on the building. The preservation of the Saenger Theatre is significant for our purposes for several reasons. Investigating the motivation behind preserving a theater in a small city enables us to compare and contrast it to larger-scale preservation efforts. Observing a preservation plan just as it is getting off the ground allows us to understand what elements of saving the past are important to people as they look forward to the preservation work (rather than when they look back at what has already been accomplished).

Part of the difficulty of preserving the Saenger Theatre is that it has experienced more than its share of disasters. According to Hood, Hurricane Georges put the current preservation plan on the fast track because the theater's roof was left with a gaping hole as a result of the hurricane's stalling "directly over the theater for several hours." But it was a fire, not a hurricane, that did the most damage to the theater and that most changed the course of its future. After an electrical transformer on the roof malfunctioned and caused a massive fire, ABC Theatres, the owners of the building, closed the doors to the Saenger in 1974. And in January 1975 the company deeded the building to the City of Biloxi for ten dollars.

The city thus acquired a building that had both fire and water damage. With approximately $0.25 million, the City of Biloxi and the organization Friends of the Saenger began an initial repair of the building. According to Gwen Gollotte, the first chairperson of the Friends of the Saenger, initial repairs and restoration were focused on the essentials, mainly repairing the elements of the theater that had been damaged. They replaced the stage curtains and re-covered the seats. They repainted the proscenium arch, ripped out the acoustical tile that covered the auditorium walls, and put in lighting and sound equipment. Gollotte explained that because there was little money for their work, much of it was accomplished through sponsorships and volunteers. The theater's chandelier, for example, was put back together by a community effort:

> An electrician found it in a cistern down at the Waterworks Department. It had been walked on, stomped on, and thrown around. It was in pieces. It was terrible. I went over to the Notre Dame High School for Boys and asked them if they could put it together as a project. Father Jim said that the band would take it on, and the kids and their parents worked and worked. They restrung the whole thing. They decided after they put it back together that it just wasn't clean enough, so they put acid cleaner on it, and all the wire corroded. They had to take it all apart and put it all back together again. It wasn't exactly like the original, but they did a good job.

Gollotte emphasized that the project of restoring the theater has required a great deal of patience over the years because of the lack of funding. "It doesn't happen over night, and although we had a five-year plan, the money dried up. So it was like taking a deep breath and waiting for the next level. Then the city came in with some money, and there was another big push, and then that pretty well dried up, so now we're into another era," Gollotte explained. "We hope, pray, and believe that we can see this to completion."

Another renovation took place in 1984, and the original stage floor was replaced in 1989. Three years later, in 1992, a computerized lighting system was installed, but it was the 1997 refurbishment and reinstallation of the theater's huge neon vertical sign that marked the beginning of the realization of a comprehensive restoration of the Saenger Theatre. The sign, which Gollotte called a "very visible symbol of the Saenger," cost $80,000 to repair, as it was in desperate need of restoration. The neon had to be completely reconstructed, and the broken and rusted enamel was rebuilt. The lighting ceremony in September 1997 was, according to Gollotte, a moving experience. "It was an emotional night when it was lit up again," she recalled. "I stood in the street and cried."

The next step in the restoration of the Saenger Theatre was stabilizing the building in 1999. The stabilization projects included replacing the roof, installing new air-conditioning units, and sandblasting the stucco off the brick exterior. Lolly Barnes, the director of Biloxi's Historic Preservation Office, explained that $0.5 million was invested in projects that the public can neither see nor touch. "Actually, they can see that the

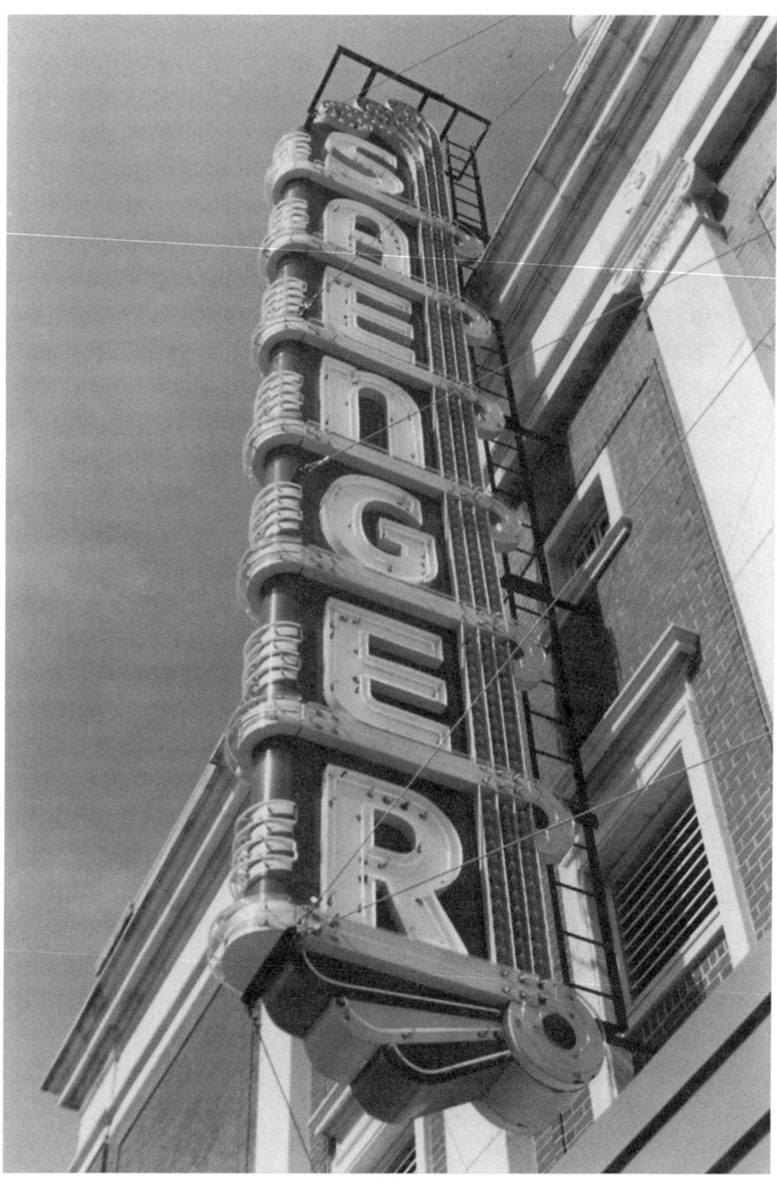

19. The Saenger Theatre marquee restoration required $80,000 and a lot of determination by theater preservationists, but the end result was a "very visible symbol" that the theater was on its way to a complete recovery. Mark Neumann, Documentary Works, Tampa, Florida.

rain is not falling on their heads," Barnes said. A makeshift garden-hose "system" on the roof had been keeping rain from dripping on the seats for ten years, but after Hurricane Georges the roof needed to be replaced entirely and immediately. "Last year after Hurricane Georges, the fellow who helps us with the cleaning came in to try to suck up some of the water out of the carpet," Barnes explained. "The ceiling tiles were apparently holding the water, as it was dripping. Bob Montgomery, our technician, poked a hole in it, and the whole thing came crashing down." Hood knew that stabilizing the structure was essential, but some people in Biloxi objected to the plan nonetheless because the repairs and restoration did nothing to beautify the building's interior. "I would sit at board meetings," Hood stated, "and even my board members would ask, 'Can't we paint the lobby? Can't we paint the dressing rooms?' I am having to constantly remind them that we have to keep the building standing first and then make it pretty."

Now that many of the elements that were jeopardizing the structural integrity of the building have been repaired or replaced, the theater recently underwent its second phase of the restoration. When I asked Hood why it had taken the city more than twenty-five years to reach the point at which they could restore the lobby and add new rest rooms, she explained that the City of Biloxi was nearly bankrupt. "The city was broke—up until the casinos moved in—now the city has caught up real well, but it also has had to fix potholes and pave roads and build more infrastructure to handle what the casinos are bringing in," she said. "For the past eight years, the city has done an admirable job. The mayor has been a conservative manager, but he took over a city that was on the verge of bankruptcy."

During the second phase of restoration, the lobby was restored; the bathrooms were completely remodeled; new bathrooms were added; and the asbestos in the boiler room was dismantled. Hood maintained that the auditorium did not lose its current "shabby chic" condition during the second phase because its restoration will cost an additional $1 million and will have to be executed in a future restoration phase. A local architect, Walter "Buzzy" Bolton, was hired to oversee the $450,000 second phase of the theater's restoration. The City of Biloxi was unwilling to hire a restoration project manager from anywhere other than Biloxi, which put a constraint on the project, but Hood believes that Bolton was appropriate for the project because he grew up attending the Saenger Theatre. "He has memories of it, and he just loves the theater," Hood explained. "He is pro–historic preservation. He has the same feelings for the Saenger as many of our board members have."

Hiring a local architect to oversee a theater restoration is clearly a different approach than we have seen at the Alabama Theatre, but because the Saenger Theatre is city owned, is run by a board, does not raise money from the private sector, and is situated in a small city, their approach to historic preservation and renovation is less grand than Whitmire's. Still, Bolton did grow up going to the theater, and the fact that he remembers what it once looked like (and probably what it felt like too) was thought to be beneficial to the restoration project. Greene contends that theater preservationists should be well grounded in theater history, and while this may not be what he had in mind, having clear memories of the theater gives Bolton a certain kind of foundation that served the theater well.

Besides the fact that the Saenger Theatre is owned by the City of Biloxi and is run by a board (on which some members have served for thirty years), there are several other factors constraining the restoration plan. With neither the financial backing nor a charismatic promoter like Whitmire to attract attention to the theater, the restoration must necessarily be on a smaller, less exact scale. The building itself has been jeopardized by poorly conceived modifications throughout its lifetime; these have diminished and at times obliterated the theater's blueprint and original craftsmanship. While some physical elements, such as the proscenium arch and the adjacent pilasters, have not been compromised, periodic water leaks have severely jeopardized much of the plaster in the building and led to the removal of the plaster ceiling in 1984. The replacement, an unattractive black dropped ceiling, severely imperils the grandeur of the auditorium.

In addition, much of the original information about the theater has been lost or was burned in the fire. Hood contended that all the original furniture has been lost or is in other city-owned buildings or in warehouses. She has only a few bits of original documentation about the theater: a 1934 photograph and a January 16, 1929, copy of the *Daily Herald,* which chronicled the theater's opening. Essentially, the restoration blueprint is guided by the memories of the few people remaining in Biloxi who remember the theater in the first half of the twentieth century. Hood admits, however, that their memories are "a little fuzzy."

At times it may seem that the entire restoration project is a little fuzzy, but there is now a growing interest in returning some of the

20. This is one of the few photographs that remain of the Saenger Theatre's original interior. Critical details such as original colors cannot be determined from early black-and-white photographs, so a certain amount of guesswork is often necessary. Biloxi Public Library, Biloxi Mississippi.

theater's elements to their original state. During my most recent visit to the theater, for example, Hood told me that George Fore, an architect from North Carolina specializing in historic preservation, had recently come to the theater for three days to analyze paint and thus determine the original paint colors. The theater board had agreed to pay a fee of $5,000 to ascertain the original color scheme of the theater. I remember that the first time I visited the Saenger Theatre, I was struck by the unusual pink color of the theater's interior walls. Hood agreed that the color was awful, but she confessed that she had no idea what the original colors were. During that visit I went to Biloxi's public library and found the 1929 newspaper article detailing the theater's design.

The article explained that the auditorium walls "are laid in beautiful decorative panels the inside of each being inlaid with a rich green and gold damask."[7] There was no mention of the lobby's colors, and although green and gold are a far cry from pink, the description was still fairly vague. When Fore came to the theater for three days to pick, peel, and analyze paint, he was able to determine the original color of the lobby by unfastening the velvet ropes from the wall (the ropes aid in the formation of audience lines). They had been taken off the wall only once in the last seventy-two years, so there was only one coat of paint over the original paint, making it fairly simple to determine the original colors. With excitement, Hood explained that the original lobby walls were cream colored, with a gold and red glaze stippled over the cream to create the illusion of stone.

The restoration of the lobby included painting the walls the original colors, using the original application technique. Hood explained that while the cost of the stippling is prohibitive, volunteers agreed to be trained at a nearby faux-finishing school in the community of Bay St. Louis. "These volunteer faux-finishers agreed to faux-finish the lobby's walls, door casings, and baseboards," Hood explained. "You know, we'd call Jeff Greene, but we can't afford it. This way, all we are out is the cost of paint. This just wasn't in the budget because we keep running into serious mechanical problems." She explained that the faux-finishing of the lobby was a stopgap step in the theater's restoration. "We want to make it look pretty so that people will get interested in refinishing the theater all together," Hood confessed. "It's cheaper to let these people learn how to do faux-finishing, and if we want to take it off when we have more money, we can." The crown molding in the lobby, which is bronze finished, is intact and needed only cleaning.

21. This sign, which hangs above a rest room at the Saenger Theatre, is one of the few original decorative details remaining in the theater's lobby. Mark Neumann, Documentary Works, Tampa, Florida.

Because of budget constraints, the lobby's restoration did not include replacing the terrazzo floor covering, which was most likely added in the 1950s, nor did it include replacing the carpet in the inner lobby or the inner-lobby doors, which had been removed at some point. However, new light fixtures that properly reflect the period of the theater were installed. The lobby had previously featured a chandelier and sconces that might look more appropriate in a 1970s Hilton Hotel. "No one remembers what the original lighting looked like," Hood admitted. "But we sure know they didn't look like those."

Although the second phase of the restoration was not as grand as Hood would have liked, she is excited about the remodeling and construction of new men and women's rest rooms, as well as a new handicapped-accessible rest room. The new bathroom fixtures have an old look, with brushed brass and chrome finishes. Since no one remembers what the original bathroom fixtures looked like, they installed new fixtures that look old. With new rest rooms, intermissions will no longer have to be thirty minutes long, and housekeeping will be easier, as the theater has a cleaning crew only three days a week. Because significant mechanical problems continued to be discovered in the theater, the aesthetic restoration of the second phase was compromised. "Every time Buzzy walked in here, he said things like 'Well, there goes your paint.

There goes your . . . ,'" Hood told me. "I told him, 'Okay, as long as you don't take away our potties.'"

The infrastructure and mechanical difficulties included such complications as the auditorium's antiquated sprinkler system. Hood remembered that two nights before the opening of *Jesus Christ, Superstar* in the spring of 2000, the sprinkler system malfunctioned and released 600 gallons of water into the auditorium. "The guy who was playing Peter was a carpet cleaner," Hood said. "He had his truck out in the parking lot. He backed it up to the theater and started sucking water out of the carpet, and he put fans out to dry it because opening night was right around the corner."

The auditorium restoration plan includes some technical improvements, such as moving the fly from the left side of the auditorium to the right, reconstructing the entire rigging system, and moving the technical booth from the auditorium floor to the projection booth area. The Saenger Theatre's board is primarily focused on restoring the auditorium's ceiling during the third phase. The ceiling was dropped five feet because the plaster work was damaged extensively in the 1974 fire. There were acoustical problems, and air-conditioning and heating ductwork needed to be covered. Since the black dropped ceiling severely compromises the aesthetics of the auditorium, everyone involved in the restoration plan is anxious to recover the original one. Once the dropped ceiling is pulled down, much of the millwork around the ceiling will once again be displayed, though some of the original decorative elements of the ceiling were destroyed in the fire. Even though Hood does not know the exact color of the original ceiling, she does know that it was light colored because she has an early black-and-white photograph of the auditorium.

George Fore, the architect from North Carolina, will come back to the Saenger to analyze the paint colors of the auditorium walls and the proscenium arch, so that most of the painted surfaces in the auditorium will be returned to the original colors. Seating will also be improved by removing some rows to create more space. Hood wants new fabric-covered seats installed also. Fortunately, the cast for the original Saenger cast-iron end caps still exists, and Hood hopes to have the end caps reproduced and fitted on the seats that line the aisles. Because the seating in the balcony remains exactly as it was the day the theater opened, nothing will be changed there. Hood added that she will press for a new air-conditioning unit during the third phase as well. "We always throw an

22. The original cast for the Saenger Theater's end caps still exists, and there are hopes that new ones will be reproduced during the auditorium restoration. Mark Neumann, Documentary Works, Tampa, Florida.

air-conditioning unit in, just for good measure," Hood said. "You know, I kind of dread summer coming because we have only one new unit up there and three twenty-eight-year-old units. They're patched and basically held together with bubble gum and duct tape."

Clearly, Hood has her share of mechanical difficulties at the Saenger Theatre. Because the building has had so many technical complications and finances are not unlimited, she has developed a pragmatic view of the building's restoration plans. She maintains two hopes for the building: she desires to restore the building as closely as possible to its original design, and she wishes for the building simply to work properly. She has a sharp sense of humor and an acceptance of the many limitations that confront the restoration plan, providing a good, practical model for undertaking the preservation of small-scale, city-owned buildings.

Even with all the obstacles facing Hood, she still wishes to have as authentic a restoration as possible. Like Jeff Greene, her desire to return to the original is not motivated by a great reverence for the original craftsmen or their work. Just as Greene contends that restored theaters are community magnets, Hood imagines that it is the people of Biloxi who will benefit from a restoration of the theater. "So much of what is known and familiar has died in Biloxi. It's not here anymore," she explains. "And we just want to keep this little corner of heaven, which was built as the 'Gem of the Gulf Coast.' It was designed with grandeur, elegance, and sophistication. You know, a lot of people in this community resist change, and we are just trying to hang on to what we can hang on to."

Biloxi is in a state of great change as a result of the casino industry, which now has a huge presence in the city. For the most part, the people of Biloxi do not resent the casinos, because they have helped the economy bounce back from its perilous state of the 1980s and early 1990s by creating a great draw for tourism and by creating many new jobs for area residents. Still, this new industry necessarily alters the fabric of Biloxi, and while the city has embraced much of the change, there is a nostalgia for the past. Hood contends that the theater restoration enables the community to maintain a small corner of the past, even as they face the inevitability of change in the present. Hood repeated several times that there are only fuzzy memories of the aesthetic details of the theater and that the "city cannot remember what the building looked like." Perhaps it could be argued that there is little reason to restore it to its original state if it really is for the citizens of Biloxi. Yet it seems that if the citizens of Biloxi are nostalgic for the past, fuzzy though it may be, and they are informed that the theater looks quite like it did in the late 1920s, they might just feel a little more secure knowing that a small bit of Biloxi is fighting the battle of time and change.

The Usable Past

Restored movie palaces represent a unique kind of historic public building because they continue to function in more or less the same way that they were originally designed to be used some seventy-five years ago. The restored movie palace remains, in other words, a lively, operating building, rather than a stagnant museum piece to be viewed from afar. A restored movie palace can help us can better understand how modern people use the past, as it is an excellent example of how we both keep the past alive and alter it to better suit our present-day needs.

As we have seen, the fact that people continue to use the movie palace causes numerous frustrations and tribulations for the preservationist, because of human erosion, carelessness, and the inevitable wear and tear on the building. It seems that the people who are committed to restoring and maintaining such structures must constantly attempt to coax the effects of time to be orderly and cooperative. Their persuasion, however, does not seem to work very well, at least not for very long. The usable past is difficult to tame, but that does not stop people from trying to uncover its mysteries.

There are various reasons for wishing to preserve the past at the picture palace. These reasons include preserving the high ideal of the original architects; protecting original craftsmanship; saving the past for future generations; conserving a corner of the past in cities where change seems to be the only constant; countering the contemporary acceptance of ephemerality; and preserving the past because it simply makes good business sense or because the preservation craft is not a bad way to make a living. It seems that the more financially secure the theater is, the more rigid the preservation effort can afford to be, as is the case at the Fox Theatre and the Alabama Theatre. However, while the Tampa Theatre and the Saenger Theatre have more financial constraints, the impulses of their preservationists are essentially the same—that is, they wish to hold on to as much of the past as possible. But rather than dwelling on what is lost or what cannot be restored, they, like Jeff Greene, believe that the preservation of a building can and should be based on an interpretation of what can be known of the past. In other words, in order for a historic building to maintain the same feeling as the original structure, the preservationists attempt to maintain the original idea of the theater.

By paying attention to and then interpreting the original ideas of the architect and the work done by original craftsmen, while at the same time keeping in mind contemporary sensibilities, the picture palace preservationist can preserve an integral aspect of the old movie theater: the illusion of the past. As John Bell and Lee Hood maintain, the movie palace was always about illusion and if that notion is preserved, then much of what was exciting and interesting about the buildings in the 1920s can be saved and maintained in the twenty-first century. Most preservation work is judged by how well the architectural visions and intentions of the people who crafted movie palaces in the first place are interpreted. Disregarding what is known of the past and simply decorating a picture palace is not considered good preservation work.

A while ago, a new movie theater opened in Ybor City, an old area of Tampa that was originally developed to house cigar factories and the people who worked in them. The area has undergone considerable revitalization, and the movie theater is part of a $45 million retail and restaurant complex. When I first entered the movie theater, I saw instantly that the design was meant to have the look of an old structure. The walls were painted as if they had an aged patina, and patches of fake bricks peeked out from the stucco on the walls, suggesting that the theater was in the early stages of becoming a ruin. The ceilings were higher than in the usual movie theater complex, and the lights were pleasantly dim, not fluorescent. All in all, it was a nice effect. Still, no one would imagine for a moment that it was an old movie theater or confuse it for the Tampa Theatre, which is only a few miles down the road. People rarely confuse a new building for an old one, and they are not going to confuse a restored building for a new one, even if the original color scheme is a shade off or if there are updated parts to the building, such as new bathrooms or new seats. Whether every artifact or brush stroke in a restored movie palace is restored accurately does not much matter, because if a good bit of the original structure is kept (rather than remodeled) and the original intentions of the building are maintained, it is still going to feel, look, sound, and even smell like the past.

Preservationists imagine that they restore, reconstruct, and safeguard our architectural history. Their attitudes and practices offer insight into how the past is interpreted, restored, and then used by contemporary society. The sociologist Barry Schwartz, in his study of collective memory and the changing attitudes toward George Washington, contends that while the idea of our founding president has changed through time, there are more continuities in his image than vicissitudes. "In most cases, as in the contemplation of Washington, we find the past to be neither totally precarious nor immutable, but a stable image upon which new elements are intermittently superimposed," Schwartz convincingly argues. "The past, then, is a familiar rather than a foreign country; its people different, but not strangers to the present."[8]

The beliefs and practices of picture palace preservationists also reveal that the usable past simultaneously stays the same and changes. Not even the most hard-core preservationists imagine that the past can be permanently fixed, and even those who put up a good fight may not be considering the many necessary technical and mechanical upgrades that enable the theaters to function in the present day. Those preservationists who choose to be or must be more pragmatic in their approach uncover what they can of the past and then interpret it in order to accommodate modern-day needs and sensibilities. None of the preservationists, however, disregards the past altogether, imagining that the history of the movie palace is simply something to be reconfigured in any whimsical or ironic fashion. Respecting both the peculiarities of the past and the vitality of the present, picture palace preservationists go about creating the illusion of an authentic past, so that modern-day audiences, like those who came before them, can savor the fantasies of the downtown movie palace.

CHAPTER 5

The Discursive Past

What the material preservation of an old theater can help us to remember is somewhat limited. The material preservation of an old picture palace primarily helps us to remember the work of early-twentieth-century architects, designers, and craftsmen. Restoring walls, ceilings, carpet, light fixtures, seating, and tile work enables us to have a partial and nostalgic sense of what it might have felt like to be an audience member in a downtown movie palace in the first half of the twentieth century. It also creates a pleasurable, sensory-based feeling of the past that is hard to describe. Yet material restoration necessarily focuses on one temporal era. In the case of a movie palace, the aim is usually to restore the building as closely as possible to its state on opening night—the moment before wear and tear began. This fixed point of time is only one moment in the history of the 1920s movie palace; such a theater has had many lives beyond its opening-night glory. And those lives reflect many significant periods of the twentieth-century city, such as the explosion of downtown development in the early decades of the twentieth century, racial segregation, suburbanization, urban renewal, racial integration, historic preservation, and downtown revitalization.

Movie palaces seem to easily generate public interest and nostalgia because of their architectural design and because they have been public sites of pleasure and popular entertainment for more than seventy years. They also hold a contextual relationship with the downtown area and the city in which they are situated. The downtown theater is a mirror of how the city and its residents have changed over time. Preserved picture palaces are made even more significant because so many buildings were lost to urban renewal. The restored movie palace is often one of the few restored public and accessible buildings in a downtown area that continues to function in much the same way as it did through most of the twentieth century. A downtown museum in a historic building may chronicle the city's history, but the public cannot use the past at a museum as easily as at the movie palace. Old theaters enable the public to touch the material past and interact with the many other pasts that exist within their walls.

While the material preservation of the movie palace is valuable, I believe that its discursive preservation is more important, for it can tell a much more comprehensive story of the movie palace. By discursive preservation, I mean the preservation of the theater's cultural and social past, the stories about the people who have moved through the building, not the building itself. In part, the past at the picture palace is a nostalgic story of the glory and romance of its heyday. But it is also a past filled with cultural dramas that hinge on elitism, racism, financial disaster, and urban decline. And, of course, the recovery of the movie palace and downtown revitalization are often-told stories of redemption, rescue missions, and aesthetic judgments. The story of the theater also includes cultural transitions and even the complications of historic preservation. In short, the life of the movie palace is a complex one that represents many of the cultural changes that city dwellers experienced in the twentieth century. While many movie palace directors have their hands full simply keeping their buildings standing, I believe that discursive preservation is as important as, if not more important than, material preservation.

Generally, the only past that gets remembered at a movie palace is the same past that is materially preserved—the rather unproblematic opening night and the happy years that followed. This "heritage syndrome," says historian Michael Kammen, is an impulse to remember only what is flattering. "Heritage is comprised of those aspects of history that we cherish and affirm," Kammen explains. "As an alternative to history, heritage accentuates the positive but shifts away from what is problematic."[1] He explains that heritage syndrome can lead to commercialization, vulgarization, oversimplification of history, and capricious memories. The heritage syndrome, Kammen asserts, can lead to a distorted and glossed-over past that denies the historical realities of certain social and cultural groups.[2] Focusing only on the theater's earliest years ignores other pasts, such as the theater's segregation and subsequent integration. When this chapter in theater history is whitewashed, African Americans are essentially discriminated against once again. If one of the objectives of restoring the downtown movie palace is to create a sense of community in the center of the city, as preservationists such as Moses and Duncan desired, then it is essential to include this segment of the theater's past in its discursive history.

While I believe that it is critical that restored movie palaces preserve their cultural pasts, I recognize that it is as difficult to preserve an authentic discursive past as a material one. In other words, if it is difficult to construct and agree upon a theater's material past, it is even more complicated to recover its social history. History is inherently revisionist and chameleon-like, notes historian Raphael Samuel. It is "a matter of quotation, imitation, borrowing, and assimilation."[3] Samuel is suggesting that history is literally in the hands of modern people, and it is subjected to their contemporary interpretations and current needs. Nonetheless, pivotal events that happened at any movie palace can be uncovered and then used by people who inhabit the theater's space in order to understand individual and collective pasts. And surely the discursive pasts of most picture palaces can be preserved more completely than they are presently. Discursive preservation can be accomplished by following a philosophy similar to the one Jeff Greene uses as he goes about restoring old buildings: embracing, rather than ignoring, the segments of the theater's cultural history that can be uncovered, while simultaneously keeping in mind that the restored movie palace must ultimately serve human beings who exist in the present.

Losing the Past at the Carolina Theatre

During the year or so that I traveled from Tampa to the other southern movie palaces, I most looked forward to visiting Durham's Carolina Theatre. Durham is not the most exciting city, and the theater is not particularly grand or spectacularly restored, but, like the Tampa Theatre, the Carolina Theatre is the only other movie palace I studied that continues to function in its original way. In other words, it is still a movie house (though it does regularly host live entertainment in Fletcher Hall). I am an only-slightly-less-than-fanatical movie buff and have never been terribly interested in live musical productions or Broadway entertainment. I am as uninterested in the opera *Le nozze di Figaro* as I am in the musical *Annie*. Most movie palace directors do not share my feelings, as live entertainment draws big crowds and greatly helps support their theaters, but I prefer the independent, foreign, and alternative films shown at the Carolina Theatre.

While I had by far the best time watching foreign films at the Carolina Theatre, I dutifully watched a live one-woman show in Fletcher Hall, performed in conjunction with the North Carolina Jewish Film Festival.[4] I also watched live productions at the other theaters as well (except for the Orpheum Theatre, which was closed both times I was there).[5] At the Alabama Theatre, I saw Lyle Lovett perform (naturally Cecil Whitmire made me pay for my ticket—with cash!); at the Saenger Theatre I watched a local symphony perform; and at the Fox Theatre I saw a ghastly ballet that attempted to interpret *The Diary of Anne Frank*.[6] But it was the chance to see movies that I had not yet seen at the Tampa Theatre that caused me to so look forward to my trips to Durham. Even though a state-of-emergency blizzard hit during my first trip to Durham and I found myself snowbound for three days in an efficiency hotel room—with nothing to eat but hamburger buns and peanut butter—I still most enjoyed myself at the Carolina Theatre because of its outstanding film programming.

Both my preference for film and my nostalgic impulses lead me to believe that a movie palace should continue to operate as a film house in order to best preserve its original function in the community. A film ticket is inexpensive, while a live performance usually costs twenty to sixty dollars more. On the other hand, the film programming shown at both the Tampa Theatre and the Carolina Theatre tends to be foreign, independent, alternative, and classic; thus it can be argued that while they preserve the original form of exhibition, they do not preserve the original middlebrow nature of the theater. Instead, the contemporary film programming transforms the movie palace into a highbrow space, violating the original democratic nature of the movie palace. Broadway-type programming actually maintains the initial middlebrow nature of the theaters, even though the tickets are much more expensive.

All of the theaters I visited do have film programming, though it is not their mainstay. The Alabama Theatre, the Fox Theatre, and the Orpheum Theatre have film series during the summer, which is the slow season for their live-production programming. The Saenger Theatre recently purchased a large screen and state-of-the-art projection equipment, which will enable them to begin showing movies four to five times a year. The Tampa Theatre and the Carolina Theatre, however, still count on movies to bring in the crowds, and by doing so have preserved the original, primary functions of the buildings. And while both theaters exhibit alternative films that may be considered highbrow, both venues also exhibit films from countries all over the world. These films are not only of interest to native-born audiences but are of particular interest to nonnative audiences, who get an opportunity to view films from the part of the world where they once lived.

The Tampa Theatre and the Carolina Theatre also create democratic spaces with an annual Gay and Lesbian Film Festival, which is heavily attended at both venues. Last year, my husband and I took a friend from Paris to view a film during the Tampa Theatre's Gay and Lesbian Film Festival. The queue to the box office snaked all the way around the corner, and we were unable to see the film because it sold out by the time we were halfway through the line. Our friend, a cultural anthropologist at the Sorbonne, was astounded to see the hundreds of people waiting in line and gathering in front of the theater. He said he had never seen such a huge audience for a gay film in Paris, much less in Tampa. The Carolina Theatre also hosts an annual North Carolina Jewish Film Festival, an annual North Carolina Nevermore Horror and Gothic Film Festival, and an annual Double-Take Documentary Film Festival.

In the case of the Carolina Theatre, the fact that the theater still exhibits films is practically the only element of the theater that has been preserved. When I went to Durham the second time, I stayed at the downtown Marriott Hotel, which is literally connected to the theater. Each night I was there, I was able to walk down a hotel corridor, open a door, and step into the theater, without ever going outside. The fact that a modern hotel was built with a direct connection to an old movie palace surely raises a few eyebrows in preservation circles; however, as a guest of the hotel, I found it terrific that I could leave my hotel room and in a matter of minutes be sitting in a theater auditorium, watching the Dutch movie *Left Luggage* (Jeroen Krabbe, 1998). In addition, the theater has two small, entirely new cinemas that were added to the original theater in 1992. Even though a decorative motif similar to one in Fletcher Hall is integrated into the cinemas, they are clearly new and were not constructed so as to fool anyone into believing that they were ever part of the old structure.

The theater was named a pivotal building in the listing of Durham's downtown district on the National Register of Historic Places in 1977; however, the theater itself is not a historic landmark. Pepper Fluke, an integral figure in the revitalization of the theater, explained that she suspected the building would have never qualified as a historic landmark because too much of the historic fabric of the building was already destroyed by the mid-1970s, including all of the theater's stairways. Nevertheless, the people involved in the early-1990s restoration, particularly Pepper Fluke, St. Clair Williams, and Monte Moses, hoped the material preservation of the building could be as authentic as possible. And while it is not my purpose in this chapter to focus on material preservation, it is important to explain the present material condition of the building and how it came to be this way, as the theater's restoration is representative of the past's ambivalent status at the Carolina Theatre.

The difficulties with restoring the theater began in 1988, with an initial renovation plan that would have left nothing but the facade of the theater intact. "It was going to be an aluminum horseshoe," Fluke remembered, "and they were going to widen the proscenium, destroy all the plaster, all of the decorative finishes. Everything in the building—gone." This initial plan was ultimately defeated with the help of outside consultants associated with the League of Historic American Theatres and a committee charged with overseeing the project. One of the largest obstacles facing Fluke and the others was that the city owned the building. Any funds raised for the project needed to come from a bond referendum. There was exactly $7.8 million to restore the building, but the first two estimates submitted to the city far exceeded that amount.

Fluke explained that the first architectural group was handed the "wish list of the century" and estimated that the restoration would cost $22.4 million. The second architect scaled down the wish list and suggested that the theater could be restored for $16.2 million. While that plan generated interest, it was impossible to implement because of the price. News of the exorbitant estimates, according to Fluke, fostered a less-than-desirable public interest in the project: "We had to overcome all the negative perception from the $22.4 million, then the $16.2 million, the fact that it was a segregated building originally and the African Americans weren't going to support this building. There was all kinds of negativism that we were working to overcome."

The restoration committee searched for an architect and finally decided on one from Chicago. Both Moses and Fluke agree that ultimately he was the wrong architect for the job. "I guess my summation of the architect we ended up with was that we had a man who was very good at new construction," Fluke admitted, "but who came into this building with a vision of a 1980s hotel and not a restored 1926 theater." Fluke explained that in hindsight the county and the city should have checked his references more carefully. "We found out later that, yes, he had worked on Radio City Music Hall, but he hadn't done any restoration. He had done something about fixing the bathrooms. We went to the Chicago Theatre to see the project there, but what we found out later was that he hadn't done the interior finishes of the restoration; he had done the office building adjacent to it."

Fluke's and the others' hope for the Carolina Theatre restoration was to maintain the original footprint of Fletcher Hall and not to turn it into something that it was never intended to be. While some of the original structure and design had already disappeared prior to the restoration, they wanted to hold on to much of what remained. In order for the building to provide a "usable history," a historic model of a 1926 movie palace and the intentions of the original architect might have served as guidelines for the restoration. They did not. While the theater is a gracious space in its own right and is well used and appreciated by many, much of the interior was wiped out during the restoration. The architect, Fluke explained, even had to be forced to maintain the original light fixtures: "It's an historic building, so we were trying very hard, but he didn't even want to keep the old light fixtures. I had to hire a company from Floyd, Virginia, that I had found to come in and say, 'Yes, these are wonderful fixtures. They can be restored. They can be brought up to code.' These sconces, all the star-burst fixtures, hanging chandeliers in the auditorium, all of that—he didn't want to use any of it." According to Fluke, he not only wanted to get rid of historic elements of the theater, he also wanted to add new structural and design elements.

"It started out fine," Fluke remembered, "but some of the ideas that he had were so off the wall. He wanted to build a gazebo little thing out in the front here. He wanted to put a half-barrel vault in the lobby downstairs that you could look at from the first balcony through end windows.

What you were going to be looking at was the back side of the concession stand!" Fluke worked for more than eight months to convince the city and county that such additions would destroy what historic integrity was left of the building. The design committee could not, for various reasons, fire the architect, but in the end, she said, they "bought him off," so that they could rid themselves of him.

Fluke admits that the architect did a good job designing the two new cinemas that are incorporated into the old theater and that there are no other movie palaces that duplicate some of the features of the restored Carolina Theatre. Unlike most other old theaters, which naturally have only one screen, the Carolina Theatre has three, and it also has four lobbies that are all rentable spaces. But Fluke says she no longer likes the way the theater feels. "It's cold. It's unfriendly. This used to be the building that everybody wanted to come to. In its awful, rinky-dink old days, they would come in an hour ahead of the film. We had little tables set up down in front of the concession area, and people would come in and meet their friends, and they would sit and talk. And there was this warmth," Fluke recalled. "Then after the film they would hang out, so they could talk about the film."

Moses, who was also an active member of the restoration process, concurs that the building lost its warmth during the restoration process. "I'm a compromiser, and I can live with things that I don't like 100 percent," Moses said. "It serves its function, but I think that it is too bad that the opportunity was missed. I think how you feel about a place—you can't describe it—it just grabs you. [That] is the difference between success and failure. This just doesn't have it." Like Fluke, Moses is pleased with the new cinemas, and he believes Fletcher Hall has a good feeling about it. He thinks that the acoustics in the hall are first rate. Moses explained that his present feeling about the theater is similar to what a father might feel for a child who grows up to be a different kind of person than the father hoped or expected. He said that he acknowledges and accepts what the theater has become.

Fluke and Moses spent many years working toward their goal of restoring the Carolina Theatre in a way that maintained its warmth by respecting the initial design intentions of the building. The restoration mishaps and compromises disappointed Fluke and led Moses to a calm acceptance of the fact that his dream for the building was not realized. Even a 1993 Historic Preservation Society of Durham newsletter intimated that the original hopes for the building's restoration were not met. After explaining that the initial plans for the restoration were far too expensive, the article notes that many compromises were made. "These compromises mean that this is not a true restoration," states the article. "Rather it is an adaptive re-use. Much of the original fabric of the building was lost over the years through insensitive remodels and is now being recreated. But the building is not being restored to its exact original design. The theater's 1926 appearance will shine forth, supported by contemporary systems and support spaces."[7]

The Carolina Theatre lacks warmth, and it simply does not have a feeling of the past like the other restored theaters that I have studied. Nonetheless, its restoration, or more appropriately, its adaptive re-use, enables the building to be a centerpiece of community and culture in downtown Durham. Both its cinematic programming and its performing arts draw many people from the Triangle area, from other parts of North Carolina, and in some cases from other states. In this important sense, the restoration was successful, because the building continues to attract audiences. Yet because much of the material past has been wiped away, the building itself is less able to provide a structural account of the past to the public.

This does not mean, however, that the past at the Carolina Theatre has been entirely forgotten. While the historic integrity of the building has been compromised, a group of people who have been deeply involved with the theater are currently struggling to retain much of its cultural past. There is both a struggle to remember and a struggle to forget at the Carolina Theatre. Deciding how and what to conserve of the theater's cultural past seems to be even more troubling and complicated than the struggles to preserve its materiality. As we have seen, preserving the material structure is complicated; there are almost as many methods and philosophies of preservation as there are old buildings. But the complications around material preservation are few compared to the complexity of discursive preservation of a theater.

When a theater's paint finishes are restored, the theater is fixed in time (for a while, anyway) and is often more beautiful than it was before it was restored, but when the theater's cultural past is restored, many pasts, some of them complex and unpleasant, are remembered. There is therefore, at most theaters, a resistance to remembering. Some theater directors simply do not bother with it at all. Interestingly, the preservationists at the Fox Theatre, who are almost militant about conserving the theater's material past, have expended no effort recovering its cultural past. They argue that they simply do not have the time to recover it because all of their energy must be used to maintain its material past.

In contrast, the Carolina Cinema Corporation—which is composed of Moses, Fluke, and St. Clair Williams—desires for the theater's past not to be forgotten by the Durham community. It seems that they are fighting a difficult battle for many reasons—some of which are simply logistical problems. But the primary problem they face is their philosophical differences with the current theater management; in many ways their disputes resemble those of the preservationists and the operating management at the Fox Theatre. It is a difference in vision, a matter of one group hoping to hold on to the past and the other group focusing on the future of the theater.

For Moses, Fluke, and Williams, the restoration of the Connie Moses Ballroom is symbolic of how the past is currently represented at the theater. As described in chapter 3, Connie Moses was considered the soul of the theater's comeback in the 1980s. The ballroom that she dreamed of and then set about creating became the focus of the social interaction at the theater. Monte Moses described it as a "charming, semi-Victorian, kooky room" when Connie was finally finished decorating it, but after the restoration the Connie Moses Ballroom could best be described as functional. While Moses has accepted the compromises and limitations of most of the building's restoration, he is disappointed with the restoration of the ballroom. "It's cold. No pizzazz, no style," Moses confided. "It looks like a gentleman's room. It's purely functional, and quite honestly, the room doesn't get a lot warmer with people in it." While the room is still called the "Connie Moses Ballroom," it seems that the name is all that is left of Connie, and that fact is a bit painful for Moses, Fluke, and Williams.

The ballroom, which was originally part of the balcony for African Americans, has obviously not been restored to its 1926 condition, but, significantly, Connie Moses's intentions for the room were also ignored. In other words, Moses, Fluke, and Williams believe that the theater has had many lives, and each of its eras is significant and should not be forgotten. If the Connie Moses Ballroom had been restored in such a way as to maintain the spirit of the woman who created it, then the theater's transitional era could have been recognized as an integral part of the life of the theater.

Of course, the state of the Connie Moses Ballroom is not the fault of Steve Martin, who did not become the theater director until the restoration was completed. And, as I said, the ballroom is only a symbol of how the past is considered at the theater today. But when I talked to Fluke and Williams, it was clear that they felt the present management at the theater made it a point to push the past out of the theater; they also felt that they were excluded. Williams explained that the "old guard" simply is not as welcome as they once were at the theater. She said, for example, that when the theater first reopened after the renovation, they tried to keep the history of the building alive. "Pepper was doing historic tours and taking people through [the theater], and then the current management wanted to do that themselves," Williams said. "And none of them knew what the building was like or anything about the history of the building."

Williams explained that at present there are very few tours of the building and that there are no local school programs or tours that focus on the history of the building and its importance to the city. The only person remaining at the theater who cares about the building and its history is in charge of its upkeep. "He's had to learn all of the ins and the outs of the old parts [of the building] and the new part [of the building]," Williams said. "He stays on because he loves the building; that's basically it." The perception that the old guard at the Carolina Theatre has been pushed out of the spotlight reminds me of the fire hoses cleaning away the past at the Tampa Theatre. There is often the feeling, when there is a change of guard, that what came before the change should be left behind. As the historian J. B. Jackson writes, "There has to be (in our new concept of history) an interim of death or rejection before there can be renewal and reform. The old order has to die before there can be a born-again landscape."[8]

Fluke believes that the people who work in an old building such as the Carolina Theatre should have not only an appreciation for the building itself but also an appreciation of all that has taken place there. "When you bring people to work in this building, you [need to] share with them that it's not just bricks and mortar—a building is a building because of everything that's gone on in the building," Fluke explained. "The people who operate this building have to be made to realize that this is not just a job, that if you don't believe in a historic structure, if you don't have a passion for what it stands for—and it stands for a lot—then you get this cold, functional building."

The members of Carolina Cinema Corporation believe that the past has been made mostly irrelevant at the theater, and while their lives have become full with other ventures, they are still determined not to let the history of the theater slip away permanently. Fluke has made several slide-show presentations about the history of the theater in the last year. She presented her program at the annual meeting of the Historic Preservation Society of Durham. While her presentation focused on the historic elements of the theater that were lost in the process of the renovation, she realized that most of the people in the audience did not know or had already forgotten about Fletcher Hall's recent restoration. "It was the first time many in the audience even realized that the auditorium as we see it today was only that way for three years," Fluke explained. She was surprised to learn that some members of the Historic Preservation Society were not aware that before the auditorium was restored, the gold leafing and other original painted finishes had been painted over; the walls had been covered with acoustic tiles and inappropriate draperies; and windows in the auditorium had been bricked.

The fact that Durham's Historic Preservation Society has hardly any memory of the Carolina Theatre's past, even its recent past, is powerful confirmation of Fluke's belief that the past is slipping away. She made a commitment to the new chair of the theater board, who happens to be a preservationist and was at her presentation, to repeat her presentation to a theater board retreat. Before Fluke made the presentation to the board, she said, "I see this as an opportunity to educate the board on what our theater once was and could be again. It remains to be seen whether the outcome [will be] successful or not." After Fluke's theater board presentation, which included the exhibition of 140 slides of the theater, she explained that, although she had received a few comments from board members, "I must admit that I feel like I am in alien territory when I go to the theater. There is so much staff turnover that I know only about four among the many."

Denise Clay, the theater's audience services manager and an employee at the Carolina Theatre for eight years, saw Fluke's board presentation. "Her slide presentation was quite amazing," Clay recalled. "When Pepper was showing the slides to the board members and the full-time staff, one man was so touched he got all weepy when he talked about it. So you know there is something there. If people knew the extent that people went to save the building—it would make a difference in the community. I really do think so." Clay, like Fluke, Moses, and Williams, does not believe that enough effort is expended to educate the public about the theater's past, and she suggested that civic groups like the Junior League should be offered the opportunity to see Fluke's slide presentation. She contends that if more people were informed about the theater's past, it would make the public more interested in the theater, and much misinformation about the theater could be corrected. "There are a lot of people who come here and ask about the history," Clay explained. "And we do have some fliers, but it is pretty basic information. I really don't think that people have a sense of the total history of this place."

Besides the philosophical differences with the current management, the Carolina Cinema Corporation members also have practical problems with preserving and presenting the past to the public of Durham. When I met with Moses and Fluke the first time that I went to the Carolina Theatre, they explained that they had many boxes of materials that I might find useful in my research, but unfortunately most of it was stored away and not accessible. Their hope, they said, was to write a book about the history of the Carolina Theatre, using the documents that they had accumulated. Months after I met with them, Fluke told me that they were trying to come to some determination about what to do with all of their records and documents: "We are all devoted to preserving the past, the history, and wishing for the potential that building could be. We are also well into the aging population, and we are among the few who really care. Durham does not have adequate space to house such an archive, which means dealing with 150 boxes of paper, files, and records. We are in conversation with the research librarian in the Carolina Room at the county library. He is very interested but recognizes the problem of storage space, working space, climate control, man/woman power, time, and money!"

Clearly the Carolina Cinema Corporation has many obstacles that they must overcome to preserve what they perceive as integral aspects of the theater's past. While they appear to wish to document all of the pasts at the theater, they seem particularly interested in preserving the transitional years of the theater—its rescue, its years as a funky art house, and its restoration. Their recognition that the cultural history of the movie palace extends beyond its nostalgia-inspiring first life is unusual, since most theater preservationists (if they concern themselves with the past at all) focus only on the first half of the twentieth century. Fluke and the others focus on the years in which they were heavily involved in the theater, and it is only natural that they would want documentation of it. Ironically, it seems that the many uphill battles that they fought in order to save and then restore the Carolina Theatre are bumps in the road compared to the struggle of making sure the public does not forget what happened at the theater during those years.

While some of the problems that the Carolina Cinema Corporation faces are logistical in nature, Fluke and Williams perceive the current management at the theater as a large part of their trouble in saving the theater's past. Martin, who has been the director of the theater for the last six years, is partially responsible for the rich and diverse programming of both film and live performances at the theater. He is committed to finding the appropriate entertainment for the unique population that the theater serves. Few areas in the country have similar demographics as Durham and the rest of the Research Triangle: 12 percent of the population have a Ph.D.; 140,000 college students live in the area; and it has the ninth largest community of African Americans in the country, including one of the biggest communities of middle-class African Americans.

Although a part of Durham's population is particularly well educated, which generally creates excellent conditions for a film and performing-arts center, Martin faces an unusual challenge in that a good portion of the Research Triangle's population turns over every five years. "We have almost a brand-new community every five years, so we have a constant struggle in making people aware of the amenities here," Martin lamented. "We consistently have to mine new customers, much more so than the historic theater in Buffalo, New York, let's say. That's an older community, and it is much less transient." The turnover in population makes it much more difficult to maintain a foundation of die-hard supporters, and, of course, it also means that the past of the Carolina Theatre is even harder to remember.

In such a culture, there are fewer long-term residents who remember firsthand the theater's past, and fewer still who perceive the theater as a significant personal identity marker. In other words, if a person's personal past does not intersect with the theater, it is less likely that the cultural past of the theater will matter as much to them. As I mentioned in the last chapter, John Ramsey, a current board member, explained that he cannot relate to the concerns that the past should be preserved at the theater. He stated that he did not wish to dwell on the past because the theater is a building for the people who come to it in the present. Ramsey also pointed to the fact that the past does not much matter to the people who are new to the Research Triangle anyway.

By the last day of my second trip to the Carolina Theatre, it was clear to me that the issue of maintaining the theater's past was a troubling one for both the members of the Carolina Cinema Corporation and the people who are currently in management positions at the theater. Martin, who has worked in several old theaters, agreed and said there is often a tension between those who saved the building and those who operate it:

> They have a different love for the building. The first one is born out of the desire to save a structure and restore it to the memory that they had of it. And the people who have to operate it have to think about how they make it relevant for today. They have to use the facility as it can be used. There is never enough money to create a museum, and if people would just be honest and say, 'We are going to raise enough money to restore this building and then keep it as a museum,' then it would be different. But that isn't what happens. What happens is they say, 'Let's save this theater because it still has life in it, and it still has relevance to downtown.' But they don't pay much attention to how it is going to operate. Their focus on restoration and recreating the past oftentimes stops at the completion of the project. That is where their foresight stops. Past that point is the real operational day-to-day problems.

Martin explained that it is not a coincidence that the focus on restoration and the lack of operational foresight cause some restored theaters to begin experiencing financial difficulty within six months to a year after the building has been reopened for operations. In addition, Martin stated that the executive directors who oversee theater restoration projects often step down within the first year of the restoration. "You have to have the respect for the past, the social graces, and the fund-raising abilities to raise money around an idea—that is restoring a theater," Martin said. "When you are operating it, you have to have an entrepreneurial spirit and a business sense in order to make it work. The conflict doesn't come from one side using the theater differently than the other. The conflict comes from a difference in vision."

Martin explained that essentially there are two kinds of directorial visions for a historic theater: one that focuses on the historic nature of the theater and maintaining it as a community-based operation, and another that focuses on making the theater a premier venue in the area. Martin made it clear that he aligns with the second perspective. "When people decide that they want to go to a cultural event in the Triangle, I don't want them to just think about Memorial Auditorium; I want them to think Carolina Theatre first, if possible; second, if not," Martin explained. "And everybody in Durham ought to be thinking about the cinemas as the place to see a movie. That's what we've set out to do, and that's what I told the board that I was going to do when they interviewed me."

Martin acknowledged that the theater has had its financial ups and downs in the six years since he has been the director. But within that time period the theater has gained a more prominent regional and national reputation, which has greatly benefited the community. He cited the fact that the theater has initiated two regional film festivals during his time as director; has begun hosting the international Double-Take Documentary Film Festival; has hosted the premiere of the national tour of *The Gin Game* in 1998; and was the only stop between California and New York and Miami of the Spanish dance and musical production *Tango Pasion*.

In terms of maintaining the historic integrity of the facility, the city is responsible for the upkeep of the building, and only a few antiques in the building need care. However, Martin noted that the building's plaster work has been a source of frustration, because the excess moisture of summer humidity attacks plaster. Two years ago, after a consultation with an air-conditioning company, he decided to reduce the humidity in the auditorium in the summer by heating the air (which dries it) as it came into the building and then cooling the heated air. Martin said that the decision to reduce the humidity in the building in the summer months has "pretty much stemmed the tide on the problem with the plaster." But it also meant a 40 percent increase in the theater's gas bill. Martin explains, "Here's the rub. We're doing that. If I were just a businessman, I wouldn't. If I were just a businessman and an entrepreneur, I would say, 'Wait a minute. The problem belongs to the city. It's their building, and it's their air-handling unit. They need to spend the $86,000 and fix it, so we don't have to spend it operationally.' I increased my business costs to protect the building. There's a conflict that Pepper Fluke doesn't recognize, but it's a conflict that I face."

Clearly, Martin is committed to the well-being of the Carolina Theatre. For the most part that commitment is focused on interesting, challenging, and diverse programming for the Research Triangle community and on sustaining a financially healthy business. But he is also dedicated to the building itself, even though he may not be as vigilant about it as Fluke would like. As much as I respect his efforts, particularly his dedication to making the Carolina Theatre a premier film festival venue in the Research Triangle, Martin is not terribly concerned with the many layers of the past that help to define the theater's identity. As much as he wishes to focus on the present and the future, and as important as that focus obviously is to the well-being of the theater, neglecting the past does not serve the theater well.

Obviously the Carolina Cinema Corporation members are refusing to let go of the theater's most recent past—its rescue and restoration. The telling and retelling of this story enables people to better understand that if old buildings that have been at the center of a community's culture are ignored and are not protected, they disappear, as so many have in the last forty years. The fact that members of Durham's Historic Preservation Society were not aware of Fletcher Hall's restoration, which was completed only a few years ago, demonstrates that the past can quickly disappear if it is not safeguarded. On the other hand, there is one past that has been ignored at the Carolina Theatre, but that has not been forgotten or reconciled by some of Durham's residents.

The past that continues to linger is the history of segregation at the theater. As we have seen, the Carolina Theatre was a primary target of desegregation efforts in Durham because the theater was city owned. It was the only theater of the six discussed here that was city owned at the time of the Civil Rights movement; consequently, it is the only theater that was a primary target of protest. The fact that the theater was regularly in the news during the efforts to desegregate it may be one of the reasons members of Durham's African American community have not forgotten that they were at one time allowed only in the theater's balcony. Some of Durham's African American community continue to resent the past at the theater. It is a wound that needs healing, and while it is difficult to know exactly how to do that, it is clear that the story of the theater's segregation and ultimate integration has not been forgotten by some people who live in Durham and that it should be part of the theater's discursive past.

Like the restoration of the Connie Moses Ballroom, which seems symbolic of how the past was handled during the theater's restoration, Fletcher Hall's ceiling is a symbolic representation of how segregation has been remembered at the theater. Once the theater was integrated in 1964, many African Americans were not interested in sitting in the balcony, where they had been forced to sit for so many years. Whites did not want to sit in the balcony either, as many of them perceived it as a black balcony. "This was the first of the movie houses to be integrated," St. Clair Williams remembered. "But they could not sell the tickets to anybody—even at a very cut rate—to climb those steps." The decision was made to build a dropped ceiling that literally covered up the tainted space of the balcony. The false ceiling completely covered the black balcony, and it also covered the auditorium's proscenium arch work and the entablature.

When I asked Fluke if the dropped ceiling was really for the purpose of erasing or covering up history (it just seemed too strange to be true), she replied, "Just erase it—that's right. The black box office was used for storage. It was just a storage room; [they] didn't use it. This whole part [of the theater] was as if it didn't exist. It also played in the restoration of the building because the African American people in this community were very offended by this whole process." The entire black balcony and much of the proscenium's decorative work was completely concealed from 1964 to 1994. An entire generation of Durham residents was unaware that there had once been a black balcony in the theater.

If the purpose of covering the black balcony was to rid the theater once and for all of its tainted history, it did not work. Resentment remains in the African American community. That became clear to me as I discussed the treatment of the past with various theater employees. Denise Clay, for example, who believes that Durham residents should have a better understanding of the total history of the theater, explained that the history of segregation at the theater has left a bitter taste in the mouths of some African Americans. "It's just one of those things. Some people say you need to forget about the past here, but how can you forget about the past when it happened?" Clay reasoned. "If it didn't affect you negatively, then maybe you can be unconcerned. But if it has affected you negatively, then that's a different story." Clay believes that the theater suffers as a result of ignoring the past, because she feels that African Americans do not perceive the theater as a place that belongs to them; to them it is a place for other people. Clay is not certain how to remedy the problem, but she thinks that it might help if the theater's history were taught to school children by means of a study packet that they would receive prior to theater tours.

Clay recalls that the theater continued to maintain an aura of exclusion for many years after it was desegregated. She explained that prior to the restoration, and Martin's directorship, programming decisions were made to turn away outside promoters who were deemed inappropriate for the building. "'This is our building. What if they did this or that to the building? *Those* people.' I've heard these things. Who are *those* people?" Clay asked incredulously. "They were referring to African Americans. 'If we offer them beer and wine, what will *those* people do?' Don't some of *those other* people have the potential to get destructive when they drink too?" Clay contends that on occasion extra security has been brought into the building, and costs have increased, when the programming promises to fill the auditorium with a predominantly nonwhite audience. "It's just not welcoming to everybody," Clay observed. "They would not say that they do that [treat nonwhite audiences differently] because they do not even realize they are doing it. On occasions I have questioned what people have said, and there are other people on the staff who have spoken up for the rights and privileges of all people. It's not just this institution. It's prevalent everywhere."

Cora Bryant, the Carolina Theatre's office manager, who began working at the theater seven years ago, also believes that the theater's racist past continues to affect African Americans' perceptions. She added, however, that since she began working at the theater, there has been an increase in African American audience members, as a result of the affordable, diverse programming that the theater offers. Bryant, a Durham native, did not come to the theater when she was young. However, her parents used to come to the theater when it was still a segregated site. "They had to come around the back door," Bryant explained. "They couldn't come through the front door. They still came because it was somewhere for them to go on a date. They came, but they were not too impressed with it."

Whether the theater's past bothers people or not, Bryant explained that it still remains in the consciousness of the community. She and some of her friends can joke about the theater's past. "I had some comp tickets for downstairs, and I was going to give them to my girl friend," Bryant said laughingly. "She said that she didn't want them because she wanted to sit in the balcony. Joking with her, I said, 'Okay, you don't have to take them, but when they made you sit up there, you didn't want to sit up there, but now you have a chance to sit downstairs, and you don't even appreciate it.' She decided she would take them after all." But Bryant said that some of her other friends still perceive the theater as a racist site and do not believe that she should even be working at the

Carolina Theatre. "Some people will say to me, 'Why are you still at that slave camp?' I told my girl friend the other day that I just bought a new house, and she said, 'Now it's time to get a new job.'" Bryant was quick to add that she enjoys working at the theater and does not pay too much attention to such attitudes.

Bryant believes that if the theater's segregated past and subsequent integration were incorporated into the theater's history, that there would still be people who would avoid the theater. "A lot of the older people, regardless of what you do, it's embedded in them. It's not going to go away," Bryant stated. "For other people, a better history of the theater would help them to acknowledge the changes that have taken place in Durham." School tours of the theater could only benefit young people, she thought. "They are going to learn about segregation in school, and the theater could play a great part. To say to them, 'This is in your town, and this is a historical site.' It's always good to know what happened."

Racial relations in Durham have improved dramatically since her parents were young, Bryant said. She remembers the marches and the demonstrations around the time of Martin Luther King Jr.'s assassination. She remembers not being able to go to particular places in Durham, and she remembers her parents' attitudes toward whites during the 1960s. But she contends that her own children do not face any of the barriers that she or her parents confronted. "I didn't attend cultural events when I was young because my parents didn't want us to be a part of certain things," Bryant said. "My children can do anything they want. There is nothing that is preventing them from doing anything. They can do it. So I think we have come a long ways."

Howard Clement, a member of Durham's city council, who was an active participant in the picketing and demonstrations that led to the theater's integration, believes that the present-day diversity of programming is an obvious sign that attitudes have changed dramatically over the years. However, he suggests that more effort still needs to be expended on the part of theater management as well as the African American community. "There have been efforts to reach out, but it's a two-way street. *We* have to demonstrate that we are willing to come downtown, to go to the theater. If there is a lack of support, it's a shared responsibility. Sometimes I think he [Martin] may be climbing up a greased pole trying to reach out to the total community."

Clement agrees that the history of the theater needs to be communicated more effectively for both younger and older residents. He claims that for younger African Americans the Carolina Theatre is just another theater. They have no barriers in front of them. Yet they should be made aware of the obstacles that once faced the generation that came before them. Clement believes that if the theater took some responsibility for its past by narrating it, older Durham residents might be more willing to go to the theater. "That railroad track still exists," Clement said. "It was a real barrier when I came to Durham, but now it's more of a stereotypical, mythical thing. It's in the mind. The theater is on the other side of town still. On the other side of the tracks. The younger professional African American lacks the scars of what I remember."

Through the years, decisions have been made at the theater to consciously forget about its history of segregation. From the lowering of the ceiling to the absences in the historical narration on theater tours, the Carolina Theatre has turned its back on its past. It is obvious, however, that some members of the African American community in Durham still remember what happened at the theater and still remain troubled by it. Though little of the material past remains at the Carolina Theatre, the theater still carries both the burdens and the triumphs of its past. The residue of history remains, and it seems that more of an effort should be made to acknowledge the hurts that were caused in the earlier part of the twentieth century. On the other hand, some parts of the theater's past—namely, the efforts to save the theater and restore it—are being quickly forgotten by Durham's residents. It is difficult to know why some pasts are more easily remembered by the public than others, but surely the scars of segregation have a more lasting effect than the reclamation of a building. Nonetheless, both chapters in the theater's past are significant to the cultural history of Durham, and the theater should preserve them for both longtime and new residents.

More recent events that have taken place at the theater are also culturally significant, and care needs to be taken so that they are not forgotten either, since they, too, mark important transitions in the life of the theater. Martin and his staff have made some extraordinary efforts in the last six years to create programming that is of interest to all—including those groups that have been routinely excluded at other cultural centers (particularly in the conservative South). When I talked with Jim Carl, the theater's film festival programmer, it became clear that the summer of 1995 marked an important transition in the theater's identity, when once again the theater became a site of protest. However, unlike the early 1960s picketing and demonstrations that took place at the theater to protest the theater's exclusionary practices, this time there was a public uproar by conservative groups because the theater announced that it was hosting a gay and lesbian film series. Thirty-two years after the Carolina Theatre was reluctantly integrated, it was a target of hostility by those who thought that the public building had become too free-thinking and liberal in its programming.

In 1995 the Carolina Theatre had been recently restored; most people in Durham were aware that their tax dollars had helped to renovate the building, and the city's residents were encouraged to view the theater as their own. Martin had been hired in April 1995, and in June, only two months later, the North Carolina Pride '95 hosted its annual march in Durham. The main site for the conference and march was the area around the downtown plaza, adjacent to the theater. Pride members and marchers stayed at the hotel that is connected to the theater. Prior to the march, organizers of Pride '95 approached the theater's film programming director, asking him to consider exhibiting a few gay and lesbian films during the weekend of the convention. "The theater was still trying to find its voice in the community and still trying to find its own niche market," Carl explained. "So the film director asked Martin's permission to secure a few titles. We're talking typical PG-13 type of titles that happened to have gay and lesbian characters in them." Martin gave the go-ahead, and four films were secured. Press announcements explaining that a gay and lesbian film series would coincide with the march were distributed in the hopes that Pride '95 participants would come to the films and generate some revenue for the theater.

Immediately following the press release, a public outcry erupted throughout the Triangle. The Christian Coalition and other conservative activists demanded that the gay and lesbian film series be canceled. The groups believed that their voices should be heard and the film series should be canceled because the Carolina Theatre is a city-owned building; thus, they insisted that their tax monies should not support programming that they found offensive. Essentially, conservative groups knew little about the films that would be exhibited. They knew only that the subject matter of the films was related to the gay and lesbian lifestyle, which they believed was perverse. An editorial in the *Herald-Sun,* for example, stated that one issue around the controversy of the film series was the fact that homosexuality was immoral. "Homosexuality is sex gone the way of perversion. It is spoken of in the Bible as an abomination. Homosexuality points to a society in decline, to morality set aside," the editorial reads. "I guess Christians and Republicans are more concerned about the assault on morality than they are about toleration. Some things morally are right and some things morally are wrong."[9]

As the series date came closer and closer, the controversy over whether the film series should be allowed to play at the theater continued. Members of the Christian Coalition and several Durham Republicans asked the Durham board of county commissioners to intervene on their behalf.[10] When the county commissioners refused, the conservative groups took their request to Durham's district attorney, Jim Hardin. Before the district attorney could make a decision on whether to cancel the series, he had to determine whether the films were obscene, as defined by state law. For materials to be categorized as obscene under state law, they must meet four tests: they depict patently offensive sexual behavior; they violate community standards; they lack literary, artistic, political, or scientific value; and they fail to be protected speech under the Constitution.[11] Hardin requested members of Durham's city council and board of county commissioners, along with the twenty theater board members, the film director, and Martin, to view the four films in order to determine if decency standards would be violated if the films were exhibited publicly.[12] After the film marathon, Hardin announced that the film series could open and that the theater would be free of the threat of prosecution, because none of the movies was obscene. "I am aware of more graphic sexual activity on daytime and prime-time national television than was depicted in any of these movies," Hardin told the *Herald-Sun*.[13]

During the weekend of the series, Christian Coalition picketers surrounded the outside of the theater. The theater was labeled the "Sodom and Gomorrah of the Triangle" by conservative community groups. "The theater obtained a reputation *immediately*," Carl explained. "The theater was automatically blackballed in the eyes of many community members who had supported it and sponsored the renovation. They refused to work with the theater anymore because of its association with the Pride '95. On the other side of it, there were others in the community who are just as influential—with just as much financial clout—who were very impressed with the fact that the theater did not back down. They subsequently came on board."

Following the decision to allow the films to be exhibited at the theater, a *Herald-Sun* editorial expressed extreme disappointment in the elected city officials' decision. "Rather than feel hate for the homosexuals in our community, we feel a deep sense of concern for them and for others in our community whose lifestyles are contrary to the will of God," an editorial proclaimed. "Isn't it ironic that both the City Council and the Board of County Commissioners use the Bible to swear people in but do not use it as a guide to set the moral standard of the community?"[14] On the other hand, twelve supporters of the film series attended a Carolina Theatre board meeting the week following the series in order to thank the theater board for standing firm in the face of controversy. "I thank you because I really think you as a board have been courageous in taking a stance that you want to see that diversity be kept alive," a supporter of the series was quoted as saying.[15] After paying distributors and subtracting overhead, the theater made a profit of $4,000 from the festival. The controversy brought free publicity to the theater as well as support from community members, which included donations totaling $650.

After all the hullabaloo of the Pride '95 film series, Martin was determined to continue his support of diverse programming. He and his staff decided to hold the First Official Gay and Lesbian Film Festival in August 1996. The festival (not just a series) was held independently; in other words, this time it was not in conjunction with a gay and lesbian conference or march. "The theater was under siege," Carl remembered. "The belief was that at least the year before, the series was happening with a gay event that was already happening downtown. This was seen as the theater's deliberate defiance." However, the Christian Coalition did not picket the festival in 1996 because city and county officials had decreased the number of government-appointed members who sat on the theater board from ten members to two. The Coalition felt that it would not be an effective demonstration. Nevertheless, they were still upset because they perceived the theater's programming as "anti-family" and continued to boycott the theater. An article about the 1996 festival in the *Herald-Sun* quoted Republican activist Virginia Bunton's disapproval of the theater. "All they show is triple-X-rated smut. If it doesn't have sex or violence in it, they won't show it. All they have to do is show a good story with a happy ending and people will come."[16]

But people did come to the festival. While the film series in 1995 attracted about 800 audience members, in 1996, 1,200 people came to the festival. By 1997, 1,800 people participated in the festival, and by the third annual Gay and Lesbian Film Festival in 1998, 2,200 attended. "By the third annual festival, there was a great deal of media coverage," Carl contended. "But the coverage was about the lack of controversy. There was report after report about the fact that there was no picketing and how things were running smoothly." The 2000 Gay and Lesbian Film Festival included 25 films, a disco-style party and reception at the theater, and a community resource room at the theater for forty organizations serving the lesbian and gay community. The audience grew from 800 in 1995 to 6,600 by the fifth year of the festival.

Carl began working at the theater a few months after the 1995 film series. He became directly involved with the planning of the 1996 festival, and by the fourth film festival, he was the curator, overseeing all aspects of it. "By the fifth year," Carl explained, "the tide had changed from this being an event that was damning to the community and lowering society's morals, to complete coverage of the festival, major reviews of the films, and the cover of the entertainment section in the state's newspapers. We are now ranked nationally as being one of the best festivals for gays and lesbians—which, I have to say, amazes film programmers in cities like San Francisco and Philadelphia, particularly since we are in Jesse Helms's backyard."

Carl contends that the story of Pride '95 has not been forgotten by the gay community. A few weeks before I talked to him, he explained, he was asked to be a speaker at a Human Rights Council gala with Barney Frank. "One of the things that was brought up immediately in this room of 500 people was the film festival," Carl said. "People were coming up to me in the lobby because the story of the festival is how they know the Carolina Theatre. They know the theater supports the Gay and Lesbian Film Festival. It's a story that has already entrenched itself. It's a true gay urban legend." While Carl does not believe that the story of the film festival will be forgotten anytime soon, he is concerned that it might get lost as more time passes. "Hopefully, somebody will come along and write it down," Carl said. And while I assured him that I would, the theater management should also be responsible for preserving the story of how the theater stood its ground against the protests of the Christian Coalition and championed the rights of gays and lesbians.

Like the theater's segregated past, and the rescue and restoration of the building, the story of the festival is significant to both the theater and to the city of Durham. Since the 1920s, the movie palace has been a reflection of the society around it, and the preserved picture palace is no different. Some efforts should be made to document and to tell and then to tell again the significant chapters of the theater's past, and that includes its most recent past. Literally and symbolically, the downtown movie palace continues to be at the center of the city, and efforts should be made to preserve the important stories of the cultural life that moves in and around it. The theater's discursive preservation, or, in other words, the remembrance and retelling of its rich and varied social history, can enable the Carolina Theatre to be a cultural site that reflects the many transitions of both the building and the community, despite the fact that the theater has lost much of its material past.

Segregation and Discursive Preservation

The Carolina Theatre is not the only theater that has a rich discursive past that deserves to be preserved. Nor is it the only theater in which management places discursive preservation as a low priority on their to-do list. However, the lack of discursive preservation at the Carolina Theatre is more apparent because the theater has what other theaters do not have—Pepper Fluke, a champion for the theater's past. Fluke and Martin do not see eye-to-eye on many topics related to the theater, but they both have the best intentions for it. While Martin's mission is more future oriented, and Fluke's is more focused on the past, if they could combine their foci, the theater would be poised to contribute even more to the Durham community. While Martin probably has days when he wishes Fluke would just forget about the past, he should be thankful that she does not. And Fluke should be thankful for Martin's eye to the future of the building. With a balance of the past and the future, the restored movie palace can be a financially healthy cultural center that provides community residents with excellent programming and an articulation of a past that is relevant to both the theater and the city.

Unfortunately, most theaters do not have a Pepper Fluke struggling to preserve the past. As I have mentioned, the preservationists at the Fox Theatre, who have taken great care to preserve the theater's material past, have made little or no effort to preserve the discursive past. Mary Catherine Martin, the restoration project manager, explained that they chose to focus on the theater's architectural past. "We talked early on about whether or not we were going to be an architectural archive or an institutional archive," she explained. "An institutional [archive] would be broader in that we would begin to maintain a history of the institution and everything that goes on here. We decided early on that we just didn't have the resources to do that. It's kind of a shame." Martin explained that theater tours led by members of Atlanta's preservation society are the only means by which the theater's cultural history is circulated. However, Martin contends that the tours are primarily theater mythology. "We're not sure where they get their information," she sighed. Martin does not object to the idea of a cultural history of the theater; however, she admits that it is a matter of the "squeakiest wheel." "It took me a long time to get people to recognize that we have a furniture collection; it's not just a bunch of furniture," Martin stated. "They had a difficult time just understanding that we have a specific collection that needs to be maintained."

I asked Martin if she considered the theater's history of segregation an integral element of the building's past that should be documented and dispersed—if not to everyone, then at least to the young people who tour the theater:

> In Atlanta, to be black is to be on top of things. Atlanta is a place where if you're black, you're in power. It seems like a dim memory; it's hard for me to even picture that possibility [segregation at the theater]. I'm not denying that it happened; it just seems way far away from the current reality. I talked about the theater to kids in Junior Achievement today. If I had told them about the segregation at the theater, I would have felt like I was burdening them with it. If they don't have the memory, why give it to them? Why load that onto their psyche if it is not there? If it would creep into a black kid's confidence, I don't want to do that. That's why I don't bring it up, because it doesn't need to be there.

With Martin Luther King Jr.'s tomb only a few miles away from the front door of the Fox Theatre, it is doubtful any school child or member of Junior Achievement in Atlanta does not already possess some knowledge of segregation in Atlanta and elsewhere throughout the South. Young African Americans in Atlanta have a right to know that their grandparents were forced to sit in the balcony at the Fox Theatre. Perhaps that knowledge would help them understand the connection between the theater and what they learn in the National Park Service Visitor Center located across the street from the memorial designating King's grave.

For all that Whitmire has done for the Alabama Theatre, he has seemingly little interest in preserving the more troubling aspects of the theater's social history. He is willing to tell a story or two about the theater's early years if it generates nostalgia in older Birmingham residents who then might be willing to contribute money to the theater. When I asked Whitmire about the integration of the Alabama Theatre, he shrugged his shoulders and said blacks have never come to the theater in great numbers, and then changed the subject by calling up the theater's website on his computer.

Fortunately, African Americans in Birmingham have worked diligently to preserve and protect the Fourth Avenue Historical District. Because of segregation and discrimination during the first half of the twentieth century, African American downtown businesses were forced into a small area along Third, Fourth, and Fifth Avenues. This area served as the cultural and social center for African Americans. This section of downtown is now a historical district, and the protected structures include three theaters: the Famous Theatre, built in 1928; the Carver Theatre, built in 1941; and the Masonic Temple, built in 1922, which regularly featured such talents as Louis Armstrong and Duke Ellington.

As you can imagine, Lee Hood at the Saenger Theatre has her hands full just keeping the building standing, but she recognizes the importance of generating a cultural history of the theater. She has hung a glass-case exhibit in the lobby, which features photographs and artifacts from the theater's earliest years. She has also set about collecting as much historical documentation about the theater as she can find, and she is trying to create a process whereby people who come to the theater can record their earlier memories of it. Her focus, at present, is the history of the theater prior to the 1960s, about which she has very little information. While it is important to preserve all of the past chapters of the theater, the focus on the early years is understandable because she is about to embark on a major renovation, and she wants to collect information that might be relevant to that project.

John Bell and Tara Schroeder have made a respectable effort to create a social history of the Tampa Theatre. Schroeder, in particular, has created the Tampa Theatre Stories Project, which is a collection of stories generated by patrons, both past and present. Schroeder and I have collected many stories from past employees and patrons during the last six years. Because some of the earliest employees have passed away since we interviewed them, we feel very fortunate that we were able to meet them and listen to their stories.[17] Presently, anyone is able to contribute a story for the project by accessing the theater's website. In addition,

Schroeder is currently constructing a self-guided theater tour pamphlet that will enable patrons to learn about both the theater's architectural and social history.[18]

Schroeder also gives bimonthly tours of the Tampa Theatre to groups and individuals. In fact, it was during one of her tours that I became interested in researching and writing about restored movie palaces. Schroeder's tour is full of nostalgia, and she tends to emphasize the fact that the theater was a site of social connections for Tampa residents prior to the 1960s. She also relates how the city bought the theater for one dollar, and then she takes the tour up to the balcony, where she tells them about Fink, the theater's ghost. While the information Schroeder shares on her tours is not wildly inaccurate, it might best be described as breezy. She aims to entertain, not educate, her audience. She also encourages older people to share their memories of the theater during the tour.[19] When I have questioned her about the accuracy of some of her statements, she just laughs and says, "Janna, it's showmanship!" Schroeder explained that most people join her tours because they are interested in the theater's architecture. "They come because the building is fascinating, but when they leave the tour, I want them to understand the humanity of the building. People in the past and people in the present," Schroeder explained, "that's what this building is about." She also wants people to enjoy themselves, gain some appreciation for the history of the theater, and hopefully donate money to the theater's preservation fund when the tour is finished.

While I do not think the tour presentation should weigh an audience down with too many facts and historic information, I do believe the tour could benefit both the theater and the people who visit it by giving them a more complete portrait of the contextual relationship between the theater and the city of Tampa. The Tampa Theatre did not even have a separate balcony; African Americans were simply not allowed in the theater at all. Within the last several months, Schroeder has constructed a study guide and tour for third- and fifth-grade students in Tampa. In both the tour and the guide, Schroeder makes connections between the theater's rise, fall, and restoration and the economic and cultural events in the United States. In addition, Schroeder discusses the theater's segregation policies with the fifth-grade students. As far as I know, this is the first time that segregation has been discussed in theater tours, and while this is a tremendous first step, I will continue to encourage Schroeder to include a discussion about the theater's segregation in her bimonthly tours.

It is important for young people to have an awareness of the social changes that have occurred in their city, but for adults it serves another purpose. As I have argued elsewhere, when the theater's historic narrative does not include the theater's past discriminatory practices, the theater becomes a site of segregated memories.[20] Though older African Americans do not have memories of going to the theater, they do have memories of not being able to go to the theater at all. To include their experience in theater's discursive past would enable African Americans to use the theater as a place for remembering past injustices. But the Tampa Theatre is not alone in this. At present, no monuments or architectural sites commemorate the struggles of the Civil Rights movement in Tampa.

Doing It Right at the Orpheum Theatre

The first time I traveled to the Orpheum Theatre to conduct research, I had an opportunity to take a tour of the building with a class of fourth graders from a public school in Memphis. I was interested in listening to the tour guides describe the building to the school children, and yet I did not anticipate that it would be any different from the dozens of other theater tours I have taken. It began as I expected; the tour guides, Mary and Robert Breymaier, explained to the students and their teachers that the theater was built in 1928. "Everything you see inside is original. Anything that is replaced has to be from the same time period," Robert Breymaier told the students. "The water fountains are really old; they are not refrigerated. Everything here is old, but it's in good shape."

As we made our way to the auditorium, the Breymaiers pointed out the six levels of the theater: the orchestra level, the mezzanine, the grand tier, the balcony, the lower gallery, and the upper gallery. Then Mary Breymaier said something that I was not expecting: "Before the Civil Rights Act, that upper gallery was the only place where African Americans could come into the theater. To get to that area, they had to buy their tickets on Beale Street, at a special ticket office. They went up a separate back stairway. Now, thank goodness, we don't have that problem. Everyone can sit wherever they want." We made our way around the various levels of the theater, and when we came to the upper gallery, she once again reiterated, "This is the section that I told you about earlier. This is where African Americans had to sit before the Civil Rights Act. They had to come the back way to get here. Memphis used to be different than it is now. If you were black you didn't have the same rights as a white person."

I was amazed. On my research trips to the various theaters, many of the theater employees I interviewed resisted even talking to me about theater segregation. Some seemed annoyed; others simply changed the subject. And then I found myself on a theater tour with fourth graders, and the guides were taking care to explain segregation to the children. I thought that perhaps the Breymaiers were an aberration, until I went on a tour with Barbara Jackson, another of the theater's guides. Jackson, for the most part, provided more specific information about the theater than the Breymeiers had. She went into detail, for example, about the chandeliers, telling the children that they are fifteen feet tall and weigh 2,000 pounds and that it takes two hours to lower them and five more hours to raise them. When she reached the point in her tour of discussing the upper gallery, she looked at an African American child who was sitting near her and said, "What's your name? Isaac? Isaac, if you had wanted to come to this theater prior to the Civil Right Act, you would have had to sit all the way up there." He looked at her for a moment, and then she explained, "That's because African Americans were forced to sit in the upper gallery. Life in Memphis was different then. Blacks were treated unfairly."

After the tour, I had an opportunity to interview Jackson, and I asked her why she included the negative aspects of the theater's history in her tour. "We don't dwell on it, but we do include it. I didn't include it the very first time I gave a tour, and one of the teachers said to me, 'We weren't allowed to come in the front door.' Well, the children, of course, wanted to hear about that, and I felt like I was keeping something back, so that's why I started to tell the story. It's part of the history, and this theater is full of history—both good and bad—so you have to be honest about it." I quickly realized that I had found a restored movie palace that was doing what I had been advocating since I began my research on the Tampa Theatre.

A tremendously successful performing-arts hall in downtown Memphis, the Orpheum Theatre has not only conserved its cultural history but also has developed a mission of educating the public about all of the various chapters of its past. Under the direction of Pat Halloran, the

23. During tours at the Orpheum Theatre, tour guides not only provide details about this fifteen-foot Czechoslovakian crystal chandelier in the auditorium, they also discuss the theater's racist practices during the first half of the twentieth century. Orpheum Theatre, Memphis, Tennessee.

theater has prospered financially and is the cornerstone of the revitalization of downtown Memphis. While Halloran has had a clear focus for the theater's future, he has not neglected its past. His leadership and commitment demonstrate that a restored movie palace can be both financially prosperous and at the same time forthcoming about its past.

The theater was purchased by the Memphis Development Foundation (MDF) from Malco Theaters Incorporated in November 1976 for a sum of $285,000. While the auditorium alone (no shops or office space) had been offered to the City of Memphis for $100,000, the city declined because it was in negotiations with the fire and police unions, and city funds were low. Halloran, who was a city councilman in 1976 and chaired the city's budget committee, explained that it simply was a matter of bad timing. It would not have been prudent for the city to have spent nearly $300,000 on an old building during a budget crunch and while the city's firemen were on strike.

Though the theater was in poor physical condition, it opened to the public less than a year after MDF purchased it.[21] Large productions such as *Fiddler on the Roof* and *The Wiz* became part of the theater's programming, and local performing-arts groups such as the opera and two of the city's three ballet companies also performed at the theater. "The place was horrendously in need of repair," Halloran remembered. "You couldn't get through a performance without the seats collapsing and somebody winding up on the floor. It was a dirty building. The carpet was thirty years old, and there was Coca-Cola syrup that had rotted into the padding. It was a mess." Halloran, who had recently lost the mayor's race in Memphis, was invited to become the general manager of the theater in 1980. Since the theater had reopened in 1977, it had been totally subsidized by Union Planners Bank, the second largest bank in the mid-South. Halloran explained that Union Planners literally wrote the salary checks and paid the theater's utility bills. The bank consistently gave the theater foundation loans and then would forgive the loans. When I expressed surprise that a bank would be so generous, Halloran told me that it was simply the nature of Bill Matthews, who was the chairman of the bank. "He was the guy who put the foundation together and told them that they were going to buy the Orpheum Theatre and then put up the money to do it," Halloran said. "He was instrumental in saving the theater."

Halloran remembers that when he became the theater's general manager, the theater foundation had only a few hundred dollars in its

24. The exterior of the renovated Orpheum Theatre, with its restored marquee. Orpheum Theatre, Memphis, Tennessee.

account, and he frequently found himself going to the bank to show Matthews how much more money he needed to borrow. A year after becoming the general manager, Halloran told Matthews it was time for the theater to become self sufficient. The theater was in the black a year later, and it has been for the last nineteen years. Halloran, whose title changed from general manager to president in 1983, explained that currently the theater brings in $10–12 million annually. "The theater by itself makes a little money or breaks even," Halloran noted. "It's the fundraising that makes it happen. It's the buffer and the subsidy that allows us to do big things." Besides a yearly silent auction that generates $160,000, a golf tournament that generates $40,000 a year, and corporate sponsorships, the theater charges a preservation fee of an additional $2 per ticket, which results in an additional $500,000 a year for the theater.

The theater has undergone two extensive renovations, the first one in 1983. Because of the nature of raising funds for such a project in a city that was not growing as fast as some in Memphis had hoped, the theater's title was transferred to the City of Memphis, and the theater foundation entered a fifty-year lease agreement with the city.[22] The $5.2 million renovation required the theater to close its doors for one year. Donna Darwin, a longtime theater employee, explained that the first renovation was essentially a rebuilding of the building. The theater was cleaned; the auditorium seats were removed so that bulldozers could level a new slant for the orchestra area; the painting finishes were decorated; improvements were made to the air-conditioning, heating, and ventilation systems; the orchestra pit was expanded; loading docks were added; and technical improvements, such as lighting and sound upgrades, were also installed. Original antique furnishings that had disappeared over the years were retrieved and then were rebuilt, refinished, and returned to their rightful places in the theater. The exterior of the theater was cleaned; fire escapes were brought up to code; the Orpheum marquee was repaired and repainted; and a new addition was built, creating a parlor, a concession area, and a box office.

The second major renovation occurred in 1996. The purpose of this renovation was to expand the stage area. "I'd call it a big renovation," the theater's technical director, Richard Reinach, explained. "We needed to add another 22 feet to the stage depth, for a total of 50 feet, which required us to knock down this 104-foot-by-80-foot wall and push it back. With the bigger stage came more rigging, lighting, and sound. We added a larger loading dock and a rehearsal hall backstage. And all of the dressing rooms are virtually brand new." Large Broadway productions, like *The Phantom of the Opera, Miss Saigon,* and *Beauty and the Beast,* which were particularly popular in the 1990s, required enormous amounts of equipment and technology to create their spectacular special effects. While such shows generated tremendous ticket sales for theaters, they also required more space and sophisticated technology than most restored movie palaces were capable of accommodating. The Orpheum, like the Fox Theatre, which also specializes in Broadway productions, was compelled to renovate the stage area as a result.

Reinach explained that the stage expansion not only changed the theater but also changed the quality of productions that Memphis residents were able to see. "Whereas we were a sleepy southern town that the big shows would pass by, now we have a facility that is big enough to accommodate them," Reinach said. "Judging by the ticket sales, Memphis really appreciated it. Every show of *The Phantom of the Opera* was sold out for five weeks." In the last two years, such immense productions are becoming less popular. However, no one at the Fox or the Orpheum is disappointed that expansions were done. "Before we did this renovation, we were having to turn away shows because we didn't have the facilities to accommodate them," Darwin said. "We did this expansion right at the peak of the megaproductions. And now they are scaling back. Yet, at the same time, *Lion King* is ready to start touring the country. And the new stage expansion is incredible as far as what it offers actors and dancers who come in."

The renovations of the building have enabled the theater to be a premier stop for nearly every major production that tours the country. That suits Halloran just fine because he is a Broadway fanatic, and yet, as I talked with him, it was clear that his commitment to the Orpheum Theatre extended beyond Broadway glitz. When I first walked into his office to interview him, I was struck by two things: the piles and piles of documents, posters, plaques, and books that were rather randomly arranged, and the bust of John Kennedy that sat near a window overlooking Beale Street. I soon learned that Halloran takes his politics seriously, and part of his mission for the theater is not only to address the city's past racial divisions, but to make an effort to mend some of the city's scars within the walls of the Orpheum Theatre.

As Halloran detailed the theater's transitional period during the late 1970s and early 1980s, he explained how the Orpheum Theatre, quite by accident, began to be the city's site for mending racial relations in Memphis:

> By this time Memphis had witnessed the assassination of Martin Luther King. They had a very low opinion of themselves; the city still does. The city has a tremendous personality conflict with itself. The Orpheum came roaring in here, and it became a very liberal place because of the liberal-thinking performing-arts groups who were using the theater. The Orpheum became a place where a large number of blacks were being hired. One of the early performances here was by a little-known dance company called Alvin Ailey, which, of course, became very famous. All of a sudden this theater that once had a colored balcony became a place where a whole lot of communication was going on between blacks and whites. The Orpheum became their place of good abode. It was the place for things to happen.

The Orpheum Theatre has geographically been situated near the center of shifting racial relations in Memphis, a city, like Birmingham, that has been a hotbed of racial controversy and discrimination. Both the Alabama Theatre and the Orpheum Theatre are beautiful and financially successful theaters with charismatic men leading their charge; however, only the Orpheum Theatre has become, both by coincidence and design, a site where the city's past and present racial relations are consciously considered to be part of the theater's responsibility. Because the racial relations of Memphis and the theater's segregated past are not forgotten, the theater's current agenda of ameliorating present-day racial relations makes for a logical next step. That the theater became a site of "good abode" in the late 1970s and early 1980s was partly coincidental; however, the fact that it has continued to take its and the city's racial relations seriously is a result of Halloran's leadership.

Halloran, whose family was in the theater business, has several strong personal characteristics and beliefs that converge to make him a strong advocate for comprehensive discursive preservation. First, he was a history major in college, and he believes that history needs to be told as honestly as possible. Second, Halloran calls himself a liberal Kennedy Democrat. "I am way out there in this city; that's the reason I didn't do well in the mayor's race," he admitted. He suggested that his political leanings shaped his desire to address the theater's past segregation and help to improve racial relations in Memphis.

Halloran, like almost all directors of restored theaters, is also utterly committed to his theater. However, he is the only theater president as of now who has written and published a theater's comprehensive history. "Because we have taken the history of the theater very seriously, I wound up working on that book for four or five years. I thought it was important for people to know the total history of the theater," Halloran said. "I was motivated to do it, so I did it." He explained that he made a commitment early on to telling people the history of the theater. "They need to know both the good and the bad," he contended. "I mean it was not only the racial conflicts and practices, there were also tremendous economic upheavals here. This theater went bankrupt, depending on how you define it, seven times. It has a star-crossed economic background that people should know about."

Halloran believes people are attracted to the theater because of its architecture and presence, and often their curiosity is piqued once they are inside the building. The logical next step, he says, is to provide a convenient way for them to learn about the theater's past. For the last twenty years, he and his staff have continued to find ways to keep the theater's history alive for Memphis. "It's kind of like *Roots,*" he told me. "The story of the family in Africa was passed on verbally for generations. We try to do that with our tours, and I routinely speak to civic groups and other groups like garden clubs. We bring in kids and classes from the University of Memphis and three or four other colleges in the area." Halloran explained that three or four times a year continuing-education classes come to the theater to learn about its history. The students gather for wine and cheese, and then Halloran takes them on a theater tour and gives each individual a copy of his book, *The Orpheum! Where Broadway Meets Beale.*

For years, Halloran said, he has gone on stage prior to each theater performance and welcomed the audience. "I try to tell them one significant historical fact about the theater, and I've got 2,000 people who are my captive audience. If I have eight shows a week, there are 16,000 people a week who learn that, oh, maybe that the theater was almost torn down in the seventies." Providing audience members with such historical facts, Halloran believes, enables them to have a better understanding of the theater and the city of Memphis. They come here and wonder why there aren't more buildings like this in the city," he explained, "and that leads them to discover that, in fact, there were three more theaters like this on this street."

Of course, Halloran's attempts to educate the public of Memphis about the history of the Orpheum Theatre do not originate solely in academic impulses. The theater needs public support, and if people are aware of the contours of its history, they are more likely to connect to it as a place that matters. Then, of course, they are also more likely to contribute financially to the theater. Compared to the transiency of Durham, Memphis has a fixed population. This fact helps the theater create a broad and dependable base of supporters. On the other hand, some of the stabilized population tends to maintain a traditional southern ideology that is difficult to shake. "There are old-line Memphis families that think and act just like their great-grandparents. That's not to condemn them; it just exists. The old South just doesn't change very rapidly," Halloran observed.

This fact, combined with Memphis's tainted reputation as the city where King was assassinated, makes Halloran's efforts to tell the complete story of the theater's past and to work toward harmonizing racial relations in the city even more of a challenge. Halloran's commitment to preserving all of the theater's history stems, he believes, from his educational background. "I'm a history major, and those kinds of things need to be told honestly, as opposed to being neglected or swept under the carpet," Halloran said. "When I give the tour, it's part of the tour, and I've instructed our tour guides to explain it in such a way that makes it clear that it's part of the history, but we are glad that it's not part of our policy today—even as a casual policy." He is aware that other theater directors choose not to talk about segregation because people may be offended by it. "It reminds me of parents that don't want to talk about sex to their kids. We've kept the lines of communication open, and I've never felt a resistance from blacks in the audience when I talk about this."

Beyond addressing the theater's segregated past, Halloran has made a commitment to theater programming that is both diverse and controversial. He aims not only to tell the past of the theater through stories and tours, but also to tell a more comprehensive past of racial relations by the shows that he books at the theater. Halloran aspires for diverse programming and makes an extraordinary effort to bring together racially diverse audiences. In 2000, Halloran made the decision to bring two highly unsuccessful Broadway shows, *Ragtime* and *Parade,* to the theater. *Ragtime* is about the economic coming-of-age of African Americans in the 1920s, and *Parade* is a true and dismal story about a Jewish pencil factory owner in Atlanta who is accused of and jailed for killing a young female factory worker. The factory owner is exonerated at the eleventh hour, but the group that would ultimately become the Ku Klux Klan broke into the jail and hanged the factory owner on a tree by the jail. "Here it is, the year 2000, and I think that these are both shows Memphis ought to see," Halloran remembered. "They are both financial disasters; they are losing money everyplace they go. *Parade* folded in New York. It was too intense and too down. *Ragtime* was on Broadway a long time, but when it went on tour, it didn't have the appeal that it did in New York."

Before *Ragtime* was scheduled to begin playing at the theater, Halloran wanted to be sure that the city's African Americans would see the show (Broadway shows do not have a strong black following). Halloran chose an appropriate commercial that he felt would appeal to the African American audience. "There were three commercials to choose from, and I chose the one that depicted a strong African American presence. I picked that commercial as opposed to the other two that were written for Des Moines and Birmingham, places where no one wants to ruffle feathers." He also devised a plan with the wife of one of his board members (she is a prominent African American medical doctor), which they hoped would encourage both blacks and whites to attend. They decided that if the opinion leaders of the African American community came to the opening night, it would not only pique interest in the show, but it would also lead the way for a more diverse audience. She coordinated the opening-night affair, and 100 of Memphis's most prominent African Americans attended the first night of the show.

The cynic could conclude that Halloran wanted African Americans to come to *Ragtime* simply because he did not want to lose money on the show. But if he had been chiefly concerned with economics, he could have simply not brought the production to the theater. What he did the following day suggests that he has a sincere desire to help heal the racial divides that exist both at the theater and in the city of Memphis. The morning after the show's opening night, he placed an advertisement in the *Commercial Appeal* that was headlined: "Something Special Happened at the Orpheum Recently." Following the headline, the advertisement reads: "*Ragtime*—the Tony Award–winning musical—was seen by the most racially diverse audience to ever see a Broadway touring production in the beautifully restored theatre." The copy then provides an outline of the production, and the final message states, "*Ragtime* tells the story of how much stronger a community can be when decisions are reached by doing what is right, fair, and best for everyone rather than the 'we don't trust or mix with "those people" attitude' that tends to destroy any sense of community. The Orpheum family was proud to have been supported by those that enjoyed this outstanding and important example of American musical theatre."

After he showed me the advertisement, Halloran observed, "That tells you how up-front we are about these things, and we all know that they still go on. When we see something that's good—we aren't looking to be sainted—we just sense that we should tell people. It goes back to why we tell people about the theater's segregated past. It's part of the history. I mean, you learn by your mistakes."

The Orpheum Theatre is an excellent model of discursive preservation, as the theater staff has made it a point to explicate many of the theater's pasts to the public. The theater's discursive past is integrated into its entertainment agenda, rather than being presented as a staid, academic presentation that exists somehow apart from the rest of the theater's programming. In other words, while preserving the past at the picture palace requires some effort, it demands little more than integrating critical historical elements into theater tours, continuing-education courses, written material (websites, brochures, press releases, magazines, newspaper articles, and books), and, perhaps most importantly, keeping the theater's past in mind when programming is being considered.

Conclusion

The material preservation of many restored movie palaces creates an atmosphere in which the public has an opportunity to interact with a particular past—the theater's earliest years. Material preservation enables the public to learn about and get a feeling for the architecture, craftsmanship, and some of the social conditions of the early-twentieth-century downtown theater; movie palaces, however, have experienced many more lives than what material preservation is capable of showing. It is only through discursive preservation that most of the chapters of the movie palace's past can be uncovered. Discursive preservation not only reveals the various cultural and economic circumstances that the movie palace has experienced through the years, it also depicts the history of the downtown in which it is situated.

Unfortunately, the social era that most theaters narrate to the public is the same era that is depicted by their material preservation. The theater's earliest years are probably the most logical and uncomplicated choice for narration because they parallel the building's restoration. It is also a period that appears to be the most uncomplicated, a period conducive to creating feelings of nostalgia. Such feelings of nostalgia are inculcated most readily in a preserved building when the focus is on an era that is the farthest away from the present.

In an effort to create a pleasant, entertaining, and nostalgic portrait of the old movie house, many theater managers have ignored what is troubling, complicated, and more recent in their theater's cultural history. Such a focus has led to a form of picture palace amnesia, which Kammen calls the "heritage syndrome." "The nation has been hankering after various imagined golden ages—for more innocent and carefree days—ever since the early 1970s," Kammen asserts. "There is nothing really wrong with nostalgia per se, but more often than not the phenomenon does mean a pattern of selective memory. Recall the good, but forget the unpleasant."[23] Heritage that is not self-deceptive, Kammen contends, "may lead people to the past for purposes of informed citizenship, or the meaningful deepening of identity, or enhanced appreciation of the dynamic process of change over time."[24] While material preservation may be necessary for saving the material and concrete past, it does not adequately reveal how buildings, cities, and culture necessarily change over time. In fact, it masks it by its very nature because it freezes one period of time; by complementing material preservation with discursive preservation, however, people are better able to understand how buildings, the urban environment, and the people who move through the city are always in the process of change.

When the complex, the disturbing, and more recent histories are forgotten or ignored at the movie palace, an opportunity to foster community connectedness is lost, which is one of the primary reasons cited for saving old buildings in the first place. An expert on local history, Carol Kammen, contends that there is both personal and social value in uncovering and narrating informed local histories. She explains that it helps community members to have a sense of connection with place and that it enables individuals to "set roots in a community." She also claims that it reaffirms the value of the environment, and, most importantly, that it is educational, because it teaches about the particularities of place and helps us to "seek the truth wherever that search may lead."[25]

While the primary mission of the restored movie palaces is naturally to entertain the public, the many pasts that are contained within them should not be forgotten, because they can help to foster a sense of community and place, and they can educate the public about social cohesiveness, cultural conflict, and the complexities of urban life.

The urbanist Dolores Hayden argues that preserved public spaces are important because both personal and collective identities are intimately connected to place. The urban landscape is a storehouse for social memories, and streets, buildings, and other city spaces frame our lives. However, places that have been significant to the working class, women, and many ethnic groups have not been adequately preserved in most cities. "Restoring significant shared meanings for many neglected urban places first involves claiming the entire urban cultural landscape as an important part of American history, not just its architectural monuments," Hayden writes. "This means emphasizing the building types—such as tenement, factory, union hall, or church—that have housed working people's everyday lives.[26] While she advocates the recovery of vernacular buildings as the path toward an inclusive urban social memory, she also advises that all of the pasts of a place be remembered, including bitter experiences and fights that communities have lost, so that their significance as historical events is not diminished.[27]

Members of the African American community most likely do not need an official narration in order to remember the past social injustices that confronted them at the picture palace. As I could see at the Carolina Theatre, the past has not been forgotten by those who experienced prejudice and segregation. Yet when stories of discrimination are included in the chronicle of a movie palace, then there is an acknowledgment, rather than a dismissal, of some of the ways in which African Americans have been denied access to the movie palace and, in a larger context, public life. For those who are too young or were not directly affected by such prejudices, a recognition of the segregated past of the movie palace provides a powerful portrayal of the ways in which racism can infiltrate even the most seemingly mundane activities of daily life.

Cities can also benefit from inclusive narratives of movie palaces' pasts, because the theaters can become a public marker of the racial injustices of the past and the struggles to overcome segregation. Other important markers of racial conflict in downtown areas, such as Woolworth's stores, are presently vacant buildings, or they have been razed. Newly built public markers of historical injustice, such as the

Birmingham Civil Rights Institute, are important memorials for remembering the social atrocities of the past, yet while the material evidence within the museum educates and memorializes, the building itself cannot. The old movie palace can easily encourage participation with the past because it literally frames it.

By memorializing other social and cultural transitions, the movie palace can also mirror nearly the entire history of the city in the twentieth century: economic prosperity, urban decline and ruin, and the more recent revitalization. As a concrete representation of these economic and cultural shifts, the movie palace has many stories to tell, and its history is contained within a building that is engaging to the public because of its fascinating architecture and its function as a place of entertainment and fantasy. Publicly acknowledging and remembering more recent social conflicts and transformations, such as the Carolina Theatre's Gay and Lesbian Film Festival, also help to mark the significant shifts in the theater's role within the community. Such cultural transformations can be meaningful to both the theater and the city, because they are reminders that, while the preserved movie palace is a historic building, it is not frozen in time. The downtown movie palace that attempts to balance the past and the future for the sake of the present will continue to have a meaningful role in the cultural and economic transformations of the twenty-first-century city.

CHAPTER 6

The Transformation of the Downtown Movie Palace

In order to gain a better understanding of how the restored theater's significance has been both preserved and transformed, it is important to remember the social and cultural function of the movie palace in the first few decades after it was designed and constructed. As you will recall, movie palaces were built in prime downtown locations because they were meant to be city showplaces. They were built to be an announcements to their cities' residents, for they were both monuments to the financial prosperity that cities were already experiencing and markers of the progress that was still to come. The theater's period-revival exterior, the protruding and highly embellished box office, and the colossal neon sign not only distinguished the theater from the buildings around it, but also gave it an appearance of a progressive place, ahead of its time. Yet, at the same time, the theater suggested a sense of tradition, for it looked like a monument to be revered.

The theater interior was really the main attraction. For as movie palace architects and owners knew, most of the people who would pay for tickets had little experience with architectural and aesthetic grandeur, but they desired to be a part of such an atmosphere nonetheless. The 1920s were, after all, the beginning of a mass-consumer culture in the United States, and the members of the emerging middle class were just beginning to understand that as potential consumers they could expect to be both entertained and fawned upon in a luxurious environment. While each picture palace was designed slightly differently, there were plenty of similarities. The interiors were opulent, if not downright garish. The Alabama Theatre, the Carolina Theatre, the Orpheum Theatre, and the Saenger Theatre could be characterized as somewhat refined in their opulence; however, architects of the Fox Theatre and the Tampa Theatre exhibited no restraint. They were designed to be outrageous, and their glitzy appeal has not lessened through the years.

The theater interior designs relied upon one common theme: the exotic past. In a country with no true castles or palaces, and certainly no ancient ones, architects simply created new palaces that were designed to look old. European and Middle-Eastern statues, paintings, and tapestries adorned the lobbies and auditoriums, and gilded mirrors and ornamented light fixtures complemented the intricately tiled and carpeted floors. Wrought-iron balustrades and carved wooden banisters led patrons to duskily lit auditoriums (complete with balconies and mezzanines) that were so large that thousands of patrons could be seated at one time. Elaborate, bedazzling proscenium arches and palatial ceilings helped to create a feeling of opulence and otherworldliness. And although the movie palace was designed to resemble an ancient and exotic world far different from the city just outside the theater's carved doors, other technologies signaled the promise of the twentieth century. The movie palace was, in many cities, the first public building to have air-conditioning, and, of course, the technology of film was itself innovative and progressive.

The atmosphere that combined the exotic, the ancient, and the modern may have dazzled patrons, but it also instructed them in appropriate public behavior. While movie palace owners claimed that their theaters were entirely democratic, the ancient and exotic art and artifacts, along with the elaborate theater design, suggested otherwise. In fact, both the original art and the reproductions that filled the theater signaled to patrons that they should learn and adopt the standards and civility associated with the high culture of the stage theater. The cosmopolitan, international imagery not only intimated that the people who inhabited the theater were positioning themselves as members of an upper social echelon, it was also a symbolic marker for the entire city. Having a movie palace was proof that a city had finally arrived.

While the interiors were intended to create an atmosphere of European high culture for the newly-middle-class patrons, the entertainment in the theaters was unequivocally Hollywood. Movie palaces exhibited mainstream movies that would draw the largest crowds, because they had literally thousands of seats that needed to be filled. The films shown at the movie palaces were rarely challenging or troubling, and usually they were neither offensive nor of great artistic merit. They usually relied on easy sentiment and formulaic plots that would appeal to mass audiences, similar to the blockbuster films of today. In a way, they were simply part of the overall experience. In fact, the present-day practice of watching a movie from beginning to end was not as important to early picture palace patrons. Using a sophisticated signaling system, ushers were able to seat hundreds of people throughout a movie's running time, as other patrons, who had also come in during the middle of the movie, vacated their seats.

When I interviewed patrons who had attended the Tampa Theatre in the early part of the twentieth century, they made it quite clear that it was both the theater and the films that made the movie palace experience special. When I asked Ann Duncan, Lee Duncan's wife, what movies she enjoyed at the Tampa Theatre when she was a young woman, she paused for a few seconds and then said, "I'm trying to think. I am trying to think." Her husband finally interjected, "It wasn't the movies. It was a social event. The going out on a Sunday. And it was the thing for people—you know, working people—to be able to go there on Sunday. Everyone went there because that was the place to go." Ann Duncan agreed with her husband and added, "I know growing up I watched anything that they showed on Sundays, and when I was going out with Lee, it was anything they showed on Fridays. It really didn't make that much difference what the movie was; they usually picked the best." The theater, it seems, was regarded as an arbiter of taste in Tampa. Ann Duncan's remark indicates that the theater management, similar to the present-day movie critic, had the authority to decide what was good.

Other people I interviewed also explained that the point of going to the theater was that it always promised to be a social event—a big afternoon or night on the town. "When you came to the theater, you were dressed—no shorts or shirtsleeves. You wore Sunday clothes," Charles Bardin, an usher at the Tampa Theatre in the 1930s, explained. "Men wouldn't think of coming to the theater without a coat." In the early years of the movie palace, it was the theater that was the center of attraction, not the movies. The theater was essentially a public space where patrons could socialize with one another in an opulent atmosphere set apart from their everyday lives. The richly adorned theaters made patrons feel, for a few hours at least, as glamorous as the Hollywood stars on the screen. Little about the movie palace reminded patrons of their daily lives, for it seemed everything pointed to either a different geography or a different time period. The movie palace's decor made it seem as if the theater were situated in an altogether different country and in a time far distant from the present. The films on the screen pointed to the excitement and glamour of Hollywood, and even the patrons themselves, dressed in their Sunday best, were somehow different, a more glamorous and sophisticated version of who they usually were outside the doors of the movie palace.

The original picture palace preservationists desired to save the giant theaters from destruction primarily because they wanted to spur downtown revitalization and protect their cities' architectural and cinematic heritage. However, they also believed that the theaters could recover, in time, their meaning to community residents. Picture palace preservationists, in other words, hoped that the recovery of the downtown movie palace would not only replenish the vitality of the downtown area but would also restore the social significance of what it meant for city residents to "go downtown."

This chapter characterizes and analyzes the restored movie palace's contemporary role within its community for the purpose of evaluating how its social meaning has been both preserved and transformed. In addition, this analysis will help determine whether the original preservationists' goal of recreating the movie palaces' social significance has been achieved. In order to do this, I examine two factors: the kind of entertainment that a restored theater presently offers its patrons and its role as preserved downtown movie palace in a city that continues its suburban spread. Just as the theaters have not been saved or preserved in precisely the same manner, they do not provide exactly the same kind of entertainment or have precisely the same function within the cities where they stand. While the theaters may differ in terms of the kind of entertainment they provide city residents, all of the theaters have achieved some success in creating downtown vitality and density. Because they are all situated in cities where the suburban lifestyle is predominant, however, they all continue to struggle against negative perceptions about what it means to go downtown.

Today, neither the Tampa Theatre nor the Carolina Theatre is exclusively a movie theater. Both facilities are routinely rented by concert promoters. The Tampa Theatre, as I have explained, has a very small stage and thus is limited in terms of the kinds of productions that will fit on its stage. Typically, singer/songwriters perform at the theater, because they do not need too much room, and they appeal to the type of audience who often comes to the theater to see films. The Carolina Theatre's Fletcher Hall has a complete season of live performances, which include music, dance, theater, and one-person performances. The 2000–2001 season, for example, included Saffire—the Uppity Blues Women; Mark Russell; *Hamlet;* the New Shanghai Circus; and *Tango Pasion*. Nevertheless, cinema exhibition has been integral to both theaters since they were rescued, and it has also been critical to the success of both theaters. In addition, the theaters' identities are largely based on the kinds of films that they show and the types of people who come to see them.

As you will recall, Monte Moses and the other members of the Carolina Cinema Corporation decided early on that the Carolina Theatre would operate as an art film cinema. Moses and Maggie Dent (who had already successfully run an art house cinema in Durham) recognized that there was a market for such films in the Triangle area. The Carolina Theatre began showing art films in 1978 and has been exhibiting them ever since. The Tampa Theatre, which reopened in 1977, had only a 16-mm film projector, which limited the kinds of films that the theater could exhibit. The theater's curator, Diane Howe Eberly, quickly realized that, although she was limited by the theater's equipment, she could create a marketing niche for the theater by exhibiting classic and foreign films. The theater relied upon Hitchcock and movies featuring such stars as Clark Gable, Humphrey Bogart, and Bette Davis; however, when cable television expansion hit the United States in 1983, attendance numbers dropped sharply. "It affected everybody, not just us—New York City even. Theater attendance just plummeted because people enjoyed the novelty of staying home and watching old films we were marketing."

The theater continued to suffer for the next five years, until a 35-mm projector was donated to the theater in 1988. Eberly explained that the donation of the projector and the concurrent growth of interest in independent films was a matter of good timing and good luck. "We lucked into the fact that the independent film market was increasing," Eberly explained. "And we lucked into having the projector donated to us at that point in time." While the Tampa Theatre has been the premier art house cinema in the city since 1988, it has had, like the Carolina Theatre, a reputation as an alternative cinema since the late 1970s.

The cultural space of both theaters has been transformed as a result of their art house film programming. During the early twentieth century, the theaters primarily exhibited blockbuster movies in order to fill their auditoriums to capacity. The cultural space of both theaters first changed with the exhibition of black exploitation films and mildly pornographic films in the early 1970s. But once the theaters were reinstated as part of the community in the late 1970s, they began to rely upon alternatives to mainstream cinema in order to create and sustain an established audience. In turn, the alternative programming helped to transform the theaters' original identities.

It is difficult to define what art film programming is exactly, particularly because the definition continues to shift as Hollywood becomes more involved with art cinema production. Art films tend to be defined by what they are not; they are not blockbusters (usually), and they are not typical Hollywood fare. "Despite the contradictions in attempts to fix the boundaries of the art film," writes Barbara Wilinsky, "one characteristic generally agreed upon is that art films *are not* mainstream Hollywood films. In fact, it often seems that art films are not defined by their thematic and formalistic similarities, but rather by their differences from Hollywood films" (my emphasis).[1] Lance Goldenberg, a film critic for Tampa's independent weekly, explained to me that the average independent American film is more conservative and less challenging than the typical art house film of thirty years ago. "Independent film has become—certainly over the last five or six years—less and less different than conventional studio products," he explained. "As Hollywood films have become stupider and stupider, basically, it becomes easier to pass off anything as an independent film, anything that doesn't entail nonstop explosions."

What separates the art film from the blockbuster is not always easy to know. While there are some general differences, the categories are more fluid than rigid, and one is not necessarily of better quality than the other. In fact, some of the mainstream films that movie palaces regularly showed in the early part of the twentieth century are now considered high culture. The cultural historian Lawrence Levine explains that popular art may be transformed into high art over a period of time, once popular culture has lost interest in it or no longer understands it. "Thus a film like D. W. Griffith's *Birth of a Nation,* which was released in 1915," Levine explains, "is transformed into high culture when time renders its 'language'—its acting styles, technology, kinetics—archaic and thus less accessible to the masses."[2]

While the definition of an art film is a bit fuzzy, most people, scholars and patrons alike, can usually distinguish one from the other. The art film tends to be perceived as more intellectually challenging for the viewer than the typical Hollywood film. In other words, the art film may favor form over function, may privilege experimental technique over theme, and may attempt to stimulate contemplation rather than identification. Generally, then, the art film portrays an aesthetic disposition that requires, or at least suggests, that viewers should distance themselves from what they see on the screen.

The general notion of how viewers experience the art film is similar to Immanuel Kant's definition of "aesthetic judgment," for the art film is often understood to stimulate contemplation of cinematic form or concepts rather than identification with the people or things represented in popular movies. A conscientious sense of "disinterest" was the sole guarantor of aesthetic contemplation, he noted. "Everyone must allow that a judgement on the beautiful which is tinged with the slightest interest, is very partial and not a pure judgement of taste," Kant wrote. "One must not be in the least prepossessed in favour of the real existence of the thing, but must preserve complete indifference in this respect, in order to play the part of judge in matters of taste."[3] Kant's definition of aesthetic judgment seems rather dour, but it does suggest that artistic contemplation requires a certain emotional distance and an active contemplation of the art object at hand.

The sociologist Herbert Gans seems to echo the Kantian aesthetic when he suggests that high culture's attention to a cultural product focuses on its construction. "[T]hey almost always place high value on the careful communication of mood and feeling," Gans writes, "on introspection rather than action, and on subtlety, so that much of the culture's content can be understood on several levels."[4] Popular culture, on the other hand, is created for a heterogeneous audience and attempts to appeal to as many people as possible. "Popular culture is more standardized, making more use of formulas and stereotypical characters and plots," Gans explains, "although even high culture is not free from standardization."[5]

General Hollywood fare does not require much, if any, intellectual contemplation, because such movies attempt to induce emotional, rather than intellectual, responses from viewers. Viewers do not expect, nor do they probably desire, to see formal experimentation when they watch a mainstream film. For the most part, the Hollywood film does not catch viewers off guard. Story lines, characters, and even settings are fairly straightforward and dependable. Characters behave in comfortable and understandable ways and are either rewarded or punished accordingly. Because such movies do not require too much intellectual engagement, cultural critics tend to perceive them as passive experiences. Goldenberg, for example, contends that some blockbusters are good, yet at the same time they tend to induce a passivity in the viewer. "They make you feel for the moment as if you are actively participating. 'Oh, look at that! Oh! I jumped!' And yet they are completely passive. They are impossible to remember, and really they are just wallpaper entertainment."

There is, of course, nothing wrong with Hollywood movies, and there is nothing wrong with viewers wanting to spend a few hours in the dark watching a film that requires little from them. People who tend to prefer mainstream cinema also view alternative movies, just as people who tend to favor art films also watch Hollywood movies. Sometimes it is difficult to know in which category a film belongs. *Crouching Tiger, Hidden Dragon* (Ang Lee, 2000), for example, played in both art house and mainstream cinemas. I happened to see it at the Carolina Theatre, but other than the fact that it had subtitles (which makes for a mainstream-movie marketing nightmare), it seemed like an enjoyable action adventure movie with a strong female lead. If, however, it had been promoted as a Hollywood action movie and had not been playing in art houses, I doubt that I would have ever made the effort to see it. In other words, the art house, for me, has become an arbiter of taste. Theaters like the Carolina Theatre and the Tampa Theatre (at times) decide for me what films are worth seeing.

Alternative films and art house cinemas tend to appeal to an audience that is searching for a more contemplative experience than mainstream films and standardized movie theaters can offer them, and the Carolina Theatre and the Tampa Theatre are not exceptions to this. As a result, the patrons and these theaters' social spaces are often distinguishable from mainstream spectators and the standard movie theater. While it is not always clear why the film programming at the Tampa

Theatre and the Carolina Theatre is considered alternative, people generally seem to believe that they can recognize the difference between an art and a mainstream product and between an alternative-film viewer and a fan of the blockbuster.

When I asked patrons and employees at both the Carolina Theatre and the Tampa Theatre to describe the type of person who generally came to see movies there, everyone seemed to have a clear classification, for they quickly and easily answered my question. "I just look at the people who come here, and they certainly look different from the people who go to the multiplex," a regular patron of the Tampa Theatre stated. "They just look different. They dress different. They act different. They probably have a higher education level than average people on the street." "They're conscious," explained another Tampa Theatre patron. "They have interests outside of their home. They travel a lot too. They are more aware. They're not just into their own little worlds." Another patron stated that Tampa Theatre patrons are more open-minded. "They are people who might actually know something outside of Florida. You know, they might actually be able to find another state or country on the map. Not that there is anything wrong with rednecks," she said, laughing.

Jim Carl, the film festival curator at the Carolina Theatre, described the typical film patron as forty to forty-five years old, with an income of $40,000–50,000 a year, and with a tendency not to be African American. He explained that the popularity of the North Carolina Jewish Film Festival has created a regular patronage of Jewish film viewers, and because of the regular exhibition of foreign films, people who used to live in such countries as England, India, and Iran also attend regularly. Denise Clay, the Carolina Theatre's audience services manager, described the typical patron as "white, hippy, arts-y, and Earth shoe–wearing, who are usually either middle or upper class and are usually either a college student or middle-aged." The typical film viewer at the Carolina Theatre, according to Steve Martin, is a film buff between twenty-five and sixty years old, well educated, with an income of $50,000 or more a year. He explained that many of the regular patrons are from the Research Triangle's college and university communities.

I have noticed that the patrons at the Carolina Theatre and the Tampa Theatre do look similar to one another. In a way, this is not a surprise, because the theaters share the same film programmer, so the same films are exhibited at both theaters. Most of the patrons seem to be in their forties or fifties. They have a tendency to be casually dressed in somewhat typical university professor attire—meaning that the men tend to be a bit rumpled, and the women are dressed in comfortable but interesting, loose-fitting dresses and pants. People do not dress, in other words, as if they are anticipating a cinematic "big night out."

There is a noticeable absence of children and teenagers at both theaters. I remember finding it unusual when I saw a middle-aged woman bringing her young son into the auditorium to see *Crouching Tiger, Hidden Dragon*. They sat near me, and she confided that she was not sure how long they would stay, because he did not yet know how to read, and so she imagined that the subtitles would pose a problem (they stayed for the whole movie). More than a few of the college-aged patrons seem to prefer black clothing, and they often dye their hair to match their wardrobes. Unlike theaters where mainstream films are exhibited, many people come to the theater alone, which suggests to me that neither theater is necessarily construed as a space where people go to be social. And it is a common sight to see only a smattering of people scattered throughout the theaters' auditoriums watching a film. Only special events such as film festivals or opening nights of popular films such as *Shakespeare in Love* or *Crouching Tiger, Hidden Dragon* fill the auditoriums and create the kind of social buzz that once characterized the movie palaces.

At times, the Carolina Theatre and the Tampa Theatre exhibit films that draw people who are not regular patrons. These moviegoers help to define the usual social space of the theater because they differ from typical patrons. A Tampa Theatre patron remembered coming to see the movie *It Came from Outer Space*. "It drew a lot of people that weren't typical Tampa Theatre people," she said. "They were just rude. They threw their feet over the seats, and I was thinking, 'they don't belong here.' They didn't appreciate the theater. Usually I feel like I'm among people who appreciate the same kind of films. But they were just rowdy." Tara Schroeder admitted that some of the employees at the Tampa Theatre were slightly irked by the preponderance of teenaged girls who recently flocked to see *The Anniversary Party*. They were apparently drawn to the movie because Gwyneth Paltrow has a role in it.

Denise Clay explained that sometimes she thinks that the Carolina Theatre should exhibit more popular films like *Crouching Tiger, Hidden Dragon* because of the tremendous revenue potential. But she acknowledged that such films bring "a different type of person" to the theater, ones who normally go to "the run-of-the-mill film houses." She explained that the theater's exhibition of *Crouching Tiger, Hidden Dragon,* for example, required more maintenance and more cinema management. When I asked her why, she told me that they were not accustomed to the rules of the facility. "Most of the people who usually come to our films take their trash out with them," Clay explained. "We've also had some facility damage, like broken chairs and things like that." Clay admitted that part of the trash and the damage could be attributed to the sheer number of people who came to the theater; nevertheless, she had a perception that the popular film drew a different type of audience to the theater. It seems that most of the people perceive that there are two types of film viewers—those who regularly attend the suburban movie theater and those who seek out the alternative to that. Just as Wilinsky asserts that art films are generally defined as nonmainstream films, patrons and employees of art house cinemas classify patrons of alternative films as those who are not patrons of mainstream films.

In order for patrons and employees to envision themselves as part of an alternative, intellectual environment, it is necessary for there to be many suburban mainstream cinemas in the Triangle area and in Tampa, and it is essential that mainstream films remain more popular than alternative films. In other words, while there is a difference between alternative and mainstream films, and there may be a difference between alternative and mainstream film viewers, the real divergence is that there is a perception that one is not the other. "In matters of taste, more than anywhere else, all determination is negation," the French sociologist Pierre Bourdieu explains, "and tastes are perhaps first and foremost distastes, disgust provoked by horror or visceral intolerance of the taste of others."[6] In other words, the Carolina Theatre and the Tampa Theatre are alternative cinemas precisely because they do not show mainstream movies and blockbusters. They are considered alternative sites to the perceived facile culture of the cineplex.

Whereas both theaters once exhibited Hollywood films for the sake of filling seats and creating a jubilant environment, by the late 1970s, both had become largely a refuge for moviegoers seeking an intellectual challenge, obscure cinematic offerings, and perhaps a sophisticated image that comes from a place on the margins of the mainstream. In the first half of the twentieth century, the theaters' distinction came from the glamour that they promised patrons. The beauty of the buildings, the attentive care of the ushers, the attractive and electrifying Hollywood stars on the screen, and the auditorium filled to capacity with people carefully dressed in their Sunday apparel provided patrons with a kind of excitement and social energy that assured them that they were at the center of the world. In both theaters, more than 1,000 people at a time were enjoying the glamorous social connection that the atmosphere provided.

Such an environment, however, could afford only a certain amount of distinction. The movie palace was touted as a democratic space where everyone could feel like royalty, but the inherent meaning of royalty is that it is for only a few. Movie palace owners could not afford to be extremely exclusive because they had too many seats to fill, so the painful practice of segregation helped to create an environment of distinction. The fact that African Americans were not allowed to enter, or were confined to the uppermost area of a particular theater, provided a signifier of exclusivity for white middle-class patrons. In order for the theaters to maintain a democratic public space that nevertheless felt aristocratic, African Americans had to pay the price.

Today the theaters' distinction comes from the fact that films and the people who attend them have a particular cultural capital. The theaters' exclusivity depends upon their films' lack of familiarity and popularity, and the fact that their regular patrons are well informed and sophisticated enough to make the choice to see films that have not been heavily advertised in popular periodicals and television. In other words, the theaters' distinction does not rely in part on purposeful exclusion. Anyone who chooses to can come to the theaters, though many people do not make that choice. They may dislike reading subtitles, or they may be unfamiliar with the film titles because they have not been well advertised. They may prefer watching films that have familiar stars for lead characters. Or they may simply want to escape for a few hours, and they imagine that the alternative film is too much work.

Going to the Tampa Theatre or to the Carolina Theatre to see a movie is an extraordinary experience to the extent that the theaters themselves are extraordinary in their design. Regular patrons attend these theaters primarily for the purpose of being entertained through intellectual engagement. The occasion is rarely marked by dressing up or eating a fine meal after the movie is over. For "certified or apprentice intellectuals," as Bourdieu describes them, art cinema and museum exhibitions are activities that "are in a sense governed by the pursuit of maximum 'cultural profit' for minimum economic cost, which implies renunciation of all ostentatious expense and all gratifications other than those given by symbolic appropriation of the work."[7] The film is the thing, in other words, and even the beauty of the theater is relegated to the background. This, of course, is quite in contrast to the early years, when the film was not the sole, or even primary, motivation for attending the theater. But today's patrons have had much more exposure to the world than earlier patrons did. While they appreciate the preservation philosophy and may even regularly contribute financially to their theater's preservation fund, most of them have traveled extensively and have seen many old theaters, museums, and churches. The preserved picture palace is simply a lovely but normal part of their intellectual and cultural landscape.

The Big Night Out: The Alabama Theatre, the Fox Theatre, and the Orpheum Theatre

While the Alabama Theatre, the Fox Theatre, and the Orpheum Theatre also exhibit films, they do not show them regularly, and the movies they do show are either classic films or popular ones that bring a wide variety of people to the theaters. These theaters are primarily known for their large live productions. The Broadway musicals and famous musicians who appear on their stages help to maintain the theaters' reputations as premier venues. Soon after the theaters were rescued and their earliest restorations began, it became clear that there would not be enough income generated by movie-ticket sales. The suburban movie theaters had already left the downtown theaters in financial ruin, and there was simply no way that thousands of people would come to the downtown theaters night after night to see a movie that they could see at a theater closer to their homes.

Besides, moviegoing was no longer a particularly special event, and since many people hoped that the theaters could once again become important and significant markers of the city, the entertainment that they provided needed to be special. Nevertheless, the theater directors of the late twentieth century had the same constraints as those in the first part of the century: they needed to provide entertainment that would fill all the seats. This meant that they needed to book shows that were popular, entertaining, and, for the most part, intellectually unthreatening. But the shows also needed to be special enough that people would make the effort to come see them. For the Fox Theatre and the Orpheum Theatre, Broadway musicals seemed to be part of the answer.

In 1986 the Orpheum Theatre, for example, showed its first profit in four years after Halloran devised a new plan for the theater, which included creating a new criterion for booking shows. "The selection process needed to be balanced with what Memphians had supported in the past by their attendance," Halloran explained, "and what was working in moderate sized cities of less than one million."[8] After he created the new booking strategy in 1986, more than 170,000 people attended the theater that same year. They came to see eight Broadway productions, which included *South Pacific,* starring Robert Goulet, and *Stop the World, I Want to Get Off,* starring Anthony Newley.

It seemed that the combination of well-known and popular entertainers and large-scale musical productions could fill theater seats, and the increasing popularity of large-scale touring productions was occurring at nearly the same time as the theaters were reopening their doors. In the 1970s touring Broadway shows became increasingly frequent across the United States. Shows such as *Annie, A Chorus Line,* and the revivals of *South Pacific* and *Oklahoma* brought the glitz and glamour of Broadway to cities across the country. Audience members who did not go to New York or London were able to see the productions closer to home. In the 1980s Andrew Lloyd Webber and Tim Rice dramatically increased the popularity of Broadway musicals with their production of *Cats.* As the years passed, the musical became something of a joke because it was a show that refused to die, but in the 1980s fans of *Cats* were fervent, and they demanded more of the same. Following the popularity of *Cats,* audiences flocked into theaters in order to see the dramatic productions of Alain Boublil and Claude-Michel Schoenberg's *Les Misérables* and Webber and Rice's revivals of *Jesus Christ, Superstar* and *Joseph and the Amazing Technicolor Dreamcoat.*

The economic upswing of the 1990s brought even larger, more technically challenging productions to stages across the country. Webber's *Phantom of the Opera,* Boublil's *Miss Saigon,* and Disney's *Beauty and the Beast* were to Broadway musicals what Pink Floyd had been to stadium rock concerts in the 1980s. The productions were enormous and dazzling, and Broadway musical fans would return to see the fanfare over and over again. The Broadway shows were the ticket to success for the renovated movie palaces. While renovations and expansions were necessary to accommodate some of the larger shows (particularly *Phantom of the Opera*), the investment seemed worthwhile because the shows brought people to the theater and then continued to bring them back for more.

Unlike the cinematic fare of the Carolina Theatre and the Tampa Theatre, the spectacular Broadway productions at the other theaters do not provoke intellectual stimulation. The shows' revelry does not create an aesthetic distance requiring audiences to be intellectually contemplative. Rather, the sentimental plots, emotive singing, and technical wizardry stimulate the emotions and senses, creating a feeling of collective participation that adds to the overall sense of excitement. "In the theatre as in cinema," Bourdieu explains, "the popular audience delights in plots that proceed logically and chronologically towards a happy end, and 'identifies' better with simply drawn situations and characters than with ambiguous and symbolic figures and actions or the enigmatic problems of the theatre of cruelty, not to mention the suspended animation of Beckettian heroes or the bland absurdities of Pinteresque dialogue."[9] In other words, Broadway productions and other popular musical programming offer spectators the promise of enchantment and fun. The shows promise theater patrons a nearly fail-safe big night out.

The Fox Theatre depends upon the blockbusters of Broadway to fill its thousands of seats, just as it used to rely upon Hollywood hits in the first half of the twentieth century. Although the origin of the theatrical illusions has changed from the West Coast to the East Coast, the formula that the shows provide is quite similar. Frank Wildhorn—the composer of *Jekyll and Hyde, The Scarlet Pimpernel,* and *The Civil War*—explained that the success of Broadway lies in its accessibility. "Audiences want music they can understand, melodies they can hum, and shows that take them on a journey," Wildhorn explained. "When the lights go down and the first note starts, they want to be moved."[10]

The Fox Theatre is the only Broadway touring house in Atlanta, and it has little competition from any other facility in the city. On occasion, a show will go to the city's civic center because of stage limitations. *Miss Saigon,* for instance, did not appear at the Fox Theatre because the production's helicopter would not have fit on its stage. Shelly Kleppsattel, the theater's office manager, remembered that years ago it was rare for a Broadway tour to stop at the Fox Theatre, but that has changed dramatically in the last ten years. "We're automatically on the stop list for all Broadway tours. Many times we're getting pre-Broadway shows. It

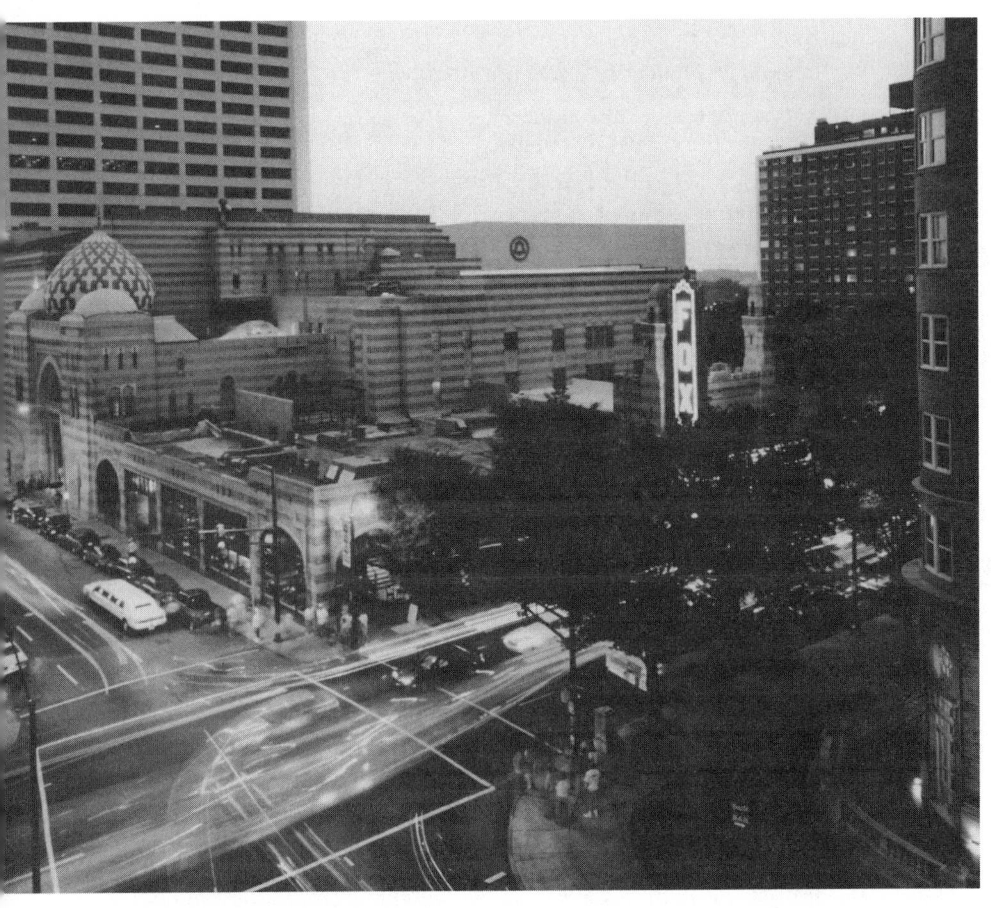

25. The enormousness of the Fox Theatre can be seen from this view at the corner of Ponce de Leon and Peachtree Streets. Notice the Bell South logo peeking over the theater. At first a threat to the theater's existence, Bell South quickly became one of its greatest supporters. Michael Portman, Atlanta, Georgia.

hasn't hurt that Elton John lives here now and previewed *Aida* here," she explained. "*Jekyll and Hyde* was pre-Broadway here, and so was *Gypsy*."

In fact, touring Broadway productions have been the mainstay of the theater's success for nearly twenty years. Yul Brynner's month-long run of *The King and I* at the Fox Theatre was the highest-grossing touring production in the United States in 1982. The same year, the theater was established as the city's premier Broadway venue. In 1989 the three-week run of *Les Misérables* at the Fox Theatre exceeded all box office records for the entire country. Major Broadway productions continue to be the anchors of the theater's programming. The 2001–2002 Atlanta Broadway Series at the theater, for instance, includes such familiar and popular shows as *South Pacific, Radio City Christmas Spectacular, The Music Man,* and *Saturday Night Fever.* Another recent Broadway hit at the Fox Theatre was the ever-popular *Titanic.*

Ed Neiss, the theater's general manager, could not be happier with the success of touring Broadway shows. He claims that the popularity of Broadway theater, the fact that the Fox is the primary Broadway theater in the city, and the tremendous financial development in the city has ensured the theater's prosperity during the last decades. It does not hurt that the theater has little competition from any other facility in the city. In fact, the Atlanta Civic Center is the only other facility in the metropolitan area that is the same size, and Neiss does not see it as a fierce competitor. "They built a big barn over there," he said, referring to the civic center. "And no one liked it. For years we have said that they are the eleventh member of our team, as long as they continue not to operate well."

Neiss stresses that it is very significant to the success of the theater that it is the primary Broadway house in Atlanta. The theater is also the home of the Atlanta Opera and the Atlanta Ballet. Neiss calls the facility "a populace theater," since they have something for everyone in Atlanta. "It might be the Atlanta Ballet one week, and the Red Hot Chili Peppers the next," he said. "We hope to fill the theater with a balance of programming consisting of everything under the sun. Right now we're operating at virtual capacity, and we hope to continue to do that." While the Fox Theatre may attribute a great deal of its success to touring Broadway shows, the Orpheum Theatre's reputation is built solely upon them. In fact, the theater has consistently set records for presenting more Broadway productions than any other theater in the United States. While most Broadway houses have a season of seven or eight shows, the Orpheum has two Broadway seasons with a total of eleven or twelve shows a year. According to the theater's 1999 annual report, Broadway shows account for 49 percent of the theater's total programming. Gospel productions come in a distant second, accounting for only 14 percent of the theater's programming. In 1999 five of the productions at the theater were the largest in terms of staging and cast size in the history of Broadway. *Sunset Boulevard, Miss Saigon, Jekyll and Hyde, Beauty and the Beast,* and *Showboat* were able to come to the Orpheum as a result of the stage expansion and enhancement that was undertaken in 1996 and 1997.

The increasing number of season subscriptions at the Orpheum Theatre attests to the popularity of Broadway with the citizens of Memphis. In 1991 there were 3,385 season subscribers, while six years later, in 1997, the number of subscribers peaked at 10,440. The tremendous amount of subscribers came as no surprise to theater management, since 1997 was the year that *The Phantom of the Opera* first appeared at the Orpheum. In order to assure seating for this popular show, people purchased an entire season subscription. *The Phantom of the Opera* enjoyed a five-week engagement at the theater, with every show completely sold out. The production is so well regarded by the theater's management that the cover of *The Orpheum! Where Broadway Meets Beale* features a picture of the theater's marquee prominently displaying the show's title.

Halloran, who is a great fan of Broadway musicals, may bring in some risky productions on occasion; however, if the second season of 2001 is any indication of what Memphis likes, it appears that they appreciate the tried and true Broadway show. *A Chorus Line, South Pacific, Cats,* and *Annie Get Your Gun* are among the season's productions. In the theater's program bulletin, Halloran describes *A Chorus Line* as a "true classic." *South Pacific* is characterized as "another one of those classics like *The Sound of Music*. They have more familiar songs than any other musical." And *Cats,* says Halloran, "needs no explanation."[11]

When I asked Richard Reinach, the theater's technical director, what he most liked about the Broadway productions, he explained that in part he likes them for their familiarity, because he was "raised on them." But he cares the most about creating the technical effects of the grand-scale productions. As we talked, I realized that people today are attracted to the dramatic illusions that appear at the Orpheum Theatre just as they were drawn to them seventy years ago, when the first talkies appeared on the theater's screen. The difference is that in the 1920s the illusion arrived at the theater in several film cans. Today it arrives by way of thirty or forty semitrailer trucks.

The Alabama Theatre has a slightly different kind of programming from the Orpheum Theatre and the Fox Theatre, since it does not rely upon a Broadway series. However, the theater regularly brings popular and well-known musicians and musical groups, as well as some plays, to its stage. Whitmire explained that the Alabama Theatre has a wide variety of shows, but that the theater is also routinely used for weddings, private parties, and corporate seminars. Whitmire found that using the theater as a rental facility helps to keep it in the black. "I always have a saying: 'If you've got the money, I've got the place,'" Whitmire quipped. The Alabama Theatre has become an extremely popular place for weddings in Birmingham. Whitmire explained that so many people are clamoring to get married at the theater that he has had to raise the price of an afternoon wedding to $1,500 and an evening wedding to $2,000. "I've found that if I'm sitting across the desk from you and your mother, and your mother has decided that you are getting married at the Alabama, then the price is no object," he said. "Even though I don't gouge, I have to have enough money to make it pay. I become Monty Hall, and it's *Let's Make a Deal* time."

Whitmire tends to book popular, accessible musicians who will attract a variety of people to the theater. I was able to see Lyle Lovett, and Whitmire explained that Fiona Apple, Jim Nabors, Cory Everson, Allison Krauss, the Drifters, the Coasters, the Miss Hard Body contest (a bodybuilding contest), and the Miss Alabama pageant were either upcoming or recent productions at the theater. During the summer of 2001, the theater hosted the production "Jazz Explosion" (featuring Will Downing, Jonathon Butler, and Chante Moore), the country superstar Dwight Yoakum, and a classic movie series. While Atlanta's and Memphis's ballet and other performing companies perform, at least part of the time, on the stages of the Fox Theatre and the Orpheum Theatre, Birmingham's performing-arts companies do not perform at the Alabama Theatre. Community organizations use the theater primarily as a seminar space, rather than a performing-arts space.

Whitmire's primary interest is for the theater to be used as much as possible. "I want this theater to last forever, and the only way for that to happen is to make it available to everyone," he said. "I've got Fiona Apple coming in. I'm not going to be happy with that concert, but there's a certain segment of people that will come to see her, and they will get to experience the theater." The theater is booked 300 nights a year, and Whitmire explained that because Birmingham is part of the Bible Belt, the theater is dark every Wednesday—which means that there are only a few nights a year that the theater is not booked. It seems that Whitmire is less concerned with creating a unified artistic vision for the theater and more interested in keeping the doors open and the seats filled as many nights of the year as possible. The wide variety of performances, from country to gospel to rhythm and blues, provides the city with a diversity of mainstream musical programming, ensuring that hundreds of thousands of Birmingham residents a year will come to the downtown movie palace to experience a big night out.

While the social spaces of the Carolina Theatre (at least the cinematic part of the Carolina Theatre) and the Tampa Theatre have been transformed, the Fox Theatre, the Orpheum Theatre, and the Alabama Theatre have for the most part maintained their original mainstream status. Even though the theaters have weathered ups and downs and made adjustments through the years to accommodate the changes that have occurred in the cities where they stand, one essential fact about them has not changed. They have and always will have a tremendous amount of seats to fill. This means that the theaters must find programming that appeals to a wide range of people. While the Fox Theatre and the Orpheum Theatre depend largely upon their Broadway Series, the Alabama Theatre depends upon one- or two-night bookings of a wide range of popular stars and musicians. Yet all three theaters fill their seats by presenting popular and emotionally appealing productions.

Interestingly, these three theaters are far more financially successful than the Tampa Theatre, the Carolina Theatre, and the Saenger Theatre. The reasons for this are varied. The Tampa Theatre, the Carolina Theatre, and the Saenger Theatre are city owned, while the other three are nonprofit organizations. I do not think that it is a coincidence that the three theaters with the most popular, mainstream programming are also the most financially successful of the six theaters discussed in this book. Hosting accessible entertainment, however, is not the only way that they have preserved their original social space.

Unlike going to see a movie at the Carolina Theatre or the Tampa Theatre, attending a concert or a Broadway production requires a certain amount of planning ahead because it is necessary to reserve a seat in advance. Such planning ahead helps to prepare the way for a big night out by creating feelings of excitement and expectation. After the tickets

26. The restored exterior of the Alabama Theatre. Birmingham residents come to the theater for a big night out. Copyright 1994, M. Lewis Kennedy, Kennedy Studios, Birmingham, Alabama.

are reserved, dinner reservations and plans for drinks after the show may be made, and, for some, deliberations about suitable attire must also be undertaken. Such big nights out are rarely an inexpensive affair. Tickets for two people (people rarely go alone) usually cost more than $100; dinner can cost even more; and the appropriate clothing can also be quite expensive. But it is important that the entire evening costs more than a night out at a movie or a play at the community theater because the cost marks the evening as a special occasion.

Bourdieu explains that people who seek intellectually engaging culture renounce ostentatious expense and any gratifications other than those provided by the symbolic profit of the work itself. However, he claims that those who seek to be merely entertained feel quite the opposite: "By contrast, for the dominant fractions a 'night out' at the theatre is an occasion for conspicuous spending. They 'dress up to go out' (which costs both time and money), they buy the most expensive seats in the most expensive theatres just as in other areas they buy 'the best there is'; they go to a restaurant after the show. Choosing a theatre is like choosing the right shop, marked with all the signs of 'quality' and guaranteeing no 'unpleasant surprises' or 'lapses of taste.' . . ."[12]

Unlike those who are seeking an intellectual cultural experience, mainstream patrons spend a good bit of money to ensure that they will have a good time. And while the production itself is familiar to them and popular enough with critics that they can be almost certain that it will be entertaining, getting dressed up and having dinner at a nice restaurant also helps to assure them that the evening will be out of the ordinary. Like early picture palace patrons, those who attend either Broadway productions or other popular entertainment at the theaters desire to mark the experience as something special. Early picture palace patrons used the downtown where the theater was located to add to their experience. They shopped in department stores, admired the merchandise displayed in windows, ate lunch or dinner in nearby restaurants, and walked up and down the city sidewalks, watching other people and conversing with acquaintances and friends. Today it is much more difficult, of course, for a big night out to be focused completely in the downtown area. Going downtown, in many cities, is, plain and simply, an inconvenience.

When patrons attend a restored movie palace to see a Broadway show or a popular musical entertainer, the buildings themselves can take on more importance. Tampa Theatre or Carolina Theatre film viewers, who may attend the theater several times a month, may forget to admire the building's unique qualities each time they go there, because it has become so familiar. On the other hand, people attending a Broadway show may go to the movie palace only a few times a year, so its unusual charm may have more of an impact. Because the building is associated with a special occasion, its fantastic design is more likely to complement the extraordinariness of the big night out.

Staying at Home: The Saenger Theatre

While the Saenger Theatre geographically and symbolically stands squarely in the center of Biloxi, Mississippi, there are plenty of opportunities for the residents of Biloxi to feel geographically distanced from their city. The theater literally sits in the shadows of the city's architectural fantasy, the Beau Rivage hotel and casino, which is owned by MGM Mirage. People from the Mississippi coast and other locations throughout the South go to the Beau Rivage to gamble, to dine, to shop, to attend the Beau Rivage Theatre, and to pamper themselves. The hotel's 1,780 rooms are large and tastefully decorated. Its twelve restaurants range from Memphis barbecues to Asian fusion cuisine; its shops bring fashions and jewelry from Italy, Miami, Los Angeles, and New York to the Gulf Coast; and its 1,600-seat theater brings in popular high-end productions like Michael Flatley's *Lord of the Dance*.

While the Beau Rivage is only two blocks from the Saenger Theatre, it seems thousands of miles away because the worlds that it references are far, far away from the small coastal city where it is situated. In fact, the Beau Rivage functions in a similar but slightly more splendid way as the Saenger Theatre did in the first half of the twentieth century, for it offers people a ticket to a more luxurious and exotic world than their daily lives usually can afford them. The Beau Rivage is designed to create the fantasy of Las Vegas glamour and big money in a modest southern city. While the Beau Rivage is not the only casino on the Gulf Coast, it is by far the most luxurious, and its towering structure seems to overshadow the rest of the area. Even as I look down from the airplane window on my way home to Tampa, the Beau Rivage looms over the rest of the city's geographical markers.

The Beau Rivage's orientation toward another world only seems to magnify the fact that the Saenger Theatre points toward home. Located in the heart of downtown Biloxi, the theater stands as a reminder of what the city was before the casinos dramatically improved the economy and drastically altered the contours of the city. The theater—which is situated near several other historic buildings in the downtown area, such as the 1907 City Hall in the neoclassical revival style, the 1847 antebellum Magnolia Hotel (which is now the Biloxi Mardi Gras Museum), and the 1895 Victorian Brielmaier home (which is now the Visitor's Center)—stands as a souvenir of a time when life in Biloxi seemed more cohesive and perhaps more genteel.

The Saenger Theatre clearly cannot compete with the casinos' theaters. The Beau Rivage brings well-known entertainers like Paul Anka and large productions like Cirque du Soleil to its stage, and at least a dozen other casinos in the Gulf Coast area also regularly have popular entertainers on their stages (Willie Nelson jogged by me one day as I was walking to the theater). The Saenger Theatre is the Mississippi Gulf Coast's performing-arts center, meaning that it is used primarily for community performing-arts groups, such as the Gulf Coast Symphony, the Gulf Coast Opera, and community theater groups. Lee Hood said that most of the productions that use the theater are "semi-professional." "It's not hokey stuff," she said, "for the most part." At times the theater does bring in nationally and internationally known performers, such as the Vienna Boys' Choir and the pianist George Winston, but such acts are rare.

Natalie Robohm, the executive director of the Gulf Coast Symphony, told me that people naturally associate the Saenger Theatre with the symphony. "They go together," she claimed. "We've tried other spots when we haven't been able to use this facility, and the closest other place would be the Biloxi High School, but it's just a high school. We lose our attendance when we don't perform here." Although Robohm has a fairly long list of complaints about the Saenger Theatre as a facility, she recognizes the economic constraints facing a city the size of Biloxi. She wishes that a new Gulf Coast performing-arts center would be built, but she acknowledged that a 2,500–seat auditorium would be a tough sell for the area. "I don't think it would be supported," she said. "With Mobile and New Orleans so close by, people can just go there for their Broadway shows."

The City of Biloxi, which owns the theater, subsidizes every community group that uses it. "They desire to keep this theater as a facility for the community," Lee Hood explained, "and so our rental fees are $300 for each performance and $75 for each rehearsal. The lights and sound

27. The restored and pristine exterior of the Saenger Theatre, which is one of the few public markers of the past in a city full of new casinos and hotels. Mark Neumann, Documentary Works, Tampa, Florida.

are thrown in as a freebie that goes with the rent." Compared to what Whitmire charges for an evening wedding at the Alabama Theatre, the Gulf Coast Symphony's $300 fee for an evening's performance is a bargain. Hood acknowledged that the theater rarely has a full house for anything other than the symphony, so it appears that the symphony and the theater are fairly dependent upon one another.

While the Gulf Coast Symphony might be considered high art, it is important to remember that the symphony members are Gulf Coast residents, not national or international performers. Hood explained that a recent symphony conductor was fired because he was scouting for talent outside of the area. "A lot of people were resentful because he brought in a lot of people from Mobile and Pensacola," Hood said. "He turned down some good local talent to bring in his people." Without the prestige of nationally, or at least regionally, known artists, the Gulf Coast Symphony lacks the pretension of more recognized symphony orchestras. When neighbors and cousins are on stage, rather than performers from other, larger cities, the Gulf Coast Symphony stays within the acceptable parameters of community artistry.

The Saenger Theatre also seems to have a strong commitment to Gulf Coast children who have a penchant for performance. Because the theater is so affordable, local theater groups are able to rent the facility, which enables children and teenagers to perform on a professional stage. June Swetman McGown, a longtime Biloxi resident and Saenger Theatre supporter, believes that this is one of the theater's most important community functions. "I think of this as a place for children to learn how to perform, to get experience, to get a feeling of self-confidence," McGown stated. "Also, it is important for kids who want to get into lighting and stage managing and things like that. This gives them a feeling of what it is like in big theaters." LeAnne Tombe Smith, a production assistant for two resident theater companies that use the theater, explained that the Saenger Theatre makes young performers feel important. "They work so hard for a couple of months in any rehearsal space we can find," she said. "When we come in here for the production, their family can come see them on the big stage. It makes them feel special, which is why I do theater for kids in the first place."

While the Saenger Theatre is an integral element of the Gulf Coast's performing-arts groups, the facility keeps community interests as its primary reference point in other ways as well. For example, Hood recently was able to purchase a state-of-the-art front and rear film projector and a large screen so that the theater could occasionally exhibit films for a minimal fee. The films that they have shown, or are planning to show, are family movies that complement a particular occasion.

During the Christmas season of 2000, for instance, the Saenger Theatre had a free viewing of *It's a Wonderful Life* (Frank Capra, 1946). There was little press for the event, but 400 people came to see the film and to eat free hot dogs and drink free hot chocolate. Included in the event was a raffle for a weekend getaway at the Beau Rivage. One family that came to the event, Hood explained, was a young, financially troubled couple and their young children. The free event enabled them to see the movie and show their children the theater. One of their children picked up a dropped raffle ticket in the lobby. And, of course, it was the winning ticket. Hood said that the child's parents were ecstatic when they realized they were going to have a weekend to themselves at the plush resort. "I would have babysat for them," Hood said, "but I guess they found somebody else to watch the kids."

The Saenger Theatre and the city of Biloxi have a great admiration for the accomplished and talented members of its own community. You will recall that the city insisted on employing a local architect to refurbish the theater, and, of course, the last symphony conductor was fired because he was scouting out talent in Alabama and Florida. One of the films that the theater has recently shown also enabled the community to pay tribute to a native son. The Saenger Theatre recently exhibited *Apollo 13* (Ron Howard, 1995) because Fred Haise, one of the original Apollo 13 astronauts, is from the area and is a hometown hero. The theater showed the movie, and then Haise spoke to the crowd of 300.

Hood is also planning to show the movie *Grease* (Randal Kleiser, 1978) during the classic-car extravaganza Cruisin' the Coast. She said that because the event will take place during the theater's restoration, she is planning to project it on the outside wall of the theater, turning the movie palace into a drive-in. Hood thinks that showing movies is important for the Saenger Theatre because it helps to develop a new, younger theater audience who can probably afford a five-dollar ticket, but may not be able to afford a twenty-dollar ticket for the Gulf Coast Symphony. She said that they will not show movies more than four or five times a year to begin with, but she likes the idea that the theater can return, at least for a few hours, to its function as a movie palace.

The theater also functions as a community center even when no one is sitting in the auditorium seats. Hood remembered that right before the 2000 presidential election, she walked into the theater one morning, only to find out that the city had designated the theater as a precinct the day before. She admitted that she was hardly thrilled to learn that she would have to be at the theater by six in the morning on election days to open the theater for the voters. However, she also said that she liked the idea of the theater serving as a community gathering spot. In addition, many of the voters who turned out at the theater for the presidential election were elderly citizens who had not been to the theater for decades. Hood said that she had the opportunity to listen to and jot down many stories about the theater in its earliest years.

Even at its most glamorous, the Saenger Theatre points to home. In February 2001 the theater presented the Gulf Coast Opera's "A Gala Evening with Raeschelle Potter." Potter, a resident of Vienna, Austria, is an international opera star. She made her operatic debut on stage at the Metropolitan Opera House. The soprano sings with many of the world's leading conductors of opera. She frequently tours Europe, and she has been featured in televised PBS and ABC concerts, as well as in documentaries and commercial soundtracks. She also has a Ph.D. from the University of Vienna and is a lecturer of cultural anthropology there.

Clearly, it was a thrill for both the theater and the Gulf Coast Opera to have Potter on stage. But what really thrilled everyone—the members of the opera, the audience, and Hood—is that Potter is a hometown girl. She is originally from Gulfport, Mississippi, a town adjacent to Biloxi. Potter, who still has family in the area, tries to get home as often as she can, despite her laborious schedule. Hood told me that her best friend's daughter came to the theater after Potter's performance and put her hand on a door and said, "Raeschelle actually touched this door!" While the community obviously has great pride in Potter's successes, Hood noted that they are most proud that she is a woman of great character and that she never forgets to make her way home.

The Saenger Theatre strives to be at the center of the Gulf Coast arts community. Because the casino theaters have more money and clout than the movie palace ever will, Hood has not attempted to compete with them; instead, she has carved an important niche for the theater. While the Saenger Theatre may have less cultural prestige than it did in the first half of the twentieth century, it has been highly effective in preserving its role as a community gathering space. In a way, the casinos scattered across the area help to define the theater as a communal place, since their theaters are attended mostly by people who travel to the area from other cities and regions. Few people who go to the Beau Rivage, for example, ever make their way to the Saenger Theatre, despite the fact that you can see the theater's marquee from some of the hotel rooms' windows. Both the people who perform on stage and those who sit in the auditorium's seats are usually Gulf Coast residents, and that seems to suit the city of Biloxi just fine. Even while most movie palaces in the late 1920s functioned similarly to one another, now that they are preserved facilities, they take on the contours and the specific needs of their cities. With imagination and passion, along with some savvy and strong marketing skills, Hood enables Biloxi's movie palace to give continual shape to the ideals of a cohesive community.

Going to the picture palace, in the 1920s, was the paramount downtown experience. Whether it was the "Gem of the Gulf Coast" or the "Showplace of the South," a movie palace generated a great deal of civic pride for city officials and residents. While a movie palace's identity was certainly intertwined with the downtown where it was situated, the thrill of the theater was that it offered passage to more glamorous and exciting places. Going downtown included the excitement of people-watching, shopping, strolling, and dining at restaurants, but once patrons were inside the theater, the city outside the theater doors disappeared. The exotic architecture and the Hollywood films created a way to travel to distant and unfamiliar regions, and the city center and everything else that was familiar vanished for a few hours.

Little has changed for movie palaces that still rely upon mainstream entertainment. Then, the movie palace promised the fantasy and romance of Hollywood; today the Orpheum Theatre and the Fox Theatre deliver the excitement and passion of New York's Forty-Second Street. Patrons at the Alabama Theatre feel the thrill of the musical hubs of Austin, Nashville, and New Orleans. In other words, contemporary patrons, like the early movie palace patrons before them, experience the excitement of arriving somewhere else. City dwellers in Atlanta, Birmingham, and Memphis can temporarily escape their own cities, by way of the movie palace. The fantasies originate from the East Coast rather than the West Coast, but the dreams they invoke are the same.

The social space at the Carolina Theatre and the Tampa Theatre has been transformed as a result of the kind of programming that they offer. No longer mainstream spaces, the theaters do not elicit the same sort of fantasies as they once did. Their alternative films do take spectators to exotic countries, urban streets, and the rustic countryside, and the familiar geography of downtown is left behind as in the other movie palaces, but what these theaters really offer is a passage to an interior, intellectual landscape. The films at these theaters lack the excitement and escape of Broadway musicals or Hollywood films, but that is not the experience their patrons are seeking. The films provide a portal for contemplation and deliberation—a way to sit quietly and wonder.

Only the patrons at the Saenger Theatre cannot forget their own city as they enter the threshold of the movie palace. Unlike the original movie palaces, with their geographical fantasies, and the five other restored theaters, the Saenger Theatre has become a genuine marker of the community where it is located. Referencing its own geography and foregrounding the city's own musical and theatrical talents, Biloxi's movie palace points toward home. If patrons want dreams of other worlds, then they will just have to go somewhere else.

Epilogue: Let's Go Downtown?

When they appeared in Atlanta, Biloxi, Birmingham, Durham, Memphis, and Tampa, all of these theaters became official markers of the economic successes of their respective downtown areas. In the 1960s and 1970s they once again served as markers; at that time, however, they were unofficial symbols of financial ruin and social upheaval. As the preservation movement gained momentum in the mid-1970s and 1980s, the movie palace once more served as an official marker, representing a step toward downtown revitalization, which included architectural renovation as well as an attempt to mend the social divisions that had plagued cities for a decade or more.

As I mentioned in the introduction, the historic American movie theater is the first item on the National Trust's list of "America's 11 Most Endangered Historic Places" for 2001. "The closing of a historic movie theater is more than the loss of a single piece of our heritage," said Richard Moe, the president of the National Trust, "it greatly affects the downtown economy as well."[13] Some twenty to twenty-five years after the rescue of the movie palaces in this book, there are still many movie palaces in downtown areas that remain standing but out of business. And it is clear from Moe's statement that there is still a great deal of hope for what an old movie theater can do for a downtown district. Moe's rhetoric sounds strikingly similar to the arguments made by preservationists such as Monte Moses and Lee Duncan; people still believe that the restored movie palace has the potential to help save both the city's heritage and its downtown.

Yet bringing a movie palace back to life is no guarantee that the downtown where it is situated will quickly follow suit. Building a movie palace as a celebration of economic prosperity was easy in the 1920s, but renovating one in an attempt to stimulate downtown rejuvenation at the beginning of the twenty-first century is more difficult. The fundamental problem that theater preservationists face is that it is unlikely that the southern downtown will ever be the center of the city again. While it is possible that a downtown area can be a vibrant pocket of redevelopment, it will not be the economic and social center of a city. Nearly every convenience that city residents desire is located in suburban areas close to their homes. Massive shopping malls, jumbo grocery stores, airport-sized Wal-Marts, twenty-screen movie theaters, and restaurant upon restaurant strung together along major roads have become natural elements of the decentered city landscape. The notion that a restored movie palace can help to change this sprawling course seems overwhelmingly optimistic.

The downtown movie palace and what it means to "go downtown" have changed dramatically over the last half of a century, yet a nostalgia for their original functions within a community still remains. Near Orlando, Florida, a town named Celebration has been planted in the swamp grass. Built by the Disney Corporation, it is a re-creation of a traditional town. Developers claim this sort of town existed prior to World War II. By building homes with porches and sidewalks in front of them, creating neighborhood streets that give priority to pedestrians, and developing an eighteen-acre downtown within walking distance of most Celebration homes, the developers hoped to create a neighborly and civic-minded way of life.

On Front Street, in the downtown area, the architect Cesar Pelli designed a movie theater called Celebration Cinema. It was created as "an ode to the showy era of the 'talkie,'" the Celebration guidebook explains, "in the decades between the two world wars—a time when going to the movies was an event, not just a routine trip to the local mall's cineplex." Celebration Cinema's design is intended to connect with a "rich past of movie houses, bringing them to the end of the twentieth century in a very contemporary form."

By resurrecting the idea of the picture palace, Celebration's planners hoped to create a sense of place within the community. But neither the downtown nor Celebration Cinema is at present flourishing. Recently, I was there on a Saturday afternoon. The theater was closed, and the area looked similar to Tampa's downtown on a Saturday afternoon—it was empty. Surprised that a movie theater would be shut down on a weekend, I asked a waiter at a nearby diner if he knew why. He shrugged his shoulders and said, "Everybody stays home and watches movies on their entertainment centers. There isn't any reason to go there that I can see." While Celebration developers may have meant to create a 1920s downtown, they constructed a turn-of-the-twenty-first-century downtown instead. The buildings are there, but the people are not. It seems that the idea of "going downtown" has been all but lost.

It is true that all of the downtowns—Atlanta, Biloxi, Birmingham, Durham, Memphis, and Tampa—are more economically stable now than they were at the time when the movie palaces were rescued. However, the downtown districts are no longer city centers. Biloxi's downtown is a few blocks of mostly empty buildings. Only one or two stores are open. The hospital a block away from the theater consistently generates the most traffic in the area.

Tampa's downtown serves as the city's Central Business District. It has plenty of pedestrian traffic and busy restaurants from noon until two during the week. But at night and on the weekend, it is a ghost town. The Tampa Theatre and the city's performing-arts center are the only destinations during evening hours, and no coffee shops or restaurants are open nearby.

The area around the Fox Theatre on Peachtree Street in Atlanta has undergone a great deal of development in the last ten years. Both the restoration of the Fox Theatre and the construction of Southern Bell's headquarters have helped to spur development in the area. And while there has been some development around the theater, it is hardly the center of the city. The theater is situated in an area that is now called Midtown, between an inhospitable downtown that features grand but fairly inaccessible buildings and Buckhead, a prosperous area that is really just a series of glorified strip malls and shopping plazas. North of the theater, Buckhead is dense with restaurants, clubs, retail shopping, and people, particularly young ones. But safely getting from place to place in Buckhead requires a car. There simply is not an area in the center of Atlanta that generates the kind of energy that pedestrian-oriented districts can invoke. Atlanta is a city built for the car, not for people. Even walking the mile or so from my downtown hotel to the theater seems strange and slightly unsafe, because I am usually one of only two or three people walking on the sidewalk along Peachtree Street.

In order to understand the present-day relationship between the movie palace and the downtown, we will look at the obstacles and possibilities that theater directors confront in Birmingham, Durham, and Memphis. The downtown districts of these three cities represent a range of promise, from somewhat struggling to reasonably thriving. In general, all six of the movie palace directors face the same problems and possess the same hopes for the downtown areas where their theaters are located; some of them have simply had more good fortune than others.

It is not for a lack of trying, but the revitalization of Birmingham's downtown has not happened as quickly or as well as Whitmire had imagined or hoped. He cannot do it by himself, and it has been tremendously difficult to attract entrepreneurs to the area around the theater. Of the six downtown areas discussed in this book, Birmingham has the most architectural potential, even if it has not been realized as of yet. There are plenty of lovely but empty buildings scattered along the streets of the downtown district. Abandoned buildings do not generally create a hospitable environment for either residents or tourists who are looking for a way to spend the day or evening. When I went to Birmingham, I stayed in two different downtown historic hotels. While I was able to walk from my hotel to the public library, I was one of only a few people on the downtown sidewalks.

Pockets of downtown revitalization are occurring. There is a trend toward revitalizing old office towers for loft living and office space. Projects such as the renovation of the 1927 New Ideal office building, which was converted into twenty-five apartments and retail space on the ground floor, even caught the attention of the *New York Times* in 1998.[14] The area around the theater, however, has not been at the forefront of the revival effort, even though the theater was the fundamental endeavor in bringing the downtown area back to life. "When we reopened this theater, the downtown was a deserted area. You could play badminton out here on Third Avenue and not have a fear of being hurt," Whitmire said. "But you wouldn't have wanted to do that because downtown was pretty dangerous."

Whitmire ackowledges that the Alabama Theatre is still the only facility downtown that generates any evening activity. That lack of density, along with the residue of fear that people feel toward downtown Birmingham, has motivated city officials and downtown merchants to create safety initiatives that will help to promote feelings of security for Birmingham citizens. The City Action Patrol (CAP) program and the Birmingham Police Department bicycle squad are heavily promoted by the City of Birmingham as friendly and beneficial methods for preventing crime in the downtown area. One article explained that the crime prevention initiatives "help to ensure downtown's crime rate is among the lowest in the metropolitan area. As more people visit the City Center, outdated perceptions that downtown is unsafe will disappear."[15]

The area around the theater has had a difficult time with revitalization because it was once the downtown retail center. Michael Calvert, who heads a public/private nonprofit organization charged with promotion and renovation in the downtown area, explained that vacant department stores are difficult to reuse. "Some are quite large, and they just don't fit what people need. It's not a good fit for a law firm or most kind of businesses," he said. "People see these vacant buildings, and they think downtown is dying, or worse, dead. But when they see restored historic buildings, they start thinking this place has some life in it." Calvert explained that downtown Birmingham must be envisioned as a "post-retail" setting. The strategic plan of the area includes, according to Calvert, making the city center the number-one choice for living, business, arts, and entertainment. "Notice I didn't say retail," Calvert noted. "Our theory is retail is gone, but the other things can still combine to create a vibrant, vital downtown."

One of the reasons Whitmire is compelled to find a way to restore the Lyric Theatre, across the street from the Alabama Theatre, is that he thinks it will create a density of people that will attract entrepreneurs. "If we can get that 1,300–seat theater open, then we can conceivably be drawing 4,000 people down here in the evening when both theaters are booked. Then it is more likely that we can get lounges open so that couples can have dinner at a white-tablecloth restaurant before or after the show. Like in New York City or Chicago," Whitmire explained. "Things like that would make the downtown a destination."

Without the other theater to help increase density, Whitmire does not believe that the area will ever be completely revived. "You've got to have the people first. It's one of those chicken and egg things," Whitmire stated. "No decent restaurateur will come into this area without the numbers that are big enough. You can't blame someone for not wanting to put a quarter of a million into a restaurant and have it sit there empty." Ultimately, all of Whitmire's plans for revitalization, including the restoration of the Lyric Theatre, come back to his commitment to the Alabama Theatre. He fears that the Alabama Theatre could eventually be threatened if new activity is not generated and businesses are not opened. "It's part of the plan to put this theater [the Lyric Theatre] to work and to generate various restaurants and things to support the after-dark business in downtown. It's foolish to think the theater can operate forever without the support that we need from various restaurants and shops."

Kathy Gilmore, the director of Birmingham's Metropolitan Arts Council, lists three steps that must be taken before the downtown area can become vibrant: add an attractive public transportation system, eliminate the area's dead zones, and increase the area's artistic activity. Gilmore describes downtown Birmingham as pedestrian unfriendly. For instance, the facilities that attract the most people, such as the Museum of Art, the Alabama Theatre, and the Civil Rights Institute, seem too far apart for people to walk from one to another. Gilmore explained that the distance between the Civil Rights Institute and the museum is only four blocks, but people drive from one building to the next. "Because you don't have attractive shops or restaurants to move people along, you've got dead zones. People who want to go from one facility to the other don't want to walk down a street with empty buildings. We are pushing very hard to get a connector to transport people from one place to the other. We want to go back to that which would be charming. Something that would be fun to ride and would connect downtown attractions."

Gilmore, who calls herself "the arts chamber of commerce," also believes that more emphasis on downtown arts activities is crucial. She stressed that without the arts, downtown Birmingham is just "a bunch of offices." "Bringing people to an arts event enlivens the city. You need to feel good when you're in a city. That's what makes cities successful. You feel good when you're there. The energy that comes from arts activities is tied to everything. The color, creativeness, and the artists themselves bring a certain vitality to the street. They have energy and bring color to the city." Like Whitmire, Gilmore hopes that, in time, the area around the theater will be lively with the opening of restaurants, antique shops, coffee shops, and art galleries. However, she does not imagine that such revitalization will happen anytime soon, because of the resistance of longtime building owners who are not interested in regenerating the area. "Unfortunately, the progress in the area is hindered by what we like to call 'curmudgeon landlords,'" Gilmore said. "They are holding on to their property and have no concern in cooperating with us."

Another obstacle to developing the area around the Alabama Theatre is that another region, Five Points, which is a mile or so from downtown, has become the restaurant and club destination for the city. It was a neighborhood streetcar stop in the 1920s and was redeveloped in the early 1980s. It has a proliferation of trendy stores, contemporary restaurants with outdoor seating, and coffee shops. A combination of new buildings, renovated structures, and well-designed landscaping and gathering areas creates a pedestrian-friendly area that is far more attractive and accommodating than downtown Birmingham. "We're happy to have it," Calvert admitted. "I just wish it was here [downtown] instead." He said that Five Points has some of the best urban streets in the country. "With the landscape treatment in Five Points, people will walk six, eight blocks down there and not think anything of it," Calvert said. "Downtown? You cannot get them to walk four blocks in either direction. There is such a heightened concern about safety down here."

The Alabama Theatre was originally constructed to be at the center of the downtown retail area. It is a concept that is no different from today's super cinemas that are strategically placed in shopping plazas that feature both well-known retail shops and high-concept restaurants. Unfortunately, in Birmingham today, as in most southern cities, there is no retail space near the theater. All that exists is the remnants of a once-thriving commercial area—large abandoned buildings that are difficult to reuse. As beautiful and as popular as the Alabama Theatre is, it cannot by itself create a high-density area. It is no wonder that Whitmire has such high hopes for the abandoned theater across the street. Although some people might argue that if one renovated theater could not spur redevelopment, it is unreasonable to think that another renovated theater will do it, Whitmire's belief is that an additional 1,500 people in the area on any given evening may create the interest that is essential for the sort of theater district that he imagines for Birmingham's downtown.

With more than 200 events per year and attendance of more than 150,000 during the 2000–2001 season, the Carolina Theatre clearly contributes a great deal to the vitality of downtown Durham, just as Monte Moses suggested that it would in 1978. "It could very well be the first step in bringing a supportive public back to the area," Moses wrote in a prospectus for the use of the theater, "and facilitate the realization of other efforts to make downtown a cultural center and a focal point of pride."[16] The city of Durham, with around 300,000 people, has approximately one-third of the people that the cities of Birmingham, Memphis, and Tampa have (their metropolitan areas all hover around the 1 million mark). For a small city, the number of people that the theater attracts is quite impressive. But even Steve Martin admits that the idea that the Carolina Theatre was at the center of the present-day revitalization efforts is a little far-fetched.

Martin describes downtown Durham as "reemerging." "It's been five years since I've come here, and in that five years, a million square feet of office space has been added," he said. "It's already begun, and at this minute we are on the cusp of it all happening." Part of downtown Durham's attraction to new developers is the tobacco warehouses that have stood empty for at least a decade. Entrepreneurs have been drawn to the warehouses, largely because of preservation tax incentives, but also because of their innate charm and adaptability. One such completed revitalization effort, Brightleaf Square, is only a few blocks from the theater. It is a high-end retail area, complemented with an assortment of upscale restaurants. It is an easy walk to Brightleaf Square from the Carolina Theatre and the Marriott Hotel adjacent to it, and I have spent several hours wandering through the trendy stores and eating at Fowler's, the upscale gourmet food store and deli.

As Martin pointed out, 1 million square feet of formerly vacant space has been purchased and renovated in downtown Durham within the last five years. Leasable office space has grown from 1 million square feet to 2 million, while at the same time occupancy has grown from 70 percent to more than 90 percent. Residential occupancy has grown from 100 units to 400 units. Downtown boosters are doing cartwheels over the $200 million renovation of the American Tobacco complex that is presently in the planning and design stage. Touted as a historic district in itself, the complex originally manufactured Bull Durham, a "roll your own" tobacco, and later manufactured Lucky Strike and Chesterfield cigarettes. The historic district will add another million square feet of office space to downtown Durham, along with retail space and restaurants. A downtown train station, a five-acre green space called Durham Central Park, and a Central Police District are also new additions to the downtown area. At present, there are 368 businesses in downtown Durham and 35 restaurants. From June 1999 to June 2000, eighty-one building permits were issued for downtown Durham, for an investment in the area of $11 million.[17]

Downtown Durham, as Martin said, is in the process of reemerging. It is not a thriving, vital place as of yet. Nevertheless, it appears to be on the upswing, and because it is a smaller area than downtown Birmingham, each additional redevelopment has a noticeable impact on the area. Unlike the problems that Whitmire is confronting with the lack of development around the area of the Alabama Theater, Martin has the advantage of the recent redevelopment of Main Street. "They're making Main Street an entertainment center with clubs and restaurants," he explained, "so the major north/south entrance is delivering people right to the Carolina Theatre." Developers in Durham, as in most other cities in the process of downtown redevelopment, recognize that it is essential to have living spaces in the area. Martin acknowledges that people have a perception that downtown is dangerous, and this belief makes it more difficult to attract both residents and developers to the area.

A zero-tolerance panhandling ordinance, Martin explained, is intended to help get intimidating people off downtown streets, but it also has the potential to displace noncriminals as well. "It is supposed to take folks who are off their medications and get them to a place where they belong and allow the truly homeless to get someplace where they can get helped," Martin explained. "Mostly it gets the criminals off the streets who are making a living intimidating people, so people can come downtown and not feel like they are being assaulted." When I asked Martin if there was a serious crime problem in downtown Durham, he explained that it was more about perception than reality. "If a man comes up and says, 'Excuse me, ma'am, do you have two dollars?' and he is 6 feet, 4 inches, tall and weighs 220 pounds, and you are not, you're going to feel intimidated whether he meant to be or not," Martin explained. "So it really doesn't matter whether he means to intimidate; the fact is you have to have a zero tolerance. It's like a broken window; you have to take immediate action every time it happens and not tolerate it. If a window gets broken, it has to be fixed immediately."

The panhandling ordinance, which is generally supported by Durham's homeless advocates, makes it illegal to solicit money on a city bus, at a bus stop, or within twenty feet of a bank or ATM. The ordinance, which aims to decrease the activity of aggressive panhandlers, defines accosting another person as approaching or speaking to someone in such a way that would cause a reasonable person to fear imminent harm.[18] Panhandling ordinances, in general, are not effective, because they are difficult to enforce and can discriminate against people who may be homeless but are not aggressively panhandling. While Martin may seem rather inflexible about panhandling near the theater, it points to his concern about how downtown is perceived by city residents and how such practices as panhandling inevitably affect business because they make people think twice about going downtown.

The perception of crime is a constant concern to all the movie palace directors with whom I spoke. The idea of "downtown" remains associated with danger. Sometimes the feeling of danger is associated with the homeless, who are attracted to downtown areas because social services, parks, and bus stations are usually located there. While city dwellers in large northern cities such as New York City or Philadelphia would most likely be less concerned with panhandlers, residents of smaller southern cities are less accustomed to urban living, because they spend a good bit of their public life protected in their cars or in malls. A 2000 survey conducted by the Durham Convention and Visitors Bureau showed that 60 percent of the people surveyed do not feel safe in downtown Durham, despite the fact that only 3.6 percent of Durham's violent crimes occur downtown.[19] Therefore, downtown business owners in smaller southern cities feel compelled to provide more police protection and tolerate less street activity in order for people to begin feeling comfortable enough to walk the streets and bring their money downtown. William Kalkhof, the president of Downtown Durham Inc., stated in a *Herald Sun* editorial that the city of Durham can increase security, lighting, and police presence, but until there are people on the streets of downtown at all hours, some people will never feel comfortable going downtown.

Like Whitmire, Martin must concern himself with operations both inside and outside the theater. It is not enough to bring excellent cinematic and live programming to the theater; Martin must also continually push for downtown redevelopment and be on the lookout for obstacles that will prevent people from coming downtown. Many people simply do not feel comfortable with the idea of downtown, no matter how it is marketed. For others, it will continue to be an inconvenience, since their homes are miles away from the city center. Going downtown may not conjure feelings of dread and fear as it did in the 1970s, but it rarely evokes a sense of community cohesiveness and social activity either. While the renovation of the Carolina Theatre may have enabled developers to imagine a rebirth of downtown, it did not open the floodgates for revitalization. As beneficial as the theater is to the Durham community, it will take more than a few movie screens and a renovated stage for people to change their attitudes about what it means to go downtown.

On a sunny weekday in early May, I ate lunch with Pat Halloran and Donna Darwin in downtown Memphis, across the street from the Orpheum Theatre. At a busy restaurant, we sat outside, underneath colorful patio umbrellas. We gossiped about other renovated theaters, watched people coming and going, and stopped our conversation more than a few times so that Halloran could introduce me to yet another notable resident of Memphis. I enjoyed myself, but most of all I was excited by the density and activity in the center of downtown Memphis. Later in the day, when I was finished working at the Orpheum Theatre, I hopped on the trolley that runs through the downtown. As I watched people on the streets and sidewalks and admired the renovation of several nice old buildings, I could not help thinking of the Memphis newspaper photographs from the 1960s that showed pockets of the downtown in ruins. It was almost impossible to believe that this was the same place. Of the six southern movie palaces that I have studied, the Orpheum seems to be the one that is situated in a downtown with the most density and vitality. And while the theater itself was one of the first revitalization efforts in downtown Memphis, other large-scale restoration projects have also contributed to the downtown's current success.

A few months before the Orpheum was purchased by the Memphis Development Foundation in 1976, Jack Belz purchased the Peabody Hotel for $75,000. Six years and $24 million later, the Peabody Hotel was reopened. The hotel, which is only two blocks from the Orpheum Theatre, is probably one of the city's most famous landmarks. But the reopening of the hotel was only the beginning of Belz's vision for downtown Memphis. He believed that the area had the potential to be a premier mixed-use city center. Over a twenty-six-year period, he developed an eight-city-block area around the hotel and created an entertainment and retail center called Peabody Place. The development, which partially opened in June 2001, includes apartment homes, a hotel, restaurants, a movie theater, retail stores, a museum, and the AutoZone headquarters. A total of $287 million of public and private funds was used to create the urban development that helped to spur a $2 billion building boom in downtown Memphis. Belz's company worked with three Memphis mayors for a quarter of a century in search of a taxpayer-funded project that would reestablish downtown Memphis as the premier city center in the mid-South.[20]

Another project that has been a tremendous boost to downtown Memphis is the revitalization of Beale Street. The street and the area around it had been home to an economically vibrant African American community during the first half of the twentieth century. Like other institutions in downtown Memphis, the area around Beale Street fell into decay in the 1960s, and much of it was destroyed during the city's urban renewal. However, in the late 1970s, the City of Memphis bought many of the properties along three blocks of Beale Street, and by 1983 the first club reopened. Little by little, the area was recharged, with businesses and clubs moving into renovated buildings. Today it is one of the most vibrant streets and tourist attractions in the mid-South, with the Elvis Presley Restaurant serving as the entryway into the area. The fact that both Beale Street and Peabody Place are within one or two blocks of the Orpheum Theatre has been a benefit to all of those involved with downtown revitalization, because it creates a density and vitality that are quite attractive to developers.

In 1991, twenty-three years after Martin Luther King Jr.'s assassination, the Lorraine Motel reopened as the National Civil Rights Museum. Situated near the revitalized area, the museum has 27,000 square feet of exhibition space, an auditorium, a courtyard, a changing gallery, and a gift shop. The permanent exhibition includes information about the Montgomery bus boycott, *Brown v. the Board of Education,* Little Rock, the march on Washington, and the Memphis sanitation workers strike. In a short time, the museum has become a significant national landmark and an important tourist attraction in a city that still suffers from its painful legacy. A $10 million fund-raising campaign is presently underway so that the museum can expand its facilities. The expansion plans include a public plaza that will strengthen its connection with the downtown.

The fact that the Orpheum Theatre sits at the center of downtown Memphis's revitalization is thrilling to Pat Halloran, but he believes that there is still much room for improvement. Halloran claims that unlike the cities of Charlotte, Dallas, and Atlanta, Memphis suffers from low self-esteem. He believes the city still languishes from the racial riots of the 1960s, Martin Luther King Jr.'s assassination, and a history of corruption and bad leadership. "The city simply cannot point to much of anything with an element of pride," Halloran said. "The town just fights and fights, and it doesn't help us any at all." Halloran explained that Memphis has also suffered from the fact that various professional sports teams have courted Memphis and then ultimately chosen other cities. (Memphis now has a professional basketball team, the Grizzlies.) In addition, only a few national corporations, such as FedEx and AutoZone, have chosen Memphis as their headquarters. Halloran contends that Memphis needs to get in the habit of marketing itself. "Marketers haven't done anything to change the way Memphis feels about itself," he lamented.

In 2001 the magazine *Black Enterprise* rated Memphis as the fifth best city in the United States for African Americans to live and work in, a far cry from the days of racial rioting in the 1960s. Downtown revitalization, rebuilding of neighborhoods, and riverfront development were listed as significant factors for Memphis's ranking. Memphis's mayor, Willie Herenton, predicted in June 2001 that Memphis will jump from a number-five ranking to a number-one ranking within the next few years, partly because he is a Memphis booster and partly because he believes that the continuance of downtown revitalization and improvements in education will further increase the city's status.[21] While racial prejudice has certainly not disappeared in Memphis, the city has made great strides in improving racial relations since the low point of the 1960s. Importantly, the revitalization efforts seem to be improving the lives of African Americans in the city.

Although *Black Enterprise* ranked Memphis highly, of their top ten ranked cities, Memphis had the worst rating in property and violent crime.[22] Unlike smaller cities such as Durham, where the perception of crime is more of a problem than the reality of it, Memphis has its share of violent crime. When I was last in Memphis, the talk of the downtown was about a homeless woman who had been killed on a downtown street in the middle of the afternoon, the day before I arrived. Halloran commented that many people who live in Memphis believe that their fellow residents are nice. "I guess that's true," he said. "But seven women have been murdered here in the last month." Because most of the Orpheum's programming is during the evening hours, Halloran continues to battle both the perceptions and the realities of the dangers of going downtown. He has quadrupled the security in and around the theater at night, so that the possibilities of crime are reduced and people will feel more secure. As downtown Memphis becomes more and more dense and Memphis residents become more accustomed to spending some of their leisure hours downtown once again, both perceptions and realities of crime will inevitably be reduced. Downtown Memphis has been tainted by a history of violence and fear, and it will most likely take a few more years before the residue of the past will be washed away.

The Orpheum Theatre, the Peabody Hotel, Peabody Place, Beale Street, and the National Civil Rights Museum have had a tremendous impact on tourism and the economic prosperity of downtown Memphis. Yet it is generally understood that for a downtown to flourish at the turn of the twenty-first century, residential density is also necessary. In southern cities, attracting both residential developers and potential downtown dwellers continues to be difficult. People are more attracted to downtown living when services such as grocery stores, laundries, dry cleaners, florists, and pharmacies are nearby. But few entrepreneurs will open such businesses if few people live in the area. This stalemate is typical and frustrating for downtown developers, and such is the case in Memphis. Approximately 20,000 people currently live in or around downtown Memphis, but still few services are available. Developers like Jack Belz have made urban living more attractive, and residential development along the Mississippi River, near the downtown area, is also enticing some people to make their homes there. Builders have been slowly but surely building new homes, renovating old buildings, and developing adaptive reuse projects for low-, middle-, and upper-income homes and apartments, further increasing the residential density of the downtown area. But the fact remains that 1 million people live in Memphis, and only 20,000 of them live around the downtown area.

Downtown Memphis is a present-day success story because it has developed into a vibrant tourist zone; it is a revitalized pocket of a vast decentered city. At the center of the idea of downtown Memphis is the movie palace. In 1928 the Orpheum Theatre was the crowning achievement of Memphis; in the late 1970s the renovated movie palace was one of the first attractions to appear within the redeveloping cityscape. Today, it is downtown's premier arts facility and stands as a tribute to the role of historic preservation in revitalization. While its role within the downtown has changed as the downtown itself has changed, it remains a monument—symbolizing what it means to go downtown. At the turn of the twenty-first century, both downtown Memphis and the Orpheum Theatre offer people what they have always desired from such places—dreamy passages to other eras and faraway worlds.

Notes

Introduction

1. See, for example, Greg Dickinson, "Memories for Sale: Nostalgia and the Construction of Identity in Old Pasadena," *Quarterly Journal of Speech* 83 (1997): 1–27; and M. Christine Boyer, "Cities for Sale: Merchandising History at South Seaport," in *Variations on a Theme Park: The New American City and the End of Public Space,* ed. M. Sorkin (New York: Noonday Press, 1992), 181–204.

Chapter 1. From Glory to Ruins

1. Douglas Gomery, "The Picture Palace," *Quarterly Review of Film Studies* 3 (1978): 26.

2. Maggie Valentine, *The Show Starts on the Sidewalk: An Architectural History of the Movie Theatre, Starring S. Charles Lee* (New Haven: Yale University Press, 1994), 29.

3. "The Alabama Theatre Souvenir Program," December 26, 1927.

4. "Tampa Theatre Opening Souvenir," October 15, 1926.

5. "New Theatre Opens, First Vitaphone Heard in Biloxi," *Daily Herald,* January 16, 1929.

6. Charlotte Herzog, "The Movie Palace and the Theatrical Sources of Architectural Style," *Cinema Journal* 20 (Spring 1981): 18.

7. Valentine, 40.

8. Qtd. in Iain Macintosh, *Architecture, Actor, and Audience* (New York: Routledge, 1993), 72.

9. David Nasaw, *Going Out: The Rise and Fall of Public Amusements* (New York: Basic Books, 1993), 230.

10. Qtd. in Valentine, 34.

11. Ibid.

12. Richard M. Kennedy, "Autobiography of Richard M. 'Dick' Kennedy," unpublished document.

13. Lawrence Levine, *Highbrow/Lowbrow: The Emergence of Cultural Hierarchy in America* (Cambridge, Mass.: Harvard University Press, 1988), 199.

14. Gomery, 28.

15. Roy Rosenzweig, *Eight Hours for What We Will* (New York: Cambridge University Press, 1977), 185.

16. "New Theatre Opens, First Vitaphone Heard in Biloxi," *Daily Herald,* January 16, 1929.

17. Rosenzweig, 205.

18. "New Theatre Opens, First Vitaphone Heard in Biloxi," *Daily Herald,* January 16, 1929.

19. "Colored Patrons Welcomed at New Orpheum Theatre," *Memphis World,* September 21, 1937.

20. "Touches on New Theatre in Preparation for Occupation," *Durham Morning Herald,* January 17, 1926.

21. "Negro Contralto to Sing Tonight," *Durham Morning Herald,* January 12, 1927.

22. Nasaw, 236.

23. Valentine, 90.

24. Letter written by Doris Keating Stafford to the Tampa Theatre, October 14, 1996.

25. Douglas Gomery, "If You've Seen One, You've Seen the Mall," in *Seeing through Movies,* ed. Mark C. Miller (New York: Pantheon, 1990), 61.

26. Loren Baritz, *The Good Life: The Meaning of Success for the American Middle Class* (New York: Harper and Row, 1982), 202.

27. Valentine, 164.

28. Baritz, 202.

29. Qtd. in Lynn Spigel, "Installing the Television Set: Popular Discourses on Television and Domestic Space," *Camera Obscura* 16 (1988), 20.

30. Valentine, 165.

31. "Alabama Theatre Is Installing CinemaScope, Books *The Robe,*" *Birmingham News,* August 19, 1953.

32. Valentine, 169.

33. Baritz, 196.

34. Clifford E. Clark, "Ranch-House Suburbia," in *Recasting America,* ed. Lary May (Chicago: University of Chicago Press, 1989), 188.

35. Herbert J. Gans, "The White Exodus to Suburbia Steps Up," in *Cities in Trouble,* ed. Nathan Glazer (Chicago: Quadrangle Books, 1970), 45.

36. Robert A. Beauregard, *Voices of Decline: The Postwar Fate of U.S. Cities* (Cambridge, Mass.: Blackwell, 1993), 124.

37. Raymond A. Mohl, *The Making of Urban America* (Wilmington, Del.: Scholarly Resources, 1997), 214.

38. Beauregard, 175.

39. Bernard J. Frieden and Lynne B. Sagalyn, *Downtown, Inc.: How America Rebuilds Cities* (Cambridge, Mass.: MIT Press, 1992), 29.

40. Frieden and Sagalyn, 27.

41. Ibid.

42. David Naylor, *American Picture Palaces: The Architecture of Fantasy* (New York: Prentice Hall, 1981), 178.

Chapter 2. The Decline of the Southern Downtown Picture Palace

1. Lee E. Bains Jr., "Birmingham 1963: Confrontation over Civil Rights," in *Birmingham, Alabama, 1956–1963: The Black Struggle for Civil Rights,* ed. David J. Garrow (Brooklyn, N.Y.: Carlson 1989), 166.

2. Bobby M. Wilson, "Racial Segregation Trends in Birmingham, Alabama," *Southeastern Geographer* 25 (1985): 31–32.

3. "South Deserves Better," *Birmingham News,* November 25, 1962.

4. Birmingham's Racial Segregation Ordinances, Section 359, 1951.

5. Glenn T. Eskew, *But for Birmingham: The Local and National Movements in the Civil Rights Struggle* (Chapel Hill: University of North Carolina Press, 1997), 128.

6. Ibid., 146.

7. Ibid., 150.

8. Aldon D. Morris, "Sustaining the Fight: The Importance of Local Movements," in *Birmingham Revolutionaries: The Reverend Fred Shuttlesworth and the Alabama Christian Movement for Human Rights,* ed. Marjorie L. White and Andrew M. Manis (Macon, Ga.: Mercer University Press, 2000), 27.

9. Eskew, 268.

10. Bains, 182.

11. Andrew M. Manis, *A Fire You Can't Put Out: The Civil Rights Life of Birmingham's Reverend Fred Shuttlesworth* (Tuscaloosa: University of Alabama Press, 1999), 5.

12. Wyatt T. Walker, "The Historical Significance of Birmingham," in *Birmingham Revolutionaries: The Reverend Fred Shuttlesworth and the Alabama Christian Movement for Human Rights,* ed. Marjorie L. White and Andrew M. Manis (Macon, Ga.: Mercer University Press, 2000), 73.

13. Wilson, 33.

14. Ibid.

15. Protests against Birmingham segregation in the downtown area were focused mainly on retail establishments and restaurants. Whitmire said that protests did occur in front of the Alabama Theatre, but it was not a focal point. Whitmire explained that once the federal government ended segregation, the theater was, at least theoretically, integrated.

16. Kennedy, no page number.

17. "Theater Will Replace Seats in $100,000 Remodeling," *Birmingham News,* January 7, 1972.

18. Garland Reeves, "Great Alabama Theatre Battles to Keep Afloat," *Birmingham News,* February 12, 1978.

19. "Theater Integration Here Said 'Not Negotiable Now,'" *Durham Sun,* March 1, 1962.

20. "City Council Asks Theater Heads to Negotiate Integration Question," *Durham Morning Herald,* March 6, 1962.

21. Ibid.

22. "Civil Rights Group Cites Segregation Status Here," *Durham Sun,* March 10, 1962.

23. "Negotiations On 'How to Integrate' Rejected," *Durham Sun,* March 14, 1962.

24. "Negro Court Suit Seen in Wake of Theater Protests," *Durham Morning Herald,* March 15, 1962.

25. "Demonstrators Line Up Again at Theater," *Durham Sun,* March 16, 1962.

26. "Court Orders Protests at Theater Halted," *Durham Morning Herald,* March 17, 1962.

27. Jean Bradley Anderson, *Durham County: A History of Durham County, North Carolina* (Durham: Duke University Press, 1990), 440.

28. The Carolina Cinema Corporation of Durham, "Prospectus: A Proposal for Use of the Durham Auditorium," May 3, 1978. Personal papers of Montrose Moses.

29. Qtd. in Clifford Kuhn, Harlon Joye, and E. Bernard West, *Living Atlanta: An Oral History of the City, 1914–1948* (Atlanta: Atlanta Historical Society and University of Georgia Press, 1990), 98.

30. Ibid.

31. Ibid., 302.

32. "An Appeal for Human Rights," *Atlanta Constitution,* March 9, 1960.

33. "A Stormy Rally in Atlanta," *Today's Speech* 11 (1963), 20.

34. Janet Feagans, "Atlanta Theatre Segregation: A Case of Prolonged Avoidance," *Journal of Human Relations* 13 (1965): 208–15.

35. "Dozen Negroes Stage Sit-In: McLellan's on Main Closes," *Commercial Appeal,* March 19, 1960.

36. "Negro Meeting Votes Boycott Monday, Thursday Absence of Downtown Approved," *Commercial Appeal,* March 23, 1960.

37."Twenty-Five Years Ago," *Commercial Appeal,* June 4, 1985.

38. Michael Honey, *Black Workers Remember: An Oral History of Segregation, Unionism, and the Freedom Struggle* (Berkeley: University of California Press, 1999), 291.

39. Ibid.

40. Ibid., 292.

41. *Time,* April 12, 1968, 18.

42."Urban Renewal Surgery Cuts Path through Downtown Area," *Press-Scimitar,* July 15, 1972.

43. "Downtown: Everything Is Waiting," *Commercial Appeal,* November 18, 1973.

44. "Malco Deserves a Happy Ending," *Commercial Appeal,* August 10, 1976.

45. "Malco Denies City's Bid on Theater," *Commercial Appeal,* August 23, 1976.

46. "Cross Burning at Residence of Beach Petitioner," *Daily Herald,* October 6, 1959.

47. "Second Wooden Cross Is Burned in Coast Area," *Daily Herald,* October 10, 1959.

48. "Not Trying to Integrate, Dr. Dunn Declares," *Daily Herald,* April 26, 1960.

49. Charles Sullivan and Murella Hebert Powell, *The Mississippi Gulf Coast: Portrait of a People* (Sun Valley, Calif.: American Historical Press, 1999), 171.

50. Qtd. in Stephen Branch, "Mass Culture Meets Main Street: Opening of Lakeland's Polk Theatre," *Tampa Bay History* 16 (1994): 33.

51. "Civil Rights Protests in Tampa: Oral Memoirs of Conflict and Accommodation," *Tampa Bay History* 1 (1979): 37.

52. Ibid., 45.

53. Ibid., 52.

54. Steven Lawson, "From Sit-In to Race Riot," in *Southern Businessmen and Desegregation,* ed. Elizabeth Jacoway and David R. Colburn (Baton Rouge: Louisiana State University Press, 1982), 281.

55. "Civil Rights Protests in Tampa: Oral Memoirs of Conflict and Accommodation," 53.

56. Judy Hamilton, "Heaven on Earth," *Florida Accent,* April 8, 1973.

57. Ibid.

Chapter 3. Rescuing the Past from the Wrecking Ball

1. Michael Putnam, *Silent Screens: The Decline and Transformation of the American Movie Theater* (Baltimore: Johns Hopkins University Press, 2000).

2. Stewart Brand, *How Buildings Learn* (New York: Viking, 1994), 95.

3. Constance M. Greiff, "Lost America from the Atlantic to the Mississippi," in *Readings in Historic Preservation: Why? What? How?* ed. Norman Williams, Edmund Kellog, and Frank Gilbert (New Brunswick, N.J.: Center for Urban Policy Research, Rutgers University, 1983), 38.

4. Ibid., 39.

5. Qtd. in Walter Muir Whitehill, "Promoted to Glory," in *With Heritage So Rich,* ed. Albert Rains and Laurance Henderson (New York: Random House, 1966), 40.

6. Greiff, 40.

7. Brand, 96.

8. Qtd. in Julia M. Klein, "How Historic Sites Can Matter in the Here and Now," *New York Times,* December 11, 2000.

9. Prys Gruffudd, "Heritage as National Identity: Histories and Prospects of

the National Pasts," in *Heritage, Tourism, and Society*, ed. David Herbert (New York: Mansell, 1995), 49.

10. The lobby and the land underneath the building are owned by separate corporations and are leased to the city.

11. Jacques Neher, "City Rejects Tampa Theatre Gift," *Tampa Times*, January 1, 1976.

12. "Decision Can Speed Cultural Complex," *Tampa Tribune*, October 27, 1975.

13. C. L. Miller, personal letter to Mayor William Poe, October 20, 1975.

14. Mr. and Mrs. Frank Lukas, "Preserve the Tampa Theatre," *Tampa Tribune*, January 28, 1976.

15. Ibid.

16. Robin Winks, "Conservation in America: National Character as Revealed by Preservation," in *The Future of the Past: Attitudes to Conservation, 1174–1974*, ed. Jane Fawcett (New York: Whitney Library of Design, 1976), 142.

17. Mrs. H. L. Culbreath, personal letter to Lee Duncan, July, 1975.

18. Ibid.

19. Qtd. in Noble H. R. Romans, "Atlanta to Have Great Shrine Home," *Atlanta City Builder*, March 1928, 5.

20. Atlanta Landmarks, Inc. "A Proposal to Save the Fabulous Fox Theatre: A National Historic Landmark," September 1, 1976, 3.

21. Georgia Legislature General Assembly, "A Resolution," adopted in the Senate, March 10, 1975; adopted in the House, March 25, 1975.

22. Atlanta Landmarks, 5.

23. "The Fox: America's Soul," reprinted in *Atlanta Journal*, March 16, 1976.

24. The Internal Revenue Service made two determinations: Atlanta Landmarks was exempt from federal income tax under section 501 (c) (3) of the Internal Revenue Code, and income derived from performances, functions, events, and the sale of concessions and the lease of building space were not unrelated taxable income. The Joint City-County Board made the determination to exempt the Fox Theatre from property taxes, effective January 1, 1976.

25. Board of Directors, Carolina Cinema Corporation of Durham, "The Story So Far," July 12, 1978, 2. Personal papers of Montrose Moses.

26. The Carolina Cinema Corporation of Durham, "Prospectus: A Proposal for Use of the Durham Auditorium," May 3, 1978, 1. Personal papers of Montrose Moses.

27. Ibid., 2.

28. Ibid.

29. Charlotte Herzog, "The Movie Palace and the Theatrical Sources of Architectural Style," *Cinema Journal* 20 (Spring 1981): 34.

30. Marshall Field and Company, "Fashions of the Hour," *Marshall Field and Company*, October 1921, 23.

31. *City of Tampa Report of the Architectural Review Commission Recommending*

the Designation of Tampa Theatre and Office Building as a City of Tampa Landmark, October 17, 1988, 12.

32. Georgia Legislature General Assembly, "A Resolution," adopted in the Senate, March 10, 1975; adopted in the House, March 25, 1975.

33. Lawrence Levine, *Highbrow/Lowbrow: The Emergence of Cultural Hierarchy in America* (Cambridge, Mass.: Harvard University Press, 1988), 234.

34. *City of Tampa Report of the Architectural Review Commission Recommending the Designation of Tampa Theatre and Office Building as a City of Tampa Landmark,* October 17, 1988, 13.

Chapter 4. Creating the Illusion of a Material Past

1. David Lowenthal, *Possessed by the Past* (New York: Free Press, 1996), 153.

2. Walter Benjamin, "The Work of Art in the Age of Mechanical Reproduction," in *Illuminations,* ed. Hannah Arendt, trans. Harry Zohn (New York: Harcourt, Brace, and World, 1968), 238.

3. Atlanta Landmarks, "Thoughts on a Policy for Preservation," April 1986, 2.

4. Ibid.

5. The jewel drop had been vacuumed only once before. In the 1970s, Joe Patten, using his Hoover vacuum and sitting on a mechanical lift, vacuumed the entire curtain. Apparently, it was so dirty prior to his vacuuming that the images on the curtain could barely be seen.

6. Kenneth Burke, *Permanence and Change: An Anatomy of Purpose* (Berkeley: University of California Press, 1954), 49.

7. "New Theatre Opens: First Vitaphone Heard in Biloxi," *Daily Herald,* January 16, 1929.

8. Barry Schwartz, "Social Change and Collective Memory: The Democratization of George Washington," *American Sociological Review* 56 (1991): 2, 234.

Chapter 5. The Discursive Past

1. Michael Kammen, *Mystic Chords of Memory: The Translation of Tradition in American Culture* (New York: Knopf, 1991), 626.

2. Ibid., 628.

3. Raphael Samuel, *Theatres of Memory* (London: Verso, 1994), x.

4. The one-woman performance was *Family Secrets,* starring Sherry Glaser. It is the longest-running one-person off-Broadway show. It depicts the lives of a Jewish family, spanning three generations.

5. Because I live in Tampa, I have had many opportunities to see live performances at the Tampa Theatre. The stage is so small, however, that the theater is severely limited in what kinds of productions can be staged. Usually, live performances are acoustical-type productions that do not require much room on the stage. Mostly, though, I go to the theater to see films.

6. The ballet was entitled *The Diary of Anne Frank* and was goose-stepped by the Ballet Contemporáneo de Caracas.

7. "The Carolina Theatre: Where Durham Comes Alive—Again," *Historic Preservation: A Publication of the Historic Preservation Society of Durham* 19 (1993): 15.

8. J. B. Jackson, "The Necessity for Ruins," in *The Necessity for Ruins and Other Topics* (Amherst: University of Massachusetts Press, 1980), 102.

9. Paul S. Gordon, "Critics of Film Festival Have Duty to Speak Out," *Herald-Sun*, June 12, 1995.

10. Julia White, "Hardin: Gay Films OK, Sex on TV More Graphic," *Herald-Sun*, June 2, 1995.

11. Ibid.

12. Julia White, "DA Asks Officials to Screen Gay Films. Their Job: Decide if Festival, Community's Decency Standards Jibe," *Herald-Sun*, May 28, 1995.

13. Ibid.

14. "Morals in Decline," *Herald-Sun*, June 19, 1995.

15. Julia White, "Board Praised for Gay Film Stance," *Herald-Sun*, June 21, 1995.

16. "Carolina Gay Festival Is on Again, Protest Isn't," *Herald-Sun*, August 1, 1996.

17. Many of these stories have been documented in Janna Jones, "The Downtown Picture Palace: The Significance of Place, Memory, and Cinema" (Ph.D. diss., University of South Florida, 1998).

18. The self-guided tour pamphlet was made possible by a grant from the Florida Humanities Council.

19. Schroeder said that many older people share their memories of the theater during tours. She asks them if they have internet access, and most reply that they do. She then asks them to go to the theater's website and write their memories so that they can be included in the Tampa Theatre Stories Project. She says few do it. She is not sure why they do not write their stories, but she suspects that they do not imagine that their stories are significant enough to be included. It might be that once they share their memories with Schroeder during the tour, they are satisfied with reliving special moments at the theater and do not need to relive them again by writing them down.

20. Janna Jones, "On with the Show: Preservation, Transformation, and Memory at the Picture Palace," *Humanities in the South* 87 (2000): 28.

21. A complete history of the Orpheum Theatre, including the history of its programming and its renovation, can be found in Pat Halloran, *The Orpheum! Where Broadway Meets Beale* (Memphis, Tenn.: Lithograph Publishing Co., 1997).

22. Halloran, 63.

23. Michael Kammen, *In the Past Lane* (New York: Oxford University Press, 1997), 219.

24. Ibid., 222.

25. Qtd. in Michael Kammen, *Selvages and Biases: The Fabric of History in American Culture* (Ithaca, N.Y.: Cornell University Press, 1987), 300.

26. Dolores Hayden, *The Power of Place: Urban Landscapes as Public History* (Cambridge, Mass.: MIT Press, 1995), 11.

27. Ibid.

Chapter 6. The Transformation of the Downtown Picture Palace

1. Barbara Wilinsky, *Sure Seaters: The Emergence of Art House Cinema* (Minneapolis: University of Minnesota Press, 2001), 15.

2. Lawrence Levine, *Highbrow/Lowbrow: The Emergence of Cultural Hierarchy in America* (Cambridge, Mass.: Harvard University Press, 1988), 234.

3. Immanel Kant, *The Critique of Judgement,* trans. James Creed Meredith (Oxford: Clarendon Press, 1961), 43.

4. Herbert J. Gans, *Popular Culture and High Culture: An Analysis and Evaluation of Taste* (New York: Basic Books, 1999), 102.

5. Ibid., 5.

6. Pierre Bourdieu, *Distinction: A Social Critique of the Judgement of Taste* (Cambridge, Mass.: Harvard University Press, 1984), 56.

7. Ibid., 270.

8. Pat Halloran, *The Orpheum! Where Broadway Meets Beale* (Memphis, Tenn.: Lithograph Publishing Co., 1997), 80.

9. Bourdieu, 32.

10. Qtd. in Kathy Henderson, "Civil Action," *Stage Bill,* March 2000, 18.

11. Orpheum Theatre, *Marquee,* March 28–April 21, 2001, 3.

12. Bourdieu, 270.

13. http://www.nthp.org/11most/theaters.htm.

14. Philip A. Morris, "Remaking Birmingham's Downtown," *New York Times,* December 13, 1998.

15. Glenda Webb, "The Center of It All," *Birmingham* (Spring 1999), 88.

16. The Carolina Cinema Corporation of Durham, "Prospectus: A Proposal for Use of the Durham Auditorium," May 3, 1978, 2. Personal papers of Montrose Moses.

17. Stephen Fraser, "Small Investors Back on Main Street," *Herald Sun,* March 8, 2001.

18. Ronnie Glassberg, "City Acting on Concerns about Crime: New Panhandling and Loitering Regulations, Curfew Ordinance Eyed," *Herald Sun,* September 1, 2000.

19. William A. Kalkhof, "Image Does Not Match Reality in Downtown," *Herald Sun,* August 10, 2000.

20. Deborah M. Clubb, "Peabody Place: Reverie Is Reality; Old, Lame-Duck Hotel Gives Flight to Urban Dream," *Commercial Appeal,* July 8, 2001.

21. Jason Greer, "Fifth Best: *Black Enterprise* Rank Recognizes City's Revitalization," *Commercial Appeal,* June 27, 2001.

22. Ibid.

Photo Credits

University of South Florida Special Collections Department, frontispiece
Tampa-Hillsborough County Public Library, figure 1, figure 2, figure 5
Durham Photographic Archives, Durham County Library, figure 3
M. Lewis Kennedy, figure 4, figure 18, figure 27
Biloxi Public Library, figure 6, figure 20
Library of Congress, Prints and Photographs Division, figure 7, figure 8
Jim Thornton/*Herald-Sun,* figure 9, figure 10
Orpheum Theatre, figure 11, figure 12, figure 23, figure 24
Mark Neumann, figure 13, figure 14, figure 19, figure 21, figure 22, figure 26
Michael Portman, figure 15, figure 16, figure 25
George Cott, figure 17

Index

Abell, Jan, 153–154
Alabama Theatre (Birmingham), 8, 11, 81, 185; cinemascope screen, 34; contemporary programming at the, 250–51; contemporary social space of, 251, 253–54; decline of, 48, 264; financial success of, 112; integration of, 47, 215, 277n.15; opening night souvenir program, 14; original interior of, 19–20; rescue of, 109–10; restoration of, 160–69; segregation of, 46; Whitmire, Cecil, 109–13, 118, 160–64, 169–73, 264–67, 277n.15
Alternative films, 237–39; viewers of, 239–44
Anniversary Party, The, 241
Apollo 13, 258
Atlanta (Ga.), 8, 10; integration of, 59–61, 61; integration of theaters in, 60; as non-pedestrian space, 263–64; race riot of 1906, 57; racial protests in, 59–61; segregation of, 58

Baines, Lee, 41, 277nn.1, 10
Baritz, Loren, 33, 276nn.26, 28
Barnes, Lolly, 175, 177
Beau Rivage Hotel and Casino (Biloxi), 254–55, 260
Beauregard, Robert, 36, 37, 276n.36, 277n.38
Bell, John, 114, 156–57, 173, 186, 215
Benjamin, Walter, 121, 281n.2
Big night out, 251, 253–54
Biloxi (Miss.), 8, 10, 174, 177–78; casino industry in, 184–85, 254–55; contemporary downtown of, 263; downtown decline of, 71; early history of, 68, 70; first movie theater in, 22; Hurricane Camille in, 71–72; racial protests of, 70–71; urban renewal in, 72
Birmingham (Ala.), 8, 10, 251; Civil Rights movement in, 42–45; downtown decline of, 45–46, 264; downtown revitalization in, 264–67; Fourth Avenue Historical District in, 215; history of, 41–44; Racial Segregation Ordinance of, 42; segregation of, 41–42; 45–46
Birth of a Nation, The, 13
Blockbuster movies. *See* Hollywood film
Broadway. *See* Live programming
Bourdieu, Pierre, 242, 243–44, 246, 253, 283nn.6, 7, 9, 12
Burke, Kenneth, 142, 281n.6

Carolina Theatre (Durham), 8, 81, 143–44, 190; contemporary African-Americans' reaction to, 204–8; and alternative films, 236–37, 239 (audiences of, 239–44); contemporary social space of, 239–44, 251, 260; decline of, 56–57, 102; dropped ceiling in, 55–56, 205, 239–44; Fluke, Pepper, 55–56, 105–7, 193–95, 197, 198, 205, 213; and gay and lesbian film programming, 209–13; integration of, 50–55, 204; and loss of the past, 11, 196–208; Moses, Constance, 101–3, 105–9, 197; Moses, Montrose, 101–3, 106–9, 193–95, 197; rescue of, 103–6; restoration of, 192–96; segregation of, 29, 49–55; transitional era of, 107–8, 197; Williams, St. Clair, 55, 193, 197–98, 205
Carolina Cinema Corporation, 103–6, 197–98, 200–202
Casey, Jack, 146–52; 160
Celebration Cinema (Orlando), 262–63
Cinemascope, 34
Civil Rights movement, 39, 78; in Atlanta, 59–61; in Biloxi, 70–71; in Birmingham, 40–45; in Durham, 49–55; in Memphis, 63–75; in Tampa, 74–75
Clark, Clifford, 36, 276n.34
Class distinction, 19–23, 26, 232–33, 242–44, 253–54
Connor, Bull, 43
Crouching Tiger, Hidden Dragon, 239, 241–42
Cultural Heritage, 113–16

Diary of Anne Frank, The, 191, 281n.6
Discursive preservation, 11; definition of, 139, 189; importance of, 212–13, 217, 228–31; model of, 224–28; struggle of, 196–208
Double-Take Documentary Film Festival, 182, 203
Downtown districts: in decline, 10, 36–39, 45–46, 56–57, 63–65, 71–72, 76–78, 102, 264; revitalization efforts of, 7, 261–62, 264–74
Drive-in theaters, 35
Duncan, Lee, 88, 92–94, 108, 145
Durham (N.C.), 8, 10, 190–91; demographics, 201, downtown decline of, 56–57, 102; integration of, 50, 52–53, 55; revitalization efforts of, 267–71; segregation of, 49–50, 52–53

Eberson, John, 20, 73, 156–57
Ellis, Jarrett, 151–55, 160
Eskew, Glenn, 43, 277nn.5, 6, 7, 9
EverGreene Painting Studios, 151, 162–63, 164–65, 168–69; Greene, Jeff, 8, 123–24, 169–73, 184, 185–86, 190

Film exhibition (contemporary), 139, 191–92, 209–13, 236–44, 258
Fluke, Pepper, 55–56, 101, 105–7, 193–95, 197–98, 205, 213
Foreign films. *See* Alternative films
Fox Theatre (Atlanta), 8, 10–11, 81, 185; damage to, 131–38; decline of, 61–62; and differences between programmers and renovators, 129–36; early history of, 94–95; effects of stock market crash on, 30; lack of discursive preservation of, 213–14; Patten, Joe, 98–101, 108, 281n.5; contemporary programming of, 246, 248–9; rescue of, 95–100; safeguarding material past of, 125–43, 196; segregation of, 58–59, 214; contemporary social space of, 251, 253–54; status of, 129
Frieden, Bernard and Lynne Sagalyn, 38, 277nn.39, 40, 41

Gans, Herbert J., 36, 84–85, 238, 276n.35, 283nn.4, 5
Gay and Lesbian Film Festival, 211–12, 231
Gay and Lesbian film programming, 192, 209–13
Gollotte, Gwen, 71, 174–75
Gomery, Douglas, 22, 32, 275n.1, 276nn.14, 25
Grease, 258
Greene, Jeff, 8, 123–24, 169–73, 184, 185–86, 190
Griffin, D. W., 13
Gruffudd, Prys, 86, 279–80n.9

Halloran, Pat, 218–20, 222–28, 245, 249, 271–73, 282n.21, 283n.8
Hayden, Dolores, 230, 283nn.26, 27
Heritage syndrome, 189–90, 229
Herzog, Charlotte, 18, 114, 275n.6, 280n.29
Historic museum, 119–20
Historic preservation, 10–12; and adaptive re-use, 193–96; American history of, 81–86; authenticity in, 124–25, 153–60, 163–73; compared to photography, 121; and contemporary sensibilities, 122, 171; criticism of, 9; and historic documentation, 124, 154–55, 160; as illusion, 9, 11, 123–25, 145, 156, 173, 186–87; limitations of, 188–90, 228–29; practical, small-scale model of, 174–85; and relevance for future, 68, 89–90, 116, 235, 261–62, 267–68, 274; and safeguarding material past, 125–43, 187; and science, 124–25, 153–54, 173; as time travel, 90, 122, 157; as usable past, 119–22, 185–87, 189
Historic American buildings survey, 83
Hollywood film, 234–35, 237–39, 242
Honey, Michael, 63, 64, 278nn.38, 39, 40
Hood, Lee, 71, 177–84, 186, 215, 255, 257–60
Huxtable, Ada Louise, 84–85

I. Weiss, 131
Illegal Trust, 34
Independent films. *See* Alternative films
Integration, 8; in Atlanta, 59–61; in Biloxi, 70–71; in Birmingham, 42–45; in Durham, 49–55; in Memphis, 63–75; in Tampa, 74–75
It Came from Outer Space, 241
It's a Wonderful Life, 258

Jackson, J. B., 198, 282n.8

Kammen, Carol, 229, 282n.25
Kammen, Michael, 189–90, 229, 281nn.1, 2, 282n.23
Kant, Immanuel, 238, 283n.3
Keillor, Garrison, 163
Kennedy, Richard M., 20, 46–47, 276n.12, 277n.16
Kennedy, Robert, 47
King, Martin Luther, Jr., 37, 43, 59–60, 62, 64–65, 272

Lawson, Steven, 74–75, 279n.54
Levine, Lawrence, 22, 115, 237–38, 276n.13, 281n.33, 283n.2
Live programming, 191, 220, 223, 226–28, 244–46, 248–51, 253–54, 255, 257–61
Lovett, Lyle, 191
Lowenthal, David, 121, 281n.1
Lyric Theatre (Birmingham), 112

Manis, Andrew, 44, 277n.11
Memphis (Tenn.), 8, 220, 222, 224, 226; downtown revitalization of, 271–74; integration of, 63–65; segregation of, 63–64; urban renewal of, 65–66
Michigan Theatre (Detroit), 39
Moe, Richard, 261
Morris, Aldon D., 43, 277n.8
Moses, Constance (Connie), 101–3, 105, 106–9, 197
Moses, Montrose (Monte), 101–3, 106–9, 193–95, 197
Movie palace, 7; architectural significance of, 114–15; class distinction in, 19–23, 26, 232–33, 244, 253–54; and consumer revolution, 13–14; contemporary film exhibition in, 191–92, 209–13; 236–44, 258; contemporary live programming in, 191, 220, 223, 226–28, 244–46, 248–51, 253–54, 255, 257–61; as cornerstone of downtown revitalization, 5, 68, 89–90, 113, 116, 235, 261–62, 267–68, 274; decline of, 5, 30, 32–35, 48, 56–57, 61–62, 66, 68, 72, 77–78, 102; as democratic space, 19–20, 192; discursive preservation of, 189–90, 196–209, 212–13, 215–17, 224–31; exteriors of, 18, 232; integration of, 39, 50–55; interiors of, 18–20, 23, 26, 232–33; and loss of the past, 196–208; material preservation of, 5, 10–12; 125–43, 160–69, 174–85, 192–96, 220–23; nostalgic feelings

Movie palace—*continued*
about, 4, 188–89, 216; ornate interiors of, 18–20, 22, 232–33; as pinnacle of urban development in the 1920s, 13–14, 18, 232, 261; rescue of, 88–94, 95–100, 103–6, 109–10, 113–18; segregation of, 29–30, 41–42, 45–46, 49–55, 58–59, 63–64, 70–71, 73–76, 214–15, 204–8, 217–18, 243; social space of, 234–44, 251, 253–54; urban renewal effects on, 39, ushers in, 23, 32

Nasaw, David, 19, 29, 275n.9, 276n.22
National Historic Preservation Act, 84
National Trust for Historic Preservation, 12, 83–84, 261, 283n.13
Naylor, David, 39, 277n.42
Neighborhood theaters, 32, 34–35, 244
Nickelodeon, 22
North Carolina Jewish Film Festival, 191–92, 240
North Carolina Nevermore Horror and Gothic Film Festival, 192

Orpheum Theatre (Memphis), 8, 11; contemporary live programming, 226–28, 245–46, 249; as contemporary social space, 251, 253–54; decline of, 66, 68; as discursive preservation model, 224–28; diverse programming at, 226–28; Halloran, Pat, 218–20, 222–28, 245, 249, 271–73, 282n.21, 283n.8; historic tours at, 217–18, 226; restoration of, 220–23; segregation of, 29, 217–18; transitional era of, 223–24
Orpheum! Where Broadway Meets Beale, The, 225, 249, 282n.21
Outkast, 142

Paltrow, Gwyneth, 241
Panhandlers, 269–70
Parade, 227–28
Patten, Joe, 98–101, 108, 281n.5
Phantom of the Opera, 139, 223, 245–46
Picture Palace. *See* Movie palace
Potter, Raeschelle, 259
Pride '95, 209–12
Putnam, Michael, 80, 113, 118, 279n.1

Racial riots, 37
Ragtime, 226–28
Rapp, George, 20
Rockefeller, John D., 83
Rosenzweig, Roy, 22, 276n.15, 17
Rothapfel, Samuel (Roxy), 18, 114

Saenger Theatre (Biloxi), 8, 11, 185; Barnes, Lolly, 175, 177; contemporary programming at, 255, 256–60; decline of, 72; discursive preservation of, 215; Gollotte, Gwen, 71, 174–75; Hood, Lee, 71, 177–84, 215, 255, 257–60; marquee of, 18, 175, opening night class distinction of, 26; restoration of, 174–85; segregation of, 71
Sagalyn, Lynne, and Bernard Frieden, 38, 277nn.39, 40, 41
Samuel, Raphael, 190, 281n.3
Scarlet Pimpernel, The, 131, 246, 249
Schroeder, Tara, 5, 215–16, 282n.19
Schwartz, Barry, 187, 281n.8
Segregation: in Atlanta, 58–59, 214; in Biloxi, 70–71; in Birmingham, 41–42, 45–46, 215; in Durham, 49–55; 204–8; in Memphis, 63–64; 217–18; in movie palaces in general, 29–30; in Tampa, 73–74, 76, 216
Shuttlesworth, Rev. Fred L., 42
Silent Screens: The Decline and Transformation of the American Movie Theater, 80
Social space, 233–44, 251, 253–54
Southern Bell, 95–96, 98–99
Southern cities, 7
Stowe House, 119–20, 122
Suburbia, 35–37
Swanson, Gloria, 5
Sweet Honey in the Rock, 87

Tampa (Fla.), 5–7, 10; Central Business District of, 263; downtown decline of, 76–78; early history of, 73; downtown revitalization of, 89–90; integration of, 77–78, 88; segregation of, 73–76, 216
Tampa Theatre (Tampa), 1, 3, 5–7, 10–11, 81, 87, 94, 185, 186, 190; and alternative films, 236–37 (audience of, 239–

44); and bank night, 32, decline of, 77–78; discursive preservation of, 215–17; and downtown revitalization, 89–90, 93; historic tour of, 5; integration of, 77–78, 88; as microcosm of downtown, 6; opening night souvenir program, 14, 23; restoration of, 11, 123, 145–60; segregation of, 75–76, 216; as social event (early twentieth century), 234; social space of, 239–44, 260; Stories Project, 215–16, 282n.19
Television, 33
Tenement Museum, 85–86

Urban renewal, 37–39, 56, 65–66, 71–72, 79

Valentine, Maggie, 14, 18, 275nn.2, 10, 276nn.23, 27, 30, 32

Walker, Wyatt, T., 44, 277n.12
Whitmire, Cecil, 109–13, 118, 160–64, 169–73, 264–67, 277n.15
Wilinsky, Barbara, 237, 242, 283n.1
Williams, St. Clair, 55, 193, 197–98, 205
Winks, Robin, 90, 280n.16
With Heritage So Rich, 83–84
Work of Art in the Age of Mechanical Reproduction, The, 121
World Theatre (St. Paul), 163

Ybor City (Tampa), 186

Janna Jones is an assistant professor of interdisciplinary studies at the University of South Florida.